TExES™
TEXAS EXAMINATIONS OF EDUCATOR STANDARDS™

ENGLISH LANGUAGE ARTS AND READING
4-8 (117)

Kathleen C. Tice, Ph.D.
University of Texas at Arlington

Research & Education Association
www.rea.com

Research & Education Association
258 Prospect Plains Road
Cranbury, New Jersey 08512
Email: info@rea.com

TExES™ English Language Arts and Reading 4–8 (117) with Online Practice Tests

Library of Congress Control Number 2018965068

ISBN-13: 978-0-7386-8829-9
ISBN-10: 0-7386-8829-0

The competencies and associated descriptive statements presented in this book are copyright © by the Texas Education Agency and were created and implemented by the Texas Education Agency and Pearson Education, Inc., or its affiliate(s). Texas Examinations of Educator Standards and TExES are trademarks of the Texas Education Agency. All other trademarks cited in this publication are the property of their respective owners.

Cover image © iStockphoto.com/monkeybusinessimages

REA® is a registered trademark of
Research & Education Association, Inc.

Contents

CONTENTS

CONTENTS

CONTENTS

About Our Author

Dr. Kathleen C. Tice is a Clinical Assistant Professor in Literacy Studies in the Department of Curriculum & Instruction at the University of Texas at Arlington. She teaches courses in literacy studies at both the undergraduate and graduate level.

Dr. Tice's research has focused upon teacher knowledge development in literacy education and service-learning in teacher preparation. She has served as the chair and annual conference program chair for the Service-Learning & Experiential Education–Special Interest Group of the American Educational Research Association. She is a co-editor of the *International Journal of Research on Service-Learning in Teacher Education*.

She taught students at the University of Illinois, Austin Community College, and at St. Edward's University, including working with migrant high school students through Rural Upward Bound.

Dr. Tice was awarded a Literacy Grant from the Honor Society of Phi Kappa Phi, the nation's oldest and most prestigious collegiate honor society for all academic disciplines. Her teaching awards include the University of Texas System Regents' Outstanding Teacher Award. She received her master's degree in reading education from the University of Houston, and earned her Ph.D. in reading and in English/language arts education from the University of Texas at Austin.

About REA

Founded in 1959, Research & Education Association (REA) is dedicated to publishing the finest and most effective educational materials—including study guides and test preps—for students of all ages. Today, REA's wide-ranging catalog is a leading resource for students, teachers, and other professionals. Visit *www.rea.com* to see a complete listing of all our titles.

Publisher's Acknowledgments

Publisher: Pam Weston

Editorial Director: Larry B. Kling

Technology Director: John Paul Cording

Graphic Design and File Prep: Jennifer Calhoun

Copy Editors: Karen Lamoreux, John Kupetz

Proofreader: Fiona Hallowell

Indexer: Casey Indexing and Information Service

Typesetter: Caragraphics

Foreword

Through years of teaching and mentoring teacher candidates, author Dr. Kathleen Tice remains abreast of how to support and differentiate preparation for aspiring teachers of English Language Arts and Reading (ELAR) in the state of Texas. Literacy experts like Dr. Tice understand that candidates' development of content and pedagogy follows a given trajectory. The organization of Dr. Tice's TExES ELAR 4–8 practice and review book supports candidates at various developmental levels. In fact, this book reminds me of Nikki, a teacher candidate who demonstrated proficiency in planning, instruction, and the learning environment, yet described the TExES ELAR test as her "Achilles' heel"!

Nikki had successfully completed several hours of required classroom observations and her initial field experience. Generally, candidates in Texas are required to pass TExES exams during the second field experience before being cleared for full clinical teaching. It was at the second field experience juncture, and out of frustration and fear, that Nikki encountered what she termed her Achilles' heel. She felt defeated at the practice stage over confusion regarding phonological awareness, phonemic awareness, and phases of literacy development. I was Nikki's site professor and chose to mentor her in the areas in which she expressed confusions.

However, I was somewhat astonished that she found the ELAR test difficult. When I observed her deliver reading and math workshop lessons, she demonstrated proficiency in the planning, instruction, and learning environment domains of the Texas-Teacher Evaluation and Support System (T-TESS). Furthermore, she maintained perfect attendance. Given this track record with addressing the needs of students and exceptional attendance, I realized that all she lacked was self-confidence and test-sophistication. She possessed the necessary qualities for impacting student achievement, so I wanted to help Nikki. By drawing upon Nikki's guided reading field experience and employing brief vignettes similar to the items contained in this practice book, Nikki overcame her Achilles' heel and scored high on the TExES ELAR test.

I am convinced there are other Nikkis out there who are passionate about meeting the needs of children but lack test-savviness. This book is a valuable tool that can support ELAR 4–8 candidates across Texas. The core of Dr. Tice's book consists of brief summaries of related research, illustrations, and realistic practice items with detailed explanations. Nikki could have benefited, for example, from Chapter 2: Proven Test-Taking Strategies to bolster her confidence. Candidates will benefit from the summaries of each domain and competency along with supporting research and examples. The two practice exams with detailed explanations of correct and incorrect choices promote independence and confidence, and can serve as a companion to literacy textbooks.

Finally, it's worth noting that teacher candidates require careful differentiation as they conceptualize literacy content and pedagogy. This book provides a wonderful road map to support candidates who require additional review, as well as for those who have mastered the content and pedagogy and choose to affirm their knowledge. I am certain you will agree that it is never the goal of a teacher educator for a learner-centered candidate to jeopardize initial licensure over lack of confidence and test-sophistication. Therefore, I strongly support the tools this book provides to strengthen future teachers' knowledge of literacy.

Deborah J. Williams, Ed.D.
Department of Curriculum and Instruction
College of Education
University of Texas at Arlington

Getting Started

Congratulations! By taking the TExES English Language Arts and Reading 4–8 (117) test, you're on your way to a rewarding career as a teacher of young students in Texas. Our book, and the online tools that come with it, give you everything you need to succeed on this important exam, bringing you one step closer to being certified to teach in Texas.

This TExES ELAR 4–8 test prep package includes:

- A **complete overview** of the TExES ELAR 4–8 test

- A **comprehensive review** of the content you are expected to know, assessed in two domains that cut across eight Texas state standards

- An **online diagnostic test** to pinpoint your strengths and weaknesses and focus your study

- **Two full-length practice tests:** available both in the book and online, where the tests come with powerful diagnostic tools to help you personalize your prep

HOW TO USE THIS BOOK + ONLINE PREP

About Our Review

The review chapters in this book are designed to help you sharpen your command of all the skills you'll need to pass the TExES ELAR 4–8 test. Each of the skills required for the two domains is discussed at length to optimize your understanding of what the test covers. Keep in mind that your schooling has taught you most of what you need to know to answer the questions on the test. Our content review is designed to reinforce what you have learned and show you how to relate the information you have acquired to the specific competencies on the test. Studying your class notes and textbooks together with our review will give you an excellent foundation for passing the test.

About the REA Study Center

At the REA Study Center (*www.rea.com/studycenter*), you will get feedback right from the start on what you know and what you don't to help make the most of your study time. Here is what you will find at the REA Study Center:

- **Diagnostic Test**—Before you review with the book, take our online diagnostic test. Your score report will pinpoint topics for which you need the most review, to help focus your study.

- **2 Full-Length Practice Tests**—These practice tests, also found in the book, give you the most complete picture of your strengths and weaknesses. After you've studied with the book, reinforce what you've learned by taking the first of two online practice exams. Review your score reports, then go back and study any topics you missed. Take the second practice test to ensure you've mastered the material.

Our online exams simulate the computer-based format of the actual TExES test and come with these features:

- **Automatic scoring**—Find out how you did on your test, instantly.

- **Diagnostic score reports**—Get a specific score tied to each competency, so you can focus on the areas that challenge you the most.

- **On-screen detailed answer explanations**—See why the correct response option is right, and learn why the other answer choices are incorrect.

- **Timed testing**—Learn to manage your time as you practice, so you'll feel confident on test day.

AN OVERVIEW OF THE TEST

What is assessed on the ELAR 4–8 test?

The ELAR 4–8 test assesses whether a candidate has the knowledge and abilities that a beginning teacher in Texas schools must possess. As you review the competencies and associated information, you will see that teachers looking to earn an ELAR 4–8 certificate are required to know how to meet a wide range of students' abilities in both oral and written language. One student in grades 4–8 could be reading on grade level while another could be reading at a much higher level. Another student may read on grade level and yet may be a reluctant writer. A student in these middle grades could also be a beginning reader and writer. As a certified teacher, you need to know how to meet the needs of every student.

The TExES ELAR 4–8 assesses skills in two domains:

Domain I accounts for 33% of the exam, or approximately 33 items, and evaluates these standards:

- **Standard I: Oral Language.** Teachers of students in grades 4 to 8 understand the importance of oral language, know the developmental processes of oral language, and provide a variety of instructional opportunities for students to develop listening and speaking skills.

- **Standard II: Foundations of Reading.** Teachers of students in grades 4 to 8 understand the foundations of reading and early literacy development.

- **Standard III: Word Analysis Skills and Reading Fluency.** Teachers understand the importance of word analysis skills (including decoding, blending, structural analysis, sight word vocabulary) and reading fluency and provide many opportunities for students to practice and improve their word analysis skills and reading fluency.

- **Standard VIII: Assessment of Developing Literacy.** Teachers understand the basic principles of assessment and use a variety of literacy assessment practices to plan and implement instruction.

Domain II accounts for 67% of the exam, or approximately 67 items, and evaluates these standards:

- **Standard IV: Reading Comprehension.** Teachers understand the importance of reading for understanding, know the components of comprehension, and teach students strategies for improving their comprehension.

- **Standard V: Written Language.** Teachers understand that writing is a developmental process and provide instruction that helps students develop competence in written communication.

- **Standard VI: Study and Inquiry Skills.** Teachers understand the importance of study and inquiry skills as tools for learning and promote students' development in applying study and inquiry skills.

- **Standard VII: Viewing and Representing.** Teachers understand how to interpret, analyze, evaluate, and produce visual images and messages in various media and to provide students with opportunities to develop skills in this area.

What is the format of the TExES ELAR 4–8 test?

The test includes a total of 100 multiple choice items. You may encounter non-scorable questions but you won't know which ones they are, so they surely aren't worth worrying about. Your final scaled score will be based only on the scorable items.

Multiple-Choice Questions

Though all the questions on the test are multiple-choice, they may not all be the type of multiple-choice question with which you're familiar. The majority of questions on the test are standard multiple-choice items. The questions are not intended merely to test your command of facts but also your critical-thinking skills. For example, you may be asked to analyze information and compare it with knowledge you have, or make a judgment about it. To acquaint yourself with all the standards and competencies covered on the test, be sure to download Pearson Education's test framework at *www.tx.nesinc.com*.

Some multiple-choice questions are self-contained while others are clustered, branching off a common stimulus. Each question will generally have four choices: A, B, C, and D. (Some questions may have more.) In most cases, the correct answer will require you to identify the single best response. Some questions, however, will require you to select *all* the responses that answer the question correctly. In such instances, you will click check boxes instead of ovals. Also be aware that this test occasionally presents non-traditional formats for multiple-choice items, both to present the information and to allow you to select the best answer. A rundown of these new formats follows.

Unfamiliar Question Types

There are several unfamiliar question types that may show up when you sit for an exam in the TExES series. First, let's look at the kind of question that asks test-takers to identify more than one correct response option to a question.

Example

1. Which of the following led to the American Revolution? Select *all* that apply.

    A. The French and Indian War

    B. The Intolerable Acts

    C. The French Revolution

    D. The Articles of Confederation

Answer and Explanation

Options (A) and (B) are correct. The French and Indian War (A), fought from 1754 to 1763, served as a powerful vehicle by which the British Empire extended its reach in North America. The British sought to impose taxation on the colonists to finance the defense of the newly acquired territory, which aggravated growing discontent with British governance. The Intolerable Acts (B) embraced measures enacted by the British Parliament in 1774 to strike back at the colonists' defiance (e.g., the Boston Tea Party in 1773) of British rule. The move backfired, spawning the First Continental Congress later that year. Simple chronology helps you root out the French Revolution (C) as an incorrect option. The French Revolution, fought from 1787 to 1799, is an anachronistic response that could not have led to the American Revolution, which ended in 1783. Finally, the Articles of Confederation instead of leading to the American Revolution actually *resulted from* it. The Articles were drafted in 1776–77 and adopted by Congress on Nov. 15, 1777, as the first U.S. constitution.

According to the Texas Education Agency, the ELAR 4–8 test may use interactive questions that may include audio or video clips instead of, say, a static map or reading passage.

Item formats may ask you to select the correct answer(s) by any of these means:

1. Click on a sentence or sentences, or on parts of a graphic representation, such as a map, chart, or figure — sometimes termed a "hot spot."

2. Drag and drop answer options into "target" areas in a table, piece of text, or graphic.

3. Use a drop-down menu.

More than anything, these innovative item types require that you read the instructions carefully to be sure you are fully responsive to the question. The TExES ELAR 4–8 test is scored based on the number of questions you answer correctly. With no penalty for guessing, you won't want to leave any item unanswered.

When should the test be taken?

Traditionally, teacher preparation programs determine when their candidates take the required tests for teacher certification. These programs will also clear you to take the examinations and make final recommendations for certification to the Texas State Board for Educator Certification (SBEC).

A candidate seeking ELAR 4–8 certification may take the test at such time as his or her Educator Preparation Program (EPP) determines the candidate's readiness to take the test, or upon successful completion of the EPP, whichever comes first. The EPP will determine readiness through benchmarks and structured assessments of the candidates' progress throughout the preparation program.

The test is generally taken just before graduation. Taking all appropriate TExES examinations is a requirement to teach in Texas, so if you are planning on being an educator, you must take and pass these tests.

How do I register for the test?

To register for the TExES ELAR 4–8 (117) test, you must create an account in the Pearson online registration system. Registration will then be available to you online, 24/7, during the regular, late, and emergency registration periods. Visit Pearson's TExES website at *www.tx.nesinc.com* and follow the instructions.

What's the passing score?

Your score on the TExES ELAR 4–8 will be reported on a 100–300 scale. A scaled score of 240 is set as the minimum passing score. To put this in context, you want to be confident you can answer between 70% and 80% of the questions correctly. As you work your way through our practice tests, scores in this range will suggest that you are sufficiently absorbing the test content. On the actual test, however, some (unknown number) of the questions will be field-tested and thus will not be scored.

If you do not get a passing score on our online diagnostic test or the practice tests, review your online score report and study the detailed explanations for the questions you answered incorrectly. Note which types of questions you answered wrong, and re-examine the corresponding review content. After further review, you may want to retake the practice tests online.

How should I prepare for the test?

It is never too early to start studying for the TExES. The earlier you begin, the more time you will have to sharpen your skills. Do not procrastinate. Cramming is not an effective way to study, since it does not allow you the time needed to learn the test material. It is important for you to choose the time and place for studying that works best for you. Be consistent and use your time wisely. Work out a study routine and stick to it.

When you take REA's diagnostic test and practice tests, simulate the conditions of the actual test as closely as possible. Turn your television and radio off, and go to a quiet place free from distraction. Read each question carefully, consider all answer choices, and pace yourself.

As you complete each test, review your score reports, study the diagnostic feedback, and thoroughly review the explanations to the questions you answered incorrectly. But don't overdo it. Take one problem area at a time; review it until you are confident that you have mastered the material. Give extra attention to the areas giving you the most difficulty, as this will help build your score. Because this TExES test covers content areas in grades 4–8, you should review the state curricula for these grades (Texas Essential Knowledge and Skills) available at *http://www.tea.state.tx.us*.

TExES ELAR 4–8 Study Schedule

Week	Activity
1	Take the online Diagnostic Test at the REA Study Center. Your detailed score report will identify the topics across the exam's two domains where you need the most review.
2–3	Study the review chapters. Use your Diagnostic Test score report to focus your study. Useful study techniques include highlighting key terms and information and taking notes as you read the review. Learn all the competencies by making flashcards and targeting questions you missed on the diagnostic test.
4	Take Practice Test 1 either in the book or online at the REA Study Center. Review your score report and identify topics where you need more review.
5	Reread all your notes, refresh your understanding of the test's competencies and skills, review your college textbooks, and read class notes you've taken. This is also the time to consider any other supplementary materials that your advisor or the Texas Education Agency suggests. Visit the agency's website at *http://www.tea.state.tx.us/*.
6	Take Practice Test 2, either in the book or online at the REA Study Center. Review your score report and restudy the appropriate review section(s) until you are confident you understand the material.

Are there any breaks during the test?

Although there is no designated break during the ELAR test, you do have a little time to use for the restroom or snacking or stretching outside the testing room. The testing time is 4 hours and 45 minutes. But the grand total for the entire appointment period is 5 hours. That leaves 15 minutes for the CAT tutorial and compliance agreement.

Bear in mind the following:

- You need to get permission to leave the testing room.

- The test clock never stops.

- Consult your test admission materials for further details, including updates from Pearson and the Texas Education Agency.

What else do I need to know about test day?

The day before your test, check for any updates in your Pearson testing account. This is where you'll learn of any changes to your reporting schedule or if there's a change in the test site.

On the day of the test, you should wake up early after a good night's rest. Have a good breakfast and dress in layers that can be removed or added as the conditions in the test center require. Arrive at the test center early. This will allow you to relax and collect your thoughts before the test, and will also spare you the anguish that comes with being late. Keep in mind that no one will be admitted into the test center after the test has begun.

Before you leave for the testing site, carefully review your registration materials. Make sure you bring your admission ticket and two unexpired forms of identification. Primary forms of ID include:

- Passport

- Government-issued driver's license

- State or Province ID card

- National ID card

- Military ID card

You may need to produce a supplemental ID document if any questions arise with your primary ID or if your primary ID is otherwise valid but lacks your full name, photo, and signature. Without proper identification, you will not be admitted to the test center.

Strict rules limit what you can bring into the test center to just your ID; we recommend that you consult the Texas Education Agency's "Texas Educator Certification Registration Bulletin" for a complete rundown. You may not bring watches of any kind, cellphones, smartphones, or any other electronic communication devices or weapons of any kind. Scrap paper, written notes, books, and any printed material is prohibited.

No smoking, eating, or drinking is allowed in the testing room. Consider bringing a small snack and a bottle of water to partake of beforehand to keep you sharp during the test.

Good luck on the TExES ELAR 4–8 test!

Proven Test-Taking Strategies for TExES ELAR 4–8

All test-taking strategies have the same practical goal: to show you the best way to answer questions and improve your score.

The strategies and tips that follow come straight from teacher education students who have passed the TExES ELAR 4–8 tests. We have consulted students just like you to see what works best.

Above all, invest the time you need to prepare fully. Studies show that teacher candidates often overestimate their preparedness for a certification exam. Even if you have achieved excellent grades in your teacher preparation program, you still may need to brush up on some concepts that may require more in-depth knowledge. Discussion and review with this book will help you crystallize your understanding and assess your knowledge. Fluency in talking about a concept or topic helps you master it.

The test requires you to supply definitions and apply concepts. To help ensure your success on the exam, take the time to examine your gaps on the questions you miss on the practice exams. Ascertain your familiarity with the concepts upon which those questions are based.

The time you devote to studying will help you on the exam, and the habit of studying will help you in your teaching career.

Remember, there is no one right way to study. Savvy test-takers sharpen their skills while minimizing such obstacles as poor time management and test anxiety. As you assess these strategies, identify what you do in your daily life and adapt your schedule to devote the time you need to address your problem areas.

To make the most of the strategies you use, have an overall plan in mind. You can adjust our strategy list to your needs. Do what best fits your style of learning and method of study.

1. Guess Away

One of the most frequently asked questions about the TExES ELAR test is: Can I guess? The answer: absolutely! There is no penalty for guessing on the test. That means if you refrain from guessing, you may lose points. To guess smartly, use the process of elimination (See Strategy No. 2). Your score is based on the number of correct answers. Answer all questions and take your best guess when you don't know the answer.

2. Process of Elimination

Process of elimination is among the most important test-taking strategies. It means looking at the choices and eliminating the ones you know are wrong, including those partly wrong. Your odds of getting the right answer increase from the moment you eliminate a wrong choice.

3. All In

Review all the response options. Even when you think you've found the correct answer or answers, look at each choice to avoid jumping to conclusions. When asked to choose the *best* answer, make sure your first hunch is really the best one.

4. Choice of the Day

What if you are stumped and thus can't use the process of elimination? Pick a fallback answer. On the day of the test, choose the position of the answer (e.g., the third of the four choices) that you will pick for any question you cannot smartly guess. The laws of probability give you a higher chance of getting an answer right if you stick to one chosen position.

5. Use Choices to Confirm Your Answer

The great thing about multiple-choice questions is that the answer is staring at you. After reading the stem, have an answer in mind. Then use the choices to *confirm* it.

6. Watch the Clock

Active time management is among the most vital point-saving skills. Keep an eye on the timer on your computer screen. Make sure you stay on top of how much time remains, and never spend too much time on a single question. Most multiple-choice questions are worth one raw point. Treat each as if it's the one that will put you over the top. Easy questions count the same as hard ones in building your raw point total. You don't want to lose easy points because you ran out of time.

7. Read, Read, Read

Really read all the multiple-choice options. Even if you initially believe answer choice A is correct, you can misread a question or response option if you're rushing. Don't linger on a question, but avoid giving it short shrift. Slow down and calm down. Verify that your choice is the best, and click on it.

8. Take Notes

Use the erasable sheet(s) you get to make notes to work toward the answer(s). If you use all the scratch paper you're given, you can get more.

9. Isolate Limiters

Pay attention to any limiters in a multiple-choice question stem. These are such words as *initial, best, most* (as in *most appropriate* or *most likely*), *not, least, except, required,* or *necessary.* Especially watch for negative words, such as "Choose the answer that is *not* true." When you select your answer, double-check yourself. Ask how the response fits the limitations established by the stem. Think of the stem as a puzzle piece that fits only the response option(s) that contain the correct answer. Let it guide you.

10. It's Not a Race

Ignore other test-takers. Don't compare yourself to others in the room. Focus on the test items and the time you have left. If someone finishes 30 minutes early, it does not mean the person answered more questions correctly than you did. Stay riveted on *your* test. It's the only one that matters.

11. Confirm Your Click

Many of us are used to rapid-clicking, whether emailing or gaming. Look at the screen to make sure your mouse-click is acknowledged. If your answer doesn't register, you won't get credit. If you want to mark it for review later, that's your call. Before you click "Submit," use the test's review screen to see whether you skipped any questions.

12. Creature of Habit? No Worries.

We are creatures of habit. It's therefore best to follow a familiar pattern of study. Do what's comfortable for you. Set a time and place each day to study for this test. Whether it's 30 minutes at the library or an hour in a secluded corner of your local coffee shop, commit yourself as best you can to a daily schedule. Find quiet places and avoid crowds. Background noise can distract you.

Don't study one subject for too long, either. Take an occasional break for 5 or 10 minutes and treat yourself to a healthy snack or some quick exercise. Then return to study.

13. Knowledge is Power

This book gives you an edge on passing the TExES ELAR test. Make the most of it. Review the sections on how the test is structured, what the directions look like, what types of questions will be asked, and so on. Take the practice tests to learn what the test looks and feels like. Most test anxiety occurs because people feel unprepared and psych themselves out. You can whittle away at anxiety by learning the format of the test and by knowing what types of questions to expect. Simulating the test even once will boost your chances of getting the score you need. The knowledge you gain will also save you time puzzling through what the directions ask.

14. B-r-e-a-t-h-e

Anxiety is neither unusual nor necessarily unwelcome on a test. Just don't let it stifle you. Take a moment to breathe. This won't merely make you feel good. The brain uses roughly three times as much oxygen as muscles in the body do: Give it what it needs. Now consider this: What's the worst that can happen when you take a test? You may have an off day, and despite your best efforts, you may not pass. Well, the good news is that this test can be retaken. Fortunately, the TExES ELAR test is something you can study and prepare for, and in some ways to a greater extent than other tests you've taken throughout your academic career. In fact, study after study has validated the value of test preparation. Yes, there will be questions you won't know, but neither your teacher education program nor state licensing board (which sets its own cut scores) expects you to know everything. When unfamiliar vocabulary appears, don't despair: Use context clues, process of elimination, or your response option of the day (i.e., choose either A, B, C, or D routinely when you need to resort to a guess) to make your choice, and then press ahead. If you have time left, you can always come back to the question later. If not, relax. It is only one question on a test filled with many. Take a deep breath and then exhale. You know this information. Now you're going to show it.

DOMAIN I:
Language Arts, Part I

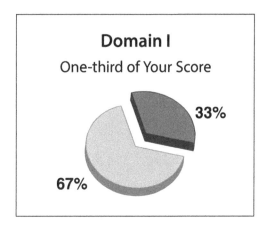

Domain I
One-third of Your Score

33%

67%

Domain I covers the following competencies, which together account for 33% of your score on the TExES ELAR 4–8 test:

- **Competency 001:** Oral Language

- **Competency 002:** Early Literacy Development

- **Competency 003:** Word Identification Skills and Reading Fluency

Domain I covers the following standards:

- **Standard I. Oral Language:** Teachers of students in grades 4–8 understand the importance of oral language, know the developmental processes of oral language, and provide a variety of instructional opportunities for students to develop listening and speaking skills.

- **Standard II. Foundations of Reading:** Teachers of students in grades 4–8 understand the foundations of reading and early literacy development.

- **Standard III. Word Analysis Skills and Reading Fluency:** Teachers understand the importance of word analysis skills (including decoding, blending, structural analysis, sight word vocabulary) and reading fluency, and provide many opportunities for students to practice and improve their word analysis skills and reading fluency.

- **Standard VIII. Assessment of Developing Literacy:** Teachers understand the basic principles of assessment and use a variety of literacy assessment practices to plan and implement instruction.

CHAPTER 3

Competency 001: Oral Language

COMPETENCY 001 (ORAL LANGUAGE)

The teacher understands the importance of oral language, knows the developmental processes of oral language and provides a variety of instructional opportunities for students to develop listening and speaking skills.

A. Knows and teaches basic linguistic concepts (e.g., phonemes, segmentation) and the developmental stages in the acquiring of oral language, including stages in phonology, semantics, syntax, and pragmatics and recognizes that individual variations occur.

B. Knows characteristics and uses of informal and formal oral language assessments and uses multiple, ongoing assessments to monitor and evaluate students' oral language skills.

C. Provides language instruction that acknowledges students' current oral language skills and that builds on these skills to increase students' oral language proficiency.

D. Plans, implements, and adapts instruction that is based on informal and formal assessment of students' progress in oral language development and that addresses the needs, strengths, and interests of individual students, including English-language learners.

E. Recognizes when oral language delays or differences warrant in-depth evaluation and additional help or intervention.

F. Knows how to provide explicit, systematic oral language instruction and supports students' learning and use of oral language through meaningful and purposeful activities implemented one-to-one and in a group.

G. Selects and uses instructional materials and strategies that promote students' oral language development; that respond to students' individual strengths, needs, and interests; that reflect cultural diversity; and that build on students' cultural, linguistic, and home backgrounds to enhance their oral language development.

H. Understands relationships between the development of oral language and the development of reading and provides instruction that interrelates oral and written language to promote students' reading proficiency and learning (e.g., preview-review, discussion, questioning).

I. Knows similarities and differences between oral and written language and how to promote students' awareness of these similarities and differences.

J. Selects and uses instructional strategies, materials, activities and models to strengthen students' oral vocabulary and narrative skills in spoken language and teaches students to connect spoken and printed language.

K. Selects and uses instructional strategies, materials, activities, and models to teach students skills for speaking to different audiences for various purposes and for adapting spoken language for various audiences, purposes, and occasions.

L. Selects and uses instructional strategies, materials, activities, and models to teach students listening skills for various purposes (e.g., critical listening to evaluate a speaker's message, listening to enjoy and appreciate spoken language) and provides students with opportunities to engage in active, purposeful listening in a variety of contexts.

M. Selects and uses instructional strategies, materials, activities, and models to teach students to evaluate the content and effectiveness of their own spoken messages and the messages of others.

N. Knows how to promote students' development of oral communication skills through the use of technology.

Oral Language Acquisition and Development

Before children start going to school, they have made strides in learning to speak and listen. Schooling offers students opportunities to expand their oral language development. Understanding oral language development can provide guidance for teachers.

By age 5, nearly all children can speak and listen in at least one language. Because acquiring oral language occurs so regularly, educators can overlook its significance. However, between birth and the start of school, children engage in the complex, abstract thinking necessary to acquire a language.

The child's environment plays a role. Parents, caretakers, and others surround a child with talking, and children acquire the language and dialect. Moreover, interactions with others provide the child with real reasons for learning how to communicate. However, these people do not formally teach a child with a sequence of lessons. Children have an innate ability to acquire language, and they actively construct their knowledge of language. Rather than just saying words they hear, children discern the underlying principles of language, which makes it possible for them to create and understand utterances they have not heard before.

Research shows that children apply these underlying principles and that adults are not consciously aware of these principles. These principles thus could not be taught. Adults know how to create messages in the language and how to reply to messages from others. But they do not know consciously how letters and words can be combined. Adults know how sounds can be combined when they speak words and how words can be combined when they talk and listen. But they cannot specify the principles.

Research also shows that children do more than just imitate the language they learn. Studies of children's language acquisition have shown that children use forms of language they have not heard. For example, they **overgeneralize** a rule they are learning. A child may say *went* but at a later point say *goed* while learning about adding *ed* to form the past tense. A child may say *feets* learning to form plurals. The child eventually uses the conventional forms, figuring the linguistic rules.

Understanding the nature of this successful language acquisition by children can provide guidance when teachers foster language development. Developing students' oral language should continue throughout their education because it is valuable in its own right, and oral language development can work in tandem with reading and writing development.

Components of Oral Language

In acquiring oral language, children gain mastery of the sounds of the language, the **phonemes**, and how sounds can be combined.

Children also learn **semantics**, or how meaning is generated in a language. This includes not only the meanings of words but also how words, phrases, and sentences combine to make sense. The semantic component includes **morphemes**, or the smallest units of meaning that can be combined. Some morphemes are **free morphemes**. They can occur alone as a word, such as *car*. Other morphemes are **bound morphemes** because these cannot occur alone as a word, such as the *-s* used to form a plural. The word *cats* consists of two morphemes, *cat* and *-s*.

Children also learn how words/morphemes can be placed together. This is **syntax**. Children can combine two words, such as "more juice," to convey meaning, but later they will learn to create complex statements and questions. Growth also includes adding prefixes, suffixes, and inflectional endings (e.g., *-s, -ed, -ing*).

Language development also includes **pragmatics**, or knowing how to use language appropriately in the context. Pragmatics is part of communicative competence, or knowing how to adjust speech depending upon what is appropriate. A person can talk about the same event in different ways, depending upon the audience and whether the setting is informal or formal.

Social Dimensions of Language Use

Children acquire language as part of communicating to connect with others and make sense of experience. The social dimensions of language growth cannot be disentangled from its cognitive growth.

Teachers can provide opportunities for students to grow in oral language when they let students use language for real reasons in the classroom and when they let students talk in different situations for different purposes. Talking also can continue to be a tool for thinking and learning.

Stages of Oral Language Acquisition

When children are around 12–18 months, they typically produce one word. When they enter the telegraphic stage, they use two or more words to create such sentence-like utterances, such as "more juice" to communicate "I want more juice" to the parent. When a child is 4 to 4½ years old, the child's language will become more complex in the statements, questions, and vocabulary (or lexicon) acquired. At 5 years, children can talk easily with others who speak the same language or dialect.

Children vary in when they start talking. Some children start before 12 months, for example. Children also can vary as they continue in oral language development. Some may use more complex sentences at 3½ years, while others may start at 4½ years.

Theories of Language Acquisition

Behaviorist theory maintains that children gradually acquire language by moving from simple to more complex utterances. Children begin with babbling and then say one- or two-word utterances until they can produce longer messages. Children can be positively reinforced in acquiring language, such as when a parent smiles or gives the child a glass of juice when the child says, "juice."

Children move from babbling to one- and two-word utterances to the more complex sentences, and people do respond, but cognitive theorists maintain that behaviorists fail to account for all language acquisition. Children produce and understand language they have never heard. More is entailed than imitation and positive reinforcement.

According to Chomsky (1965), children would not be equipped to produce and understand the infinite number of possibilities of sentences if they relied solely upon input from the environment. Chomsky proposed the notion of humans having a **Language Acquisition Device**. Children are born with Universal Grammar, which is innate and contains all the information needed to acquire the grammar of a language. Children then can acquire the language they hear.

Subsequently, psycholinguists did not totally accept Chomsky's assertion that children are born with Universal Grammar, and they said children might use more general cognitive principles. Children are born with the ability to acquire language, and the development is gradual. When a child hears enough linguistic constructions, the child will discern the patterns.

Important Factors of Oral Language Development in Schooling

Educators can assume that when students reach the middle grades, they know enough about speaking and listening. Teachers can assume that even younger children know enough. Since much must be accomplished in reading and writing, educators may see oral language development as a low priority. However, theory and research shows that students' oral language development affects their development in reading and writing. Effective instruction does not skip oral language development. Students also need school to provide opportunities to grow in using oral language because those opportunities can differ from everyday uses of oral language.

Students proficient in reading and writing have had certain oral language experiences that prepare them for successful reading and writing development. Many students can engage in everyday speaking and listening, but their vocabulary is not strong enough for reading and writing in school. However, a strong vocabulary is only part of what they need for successful reading and writing. Students also must know how to create meaning by learning how to combine words, sentences, or thoughts to develop a mental representation of the message. A thought or sentence mentioned in one part of the text must be combined with others to create meaning.

When students engage in everyday listening, they are not required to understand longer texts. In everyday speaking, students also do not have to compose longer texts. If students listen to longer texts, such as books read aloud, they gain the listening comprehension needed for reading. If students gain experiences in talking when they can compose their thoughts in longer ways, they gain a proficiency needed for writing.

Oral language development also is valuable on its own. The language opportunities that education provides can help expand the oral language at home. As students continue their education, their opportunities for growth in speaking and listening should continue. Education fosters growth by providing opportunities to use everyday and academic language as students learn in subject areas. Education can also contribute in special ways because students also engage in speaking and listening settings that expand audiences, purposes, and situations.

Planning for oral language development does not require teachers to add another subject area. Speaking and listening should be integral to students' experiences. Teachers can ensure that students engage in speaking and listening that enhances the learning of reading and writing as well as specific subjects.

Audience

Teachers can incorporate opportunities for students to engage in situations that vary according to audience. The audience can vary in **size**, for example. The demands of using language differ when talking to another individual, in a small group, or in a whole-class or large group. Audience also can vary in **familiarity**. How well a speaker knows a person provides differences across oral language situations. The audience's **age** also plays a role. Speakers may need to adjust their comments depending upon the age and familiarity of the listeners.

Functions of Language

Halliday (1975) has provided a description of different functions of language, and teachers can use these descriptions to ensure that students engage in using language for different purposes. By engaging in these different functions, students can gain proficiency if they get scaffolding and support:

- Instrumental—to obtain something

- Regulatory—to request or control

- Personal—to express self

- Heuristic—to gain information or explore

- Imaginative—to create

- Representational—to inform

Language Register

In oral and written language development, growth includes knowing how to adjust the level and style of language to the situation. A more formal register is appropriate for some situations, while informal registers are appropriate when communicating with family and friends. By providing students with multiple opportunities to use language in informal and formal settings, students can gain proficiency in using registers.

Fostering Oral Language Development

The curriculum requires speaking and listening development, but teachers often view reading and writing development as the legitimate areas. Educators often assume that native speakers already know what they need for speaking and listening. Students are often expected to work quietly on their own. Although students need to know how to work independently and be productive, they also must learn how to work with others. In the community and the workplace, successful interaction with others—which includes getting and keeping a job—can depend upon proficiency in speaking and listening. Oral language development is thus valuable on its own, and English learners especially can rely upon teachers to help them become proficient. Proficiency in oral language depends upon using language for different purposes, situations, and audiences.

The following guidelines discuss how to foster students' abilities in speaking and listening:

- **Speaking and listening can be developed without sacrificing the learning of subject matter.** Teachers may determine that they do not have time to add speaking and listening to their classes. Teachers also know that formal assessments focus on reading and writing. However, written language experiences can include talking and listening. Learning experiences in which each student works alone by writing can be presented so that students talk about ideas before and after writing, which can make it easier for students to formulate thoughts. Students can work with the teacher and other students in completing various written learning tasks and incorporate speaking and listening. The demonstrations and collaboration provided by speaking and listening can enhance learning. Students can achieve proficiency faster if oral language situations offer support while developing oral language abilities.

- **Make a conscious effort to provide students with opportunities to engage in authentic speaking and listening.** Talking easily with family and friends does not mean a person can talk easily with a potential employer in a job interview. Different language situations place different demands on speakers and listeners. Think about how to let students use language for different purposes and in formal and informal situations. For example, include conversations with other classmates about a reading and then have a panel discussion about the same reading. Provide ways of communicating with different audiences. These include people who are familiar or less familiar with the subject, who are the same age as the students, and who are younger or older. Audiences also can vary in size.

- **Provide modeling.** Students benefit when teachers engage in discussions with them as a group or as individuals. The teacher's modeling expands the adult models in the home and the community. In school, the uses of language can differ, and the adult modeling for a given purpose or type of situation thus may not exist at home.

- **Provide helpful growth in using conventional language rather than focusing upon errors.** Students should learn conventional speech, but teachers should avoid criticizing their dialect or an unconventional way of saying something. Rather than call what the student said "wrong," the teacher can use the conventional language to reply. For example, a student sharing a past event may say, "He goed with me." The teacher could reply, "Oh, it's great that he went with you." The student hears the conventional form but feels safe talking with the teacher. The expressions students use could be what their parents and other loved ones use. Over time, students can acquire more conventional uses of language when given opportunities to use it in school.

- **Let students engage in talking and listening daily as part of routines.** Research on language development tells us that growth in language comes by using language daily. Talking and listening can help students form personal connections, and the social dimensions of learning cannot be disentangled from the cognitive.

- **Focus on what students can do over what they cannot do.** Most students have acquired at least one language by age 5. A student may mispronounce a word or fail to use it conventionally, but most students will eventually use the more conventional forms by talking and listening. Some students are more reticent, and some are more talkative, especially in certain situations. As speaking situations become more familiar, reticent students are apt to talk more, and such students do gain from listening. If teachers let students engage in a range of authentic talking situations, students will grow in using language.

- **Seek advice when needed.** If a student has difficulty hearing or remains far behind peers in communicating, the teacher should seek advice. The student may need the help of professionals who specialize in speech and hearing.

- **Remember that students rely upon their speaking and listening knowledge of a language when learning to read and write in that language.** They do not need to wait to achieve proficiency in speaking to begin reading and writing instruction. But students draw upon known vocabulary as well as how to combine sounds and words when they read and write. Short-changing oral language development hampers growth in reading and writing.

Conditions for Learning Oral and Written Language

Brian Cambourne delineated conditions for learning language based upon his study of children's language development. When these eight conditions for learning exist, children acquire oral language most easily. These following conditions also guide the acquisition of written language:

1. **Immersion**—Students should be immersed in using oral and written language in such authentic ways as reading aloud to students, letting students work in small groups, and providing students with daily opportunities to write.

2. **Demonstrations**—Students need demonstrations of oral and written language. The modeling by the teacher and other students as well as the language of books makes it possible.

3. **Engagement**—Regardless of their proficiency levels, students can engage and see that they can read and write when they use language in a supportive environment.

4. **Expectations**—Maintain high but realistic expectations for each student, knowing they will gain in language development over time.

5. **Responsibility**—With meaningful support, students can be responsible for their learning and make choices about what they read and write even as they adhere to curriculum guidelines.

6. **Approximation**—Students will gain proficiency in using oral and written language when their efforts are valued and they are guided toward accuracy and self-correction.

7. **Use**—Students need multiple opportunities to use oral and written language in a different ways for real reasons.

8. **Response**—Students will gain most when teachers and others listen to them, read their writing, and provide genuine comments.

How Oral and Written Language Development Can Work in Tandem

Speaking and listening contributes to students' growth in reading and writing. By incorporating effective daily instructional practices, teachers can capitalize upon speaking and listening to help their students grow as readers and writers. The practices make an impact when they become part of the routines in classrooms. The growth will take place over time. Gains can be seen immediately, but gains are greater when students become familiar with the instructional practices. Teachers should provide oral language experiences that vary **audiences** and **purposes** as well as call for informal and formal **registers**.

Reading Aloud

A successful reader does more than identify words. Students may pronounce words correctly, but many cannot understand what they are reading when they reach third and fourth grades where the content is longer and fewer pictures provide support. A major cause of difficulty is that students have not always developed the abilities needed for reading longer texts. Developing students' listening comprehension can help them navigate longer texts. They developed the thinking they need when they gained listening comprehension.

When students talk with others outside of school, they encounter brief segments of language. With friends and family, the exchanges are often short. Through these oral language experiences, students gain much, but they do not gain the listening comprehension for successful reading. Without developing listening comprehension, students cannot sustain attention or combine ideas to create understanding when they encounter longer segments of language.

Students' oral language experiences will not offer them the range of vocabulary they encounter in reading. However, students can develop listening comprehension and vocabulary by reading quality literature aloud. Quality literature for youth will engage students and develop vocabulary and comprehension.

By reading different types of quality literature aloud to students, teachers can help them sustain attention and create understanding as they encounter longer passages and different literature. Students should read on their own daily, but they also gain when they hear teachers read aloud daily. Their listening comprehension will also increase over time.

Reading aloud is also critical for showing students that reading can be rewarding. Assigned reading may not work with reluctant readers. Conversely, if teachers read quality literature that students enjoy hearing, reluctant readers can see a reason to read on their own.

Writing Conferences

Writing conferences with students can help students talk about a topic. This provides scaffolding for writing. Besides the individual conference, whole-class writing conferences can support writing development. Classmates tell one another what they liked or learned and then ask genuine questions. This helps the writer see passages that need development.

Buddy Reading or Partner Work

Reading with partners lets students participate in productive reading while providing oral language development. When the students and teacher work together or when students work in small groups, they can learn content as well as how to learn.

Grand Conversations

Traditionally, reading assignments to measure understanding have entailed writing answers to questions or completing packets. The same learning objectives can be met by engaging daily in grand conversations with students. Instead of question-answer recitations, the teacher and students share their thoughts that emerge from the reading. This works well when the teacher models sharing and participates in the conversation.

Students enjoy talking about books. Students' comments often show they can think at high levels about what they have read. In sharing their personal responses, students make inferences, evaluate ideas, and share connections to their lives and other readings. These conversations also can provide the basis for subsequent discussions of literary elements in a work.

Talking also can provide support for students as they learn how to write about what they have read. The students' development in oral composing will help them to compose when writing because they have gained practice in formulating their thoughts.

Retelling

After students have read a selection independently, the teacher can ask the group to retell what was read before having a grand conversation as a way of ensuring the students understand and remember what took place in the reading selection. This should be a casual conversation so that students feel safe to talk. If students omit a part, the teacher can add it to provide modeling and accuracy (e.g., "Yes, that happened, and just before that . . ."). If students stop, the teacher can provide a prompt, such as "What happened next?" to encourage them. If students are reluctant to start, the teacher can first model and then invite them to share.

Retelling can encourage students to pay attention to the text when they read. If teachers do this with each reading, students can gain in proficiency in remembering and retelling.

Retelling also can be used to assess whether students have understood a reading. In retelling, a student may not show higher levels of comprehension, but they can be developed through the conversations. Recalling what was read through retelling also helps to make inferences, evaluations, synthesis, and applications.

Technology and Audio-Assisted Reading

Students can get additional experiences by listening to audiobooks, which provide opportunities to expand vocabulary as well as listening comprehension.

Cooperative Learning

Students can make greater gains in vocabulary and overall oral language development by participating in small-group work and by working in pairs. These learning experiences also can provide scaffolding for students who need more help before completing a task independently. English learners as well as other students can profit from cooperative learning.

"Turn and Talk"

Traditionally, teachers have asked an entire group of students a question or set of questions to foster learning. Although students are often reluctant to share because they lack confidence in talking to a whole group, they can gain confidence and improve ability when first talking and listening with another classmate.

Teachers can use "turn and talk" when they want students to think more about a topic. Instead of answering the teacher's question, students turn and talk to a partner to help crystallize their thinking and develop their oral language abilities. After talking with a partner, they can share their conversation with the whole group.

For instance, after students have learned in science about the function of the bark of the tree, the teacher could ask them to turn and talk about one thing they learned. Then the students could share and talk as a group. The teacher also could list ideas to review in later lessons of the unit on trees.

"Turn and talk" works best when the teacher makes sure all students have partners who can help them grow in speaking and listening. It may be best to place a reticent student with one who is confident and supportive. Teachers also should help students learn about how to listen politely.

A demonstration of how to "turn and talk" also helps students. Many teachers use this strategy when students can address this topic in 30 to 60 seconds. Letting students talk with a partner or work together could also be done for a longer time.

Assessing Listening and Speaking in K–12

Performance-based activities can provide students with opportunities to use language. They also can provide a context for gathering information about a student's proficiency in listening and speaking. These listening and speaking activities work best as an ongoing part of learning in the class. Students' speaking abilities also can be assessed in the classroom with a structured checklist identifying specific features that teachers want to observe. The checklist could be organized to include social as well as academic situations and/or proficiency levels.

Example of a Speaking and Listening Checklist:

- ✓ Listens to others during whole-class conversations

- ✓ Listens to others during small-group conversations

- ✓ Contributes to whole-class conversations

- ✓ Contributes to small-group conversations

- ✓ Talks with individual students

- ✓ Speaks clearly

- ✓ Uses courteous language

- ✓ Uses appropriate social registers

- ✓ Provides comments that relate to the topic

- ✓ Asks questions related to topic

Language Assessment of Limited English Proficient Students

The Texas Education Agency (TEA) designed the Texas English Language Proficiency Assessment System (TELPAS) to assess the progress that limited English proficient (LEP) students make in learning the English language. The federal government requires English language proficiency assessments in grades K–12 to evaluate the progress of English language learners (ELLs).

The TELPAS assesses proficiency in listening, speaking, reading and writing. For students in grades K–1, the TELPAS includes ratings based upon classroom observations. Students in grades 2–12 get a score on the multiple-choice questions of the TELPAS reading test. Speaking and listening proficiency ratings are based upon classroom observations, and writing scores are based upon a collection of each student's writing.

Students get a rating based upon four levels of English proficiency:

Beginning—These students have a small vocabulary of common words and little ability to use English in academic settings. Students often communicate by using English they memorized.

Intermediate—These students can communicate about familiar topics and understand some conversations, but they may not understand all the details. They can use basic English, and they need language support to understand.

Advanced—These students can understand most of what they hear in social situations, but they may have difficulty with unfamiliar vocabulary and grammar. They can understand and use grade-appropriate academic English when they have support.

Advanced High—These students can communicate in most situations. They can use grade-appropriate academic English with little support even when encountering new information.

English Language Proficiency Standards (ELPS)

ELLs can learn English and new subject matter of disciplines. English Language Proficiency Standards (ELPS) delineate what ELLs must know and do to become proficient in academic English. The ELPS are used across the curriculum for learning in disciplines, and the TEKS requires teachers to integrate these student expectations as they teach subjects to ELLs.

The ELPS address expectations for student mastery of such learning strategies as listening, speaking, reading, and writing. ELLs thus must be able to learn in a discipline and make gains in speaking, listening, reading, and writing. Supporting ELLs requires making sure ELLs have many targeted opportunities to use English across the curriculum.

Using pictures and gestures can help ELLs new to English. Providing scaffolding and support for learning in disciplines is necessary for all students, but especially ELLs.

Supporting students includes making sure of the following:

1. Students use language daily.

2. Language use builds upon what is known in English and about a topic.

3. Students experience interesting learning opportunities.

4. Students can participate because the pacing and level of difficulty of the learning experiences is appropriate.

These methods support work for all students. ELLs and native speakers thus can participate in the same learning experiences, but more scaffolding will be needed for ELLs, depending upon each student's language proficiency.

Competency 002: Early Literacy Development

COMPETENCY 002: EARLY LITERACY DEVELOPMENT

The teacher understands the foundations of early literacy development.

A. Understands the significance of phonological and phonemic awareness for reading and typical patterns in the development of phonological and phonemic awareness and recognizes that individual variations occur.

B. Understands elements of the alphabetic principle (e.g., letter names, graphophonemic knowledge, the relationship of the letters in printed words to spoken language) and typical patterns of students' alphabetic skills development and recognizes that individual variations occur.

C. Understands that comprehension is an integral part of early literacy.

D. Understands that not all written languages are alphabetic and that many alphabetic languages are more phonetically regular than English and knows the significance of this for students' literacy development in English.

E. Understands that literacy acquisition generally develops in a predictable pattern from pre-reading (emergent literacy) to conventional literacy and recognizes that individual variations occur.

F. Understands that literacy development occurs in multiple contexts through reading, writing, and the use of oral language.

G. Knows characteristics of informal and formal literacy assessments (e.g., screening devices, criterion-referenced state tests, curriculum-based reading assessments, informal reading inventories, norm-referenced tests).

H. Knows how to select, administer, and use results from informal and formal assessments of literacy acquisition.

I. Knows how to use ongoing assessment to determine when a student needs additional help or intervention to bring the student's performance to grade level, based on state content and performance standards for reading in the Texas Essential Knowledge and Skills (TEKS).

J. Analyzes students' errors in reading and responds to individual students' needs by providing focused instruction to promote literacy acquisition.

K. Selects and uses instructional materials that build on the current language skills of individual students, including English-language learners, to promote development from emergent literacy to conventional literacy.

L. Selects and uses instructional strategies, materials, activities and models to teach students listening skills for various purposes (e.g., critical listening to evaluate a speaker's message, listening to enjoy and appreciate spoken language) and provides students with opportunities to engage in active, purposeful listening in a variety of contexts.

M. Selects and uses instructional strategies, materials, activities and models to teach students to evaluate the content and effectiveness of their own spoken messages and the messages of others.

N. Knows how to promote students' development of oral communication skills through the use of technology.

Phonological and Phonemic Awareness

Before children learn to read print in an alphabetic language, such as English and Spanish, they must understand that words consist of speech sounds, or phonemes. In reading, they must account for the sounds as they remember the word. **Phonemes** are the smallest parts of a spoken word's sound to make a difference in the word's meaning. For example, changing the first phoneme in the word *mop* from /m/ to /t/ changes the word from *mop* to *top* and thus the meaning. (A letter between slash marks shows the phoneme, or sound, that the letter represents, not the name of the letter. For example, the letter *h* represents the sound /h/.)

In learning to speak, children learn the phonemes of their language and which sounds can be combined to create words. This knowledge is not conscious. In learning to read and write, however, children must have a conscious knowledge that words consist of sounds because they must account for the sounds when they relate letters to them. Children can use letter–sound knowledge for reading if they know that words consist of blended sounds and that words can be segmented into individual sounds.

Phonological awareness is understanding that spoken language can be divided into smaller parts as well as knowing how to manipulate these parts. Phonological awareness moves on a continuum from larger to smaller and from less to more complex language units as follows:

1) word level, including appreciation of **rhyme and alliteration**

2) syllable-level counting, and blending and segmenting **syllables** of words

3) phonemic awareness—hearing, identifying, and blending and segmenting **onset** (all sounds before the vowel) **and rime** (e.g., "b" and "at" for "bat")

4) blending and segmenting individual phonemes of words or changing individual phonemes in words to create new words

Phonemic awareness is the highest level of phonological awareness, and phonemic awareness activities are those that focus upon individual sounds of words and manipulating the sounds. Phonological awareness activities feature words and syllables, including onset and rime.

Development of phonological awareness in rhyming can begin when children are 4. Children in kindergarten typically start activities in which they blend and then segment onset and rime. Between kindergarten and first grade, children typically can blend and then segment individual phonemes of words.

Phonological awareness can be assessed to determine such specific skills as follow:

Rhyming: Which word rhymes with "cat"? → **"bat"**

Syllable Splitting: The teacher says "running" and the child taps a finger two times.

Onset and Rime: → The onset of "cat" is /**k**/, the rime is /**at**/.

Phonemic awareness can be assessed to determine such specific skills as these:

Phoneme identity of initial sounds: Which word has a different beginning sound?

Phoneme identity of final sounds: Which word has a different ending sound?

Blending: What word is made from the sounds /k/ /a/ /t/? → **"cat"**

Phonemic segmentation: What are the sounds in "cat"? → /**k**/ /a/ /t

Phoneme deletion: What is "cat" without the /k/? → **"at"**

Phoneme manipulation: What word do you have when you change the /t/ in **"cat"** to an /n/? → **"can"**

Both phonemic awareness and phonological awareness deal with sounds in oral language. **Phonics** relates sounds to print, however, and early writing experiences can **foster phonemic awareness**. When children use **"invented" spelling,** they write a representation of each sound in a word even if the word is misspelled conventionally (e.g., *mkrone* for *macaroni*). If children cannot hold a pencil, they can use letter tiles or word processing to spell. Reading poems daily for shared reading can foster sensitivity to rhyming. Early instruction in letter-sound correspondences and seeing word families (e.g., *bat, cat, hat, sat*) as part of phonics instruction strengthens phonemic awareness.

Phonemic awareness can be assessed and developed. Recognizing the same initial sounds is easier than isolating a sound. Blending sounds to say a word is easier than hearing a word and then segmenting the word into its individual sounds. Phonemic awareness can be refined by the following steps:

- Recognizing words that start with the same sound

- Isolating the initial sound of a word

- Isolating the final sound of a word

- Blending or combining individual sounds to say a word

- Segmenting or breaking down a word to say the individual sounds

Guidelines for Assessment and Instruction

- Oral language abilities are a prerequisite for phonological awareness. Children must have listening skills, understand what others say, share their ideas, and produce sentences.

- Teachers often use a puppet or stuffed animal for phonemic awareness activities. For example, the teacher may say, "Mr. Dog speaks slowly. Let's see if we can tell what he says: /s/ /u/ /n/." Children say the word or point to a picture to show they can blend individual sounds.

- Before an activity, teachers should model so that children understand the task. Children may seem to lack phonemic awareness when they just fail to understand what the teacher asked them to do.

- Children's abilities vary, but many will progress with instruction, and the child thus may not have a disability. If they are uncertain, teachers should seek advice from specialists if a child fails to progress.

- Phonemic awareness activities can be beneficial but should not replace early literacy instruction. Children need classroom experiences with print. Children gain phonemic awareness as they encounter print and account for such sounds, as the following: using "invented" spelling at the writing center, engaging in shared reading and choral reading in which word patterns and rhyming words are seen and heard, and learning letter–sound correspondences.

- Start with continuous sounds that are easier to blend and can be held continuously, such as *a, e, f, i, l, m, n, o, r, s, u, v, w, y, z*. Stops sounds are not held continuously but rather have an "uh" sound: *b, c, d, g, h, j, k, p, q, t, x*.

- Start with easier tasks, such as rhyming, then move to noting syllables, onset and rime, and phonemic awareness activities.

- Start with larger units of language, such as onset-rime, and move to individual phonemes.

- Children's "invented" spelling should not be discouraged. Accounting for each letter in a word develops phonemic awareness.

- Some teachers assume that misspelling the word will impede spelling development, but children who use "invented" spelling make strong progress in spelling. The "errors" drop as children encounter conventional spelling. Children also account for many of the letters that do belong in the correct spelling of the word. They are thus making progress in learning to spell with "invented" spelling.

Alphabetic Principle

With understanding that words consist of individual speech sounds, children must understand that speech sounds are represented in print by letters or a group of letters. This is the alphabetic principle. Children learn that they represent speech sounds through letters when they read and write. A group of graphs or characters represents the phonemes (sounds) of the language. Spanish also relies upon the alphabetic principle, and the letters used in English and Spanish are based upon the Latin alphabet. Spanish is highly regular in how sounds relate to letters. English and French, however, are examples of languages in which the relation between sounds and symbols can be irregular. Other alphabet systems of the world include Russian, Korean, Hindi, and Greek.

Arabic and Hebrew are consonant-based systems whose alphabet represents consonants and some vowels, and vowels can be represented by diacritics. A syllabary writing system represents syllables, which typically is a consonant and a single vowel. Pictographs and ideographs are complex systems in which symbols represent sounds and meaning, objects of the world, ideas, and abstractions.

As children acquire the alphabetic principle in English, they learn the sounds associated with specific letters—or phonics, which relates sounds to letters. Through phonics instruction, children learn to apply the alphabetic principle as they learn relationships between sounds and letters. Not all words in English have regular spellings that apply phonics generalizations. Students then identify words in other ways, such as knowing the word automatically or reading parts of the word to decode the entire word (e.g., *disappear,* which can split into "dis," meaning "to do the opposite of," and "appear," meaning "to come into view." Thus, *disappear* is the opposite of "becoming visible."). However, students must understand the alphabetic principle to progress in reading.

To progress in the alphabetic principle, students must identify letters easily. Before students can improve their reading vocabulary, they must learn to **identify lowercase and uppercase/capital letters.** Learning to write letters is the best way to help children learn to identify them. Beginning readers can read words without identifying any of the letters. However, remembering a large stack of words requires knowing the letters of the word to aid retention. Identifying letters is thus part of early reading instruction.

Stages of Reading Acquisition

Students move through stages of reading development and develop at different paces. Within a given classroom, students can be at different stages and their knowledge can vary.

In the first stages of reading development, students learn to decode words. Instruction in spelling and reading focuses on making gains in letter and word identification skills: sight vocabulary, phonics, structural analysis or word parts, and using context. Students learn to use sources of information or cues as well as learning strategies. **Emergent**, **Progressing**, and **Transitional** Stages are the first stages characterized by learning how to identify words. At the **Fluent** Stage, students have mastered word identification.

When students reach the Fluent Stage, they then still profit from guided reading or small-group instruction. Instruction focuses on vocabulary development and sophisticated reading abilities because students know how to decode well. Students should be reading a variety of types of literature, including informational texts. Teachers should devote more time to independent reading, but students still gain from hearing books read aloud because it increases their listening comprehension and shows them what books offer. Students also must be shown how to read to learn in different disciplines and shown that literary nonfiction can be just as enjoyable as fiction.

After a teacher introduces a text, students in beginning stages read softly or silently. Fluent readers may read the section independently, and the group then meets later to discuss the selection. Instruction also focuses on understanding literary terms and techniques as well as how to read informational texts.

Emergent Stage

Emergent readers:

- know that written language presents a message
- have progressed in concepts of print in knowing that print moves from the left, from the top, and can make a return sweep
- may be able to distinguish a letter from a word
- can make a voice-print match by pointing with a finger
- can turn pages and pretend read (i.e., imitating reading behaviors, a practice that serves to develop children's interest in reading by having them attend to the details involved in reading)
- may use some letter sounds for the beginning and ending of words
- may know some high-frequency words
- can use picture clues

- can connect to the text by using oral language and knowledge of story structure

- start by reading books with one or two lines of print with predictable sentence patterns and illustrations that provide support.

Progressing Stage

Progressing readers:

- are developing a knowledge of high-frequency words they know automatically

- may begin by reading simple sentences but later include more sentence patterns

- can read stories with a beginning, middle, and end

- attend to punctuation

- can search for cues and self-correct

- start by reading multiple lines of print with some similar sentence patterns and illustration with support.

Transitional Stage

Transitional readers:

- know a large number of high-frequency words automatically

- are more adept at using phonics (letter-sound correspondences) and structural analysis (word parts) for word identification

- use sources of information as they identify words by using knowledge of visual cues, meaning cues, and language structure (how words go together)

- become more proficient at monitoring their reading

- understand how to use punctuation marks in reading fluently

- read longer, complex texts with some support from illustrations

- read fiction, poetry, and informational texts.

Fluent Stage

Fluent readers:

- use all sources of information to identify words quickly and self-correct

- consistently monitor for understanding

- read fluently

- can read challenging vocabulary

- adjust their reading rate depending upon the purpose

- read different genres

- can discuss the text and use details from the text to support comments

- understand and apply literary terms

- become more proficient in reading to learn from informational texts

Role of Instruction

Students rely on effective instruction to reach their potential as readers. Teachers can provide sound learning experiences that meet students' needs while showing them that literacy experiences can be rewarding. Effective instruction accounts for the **student's ability** and the **demands of the text** while also **providing support to help the student succeed.**

Through **reading aloud,** teachers can help students gain an understanding of how written language works and how reading can be rewarding. Through **small-group instruction,** teachers can help students increase their ability to identify words, read independently, and discuss texts. Students can apply skills by **reading independently** daily. When students cannot read independently for long periods, they can engage in reading through other experiences, such as **buddy reading** or **audio-assisted reading.**

Importance of Comprehension Development

Comprehension development is important from the outset. If instruction fails to focus on comprehension as part of early literacy instruction, students risk becoming "word callers" who can identify words with little or no understanding of what they read.

Beginning readers will read simple texts with words repeated because of their limited ability to decode. Repeated words help them to gain a sight vocabulary or know a word immediately. These shorter texts, which are often supported by illustrations, do not make the demands on comprehension that longer texts will make in middle and upper grades.

Teachers can develop comprehension by reading aloud texts longer than those which students can read. Teachers also can encourage students to monitor their understanding as they decode by thinking about what would make sense rather than solely focusing upon print. By asking students to retell what they read, teachers can show students that comprehension is needed for reading.

Sources of Information in Proficient Reading

Proficient readers use sources of information or use cues when they read. Teachers can help students use all sources of information or cueing systems when they know what these sources of information are and can assess students' oral reading.

- **Visual cues** entail using print for word identification. Phonics, structural analysis (or morphemic analysis), and sight words help students use **visual cues** to read.

- **Meaning** entails paying attention to what would make sense in identifying a word. When students rely on what they know about the **semantics** of language, they are using **meaning cues**. They are paying attention to what makes sense.

- **Structure cues** (or language structure cues) entail using knowledge of **syntax** or how words can be combined in English.

If students are learning to speak in English, they will have more difficulty using their knowledge of semantics of English or meaning cues. English language learners also will not be as adept at using knowledge of syntax or language structure. They are less certain of how words can be combined in a language. However, if teachers read aloud to students and provide oral language development experiences, students learning English will progress in using meaning and structure cues.

Analyzing Oral Reading Errors

Teachers can help students use all sources of information or cueing systems when they know what to observe when assessing students' oral reading. Students' oral reading errors are miscues that can reveal which cues a student is not using.

- **Visual cues** entail using print for word identification. The student will notice the letter-sound correspondences in the initial, middle, and final position of words in using phonics. The student may use structural analysis or word parts to identify a word, and a student may identify the word by using sight words.

In this example of a miscue, the student is not paying attention to print in word identification.

> **Student:** After school, Fred **wanted** to go to the mall.
> **Text:** After school, Fred **decided** to go to the mall.

The student substituted the word *wanted* for *decided*. The student **did not use any visual cues** in identifying this word.

In this example of a miscue, the student **pays attention to some, but not all, visual cues in identifying a word.**

> **Student:** Next week we will **combine** leaves we find for our science unit.
> **Text:** Next week we will **collect** leaves we find for our science unit.

The student substituted the word *combine* for *collect*. The student made a miscue or oral reading error, but the student **did use some visual cues** in identifying this word.

- **Meaning cues** entail paying attention to what would make a sentence, given the sentence the student is reading as well as the context of the story.

In this example of a miscue, the student **is paying attention to meaning**.

> **Student:** After school, Fred **wanted** to go to the mall.
> **Text:** After school, Fred **decided** to go to the mall.

The student **is not using visual cues**, but the student **is using meaning cues**.

In this example of a miscue, the student **is not paying attention to meaning**.

> **Student:** After school, Fred went to the mall with his **freeze**.
> **Text:** After school, Fred went to the mall with his **friends**.

The student is using some visual cues (i.e., the consonant blend *fr*), but the student is not using meaning cues because what the student says does not make sense.

- **Structure cues** entail using language structure or how words can be combined in conventional language.

In this example of a miscue, the student **is not using (language) structure cues.**

> **Student:** After school, Fred **depended** to go to the mall.
> **Text:** After school, Fred **decided** to go to the mall.

The student is using some visual cues (i.e., the *de* and the *ed)*, but the student is not using structure cues. What the student says is not how words are combined in conventional English.

The student also is not using meaning cues. What the student says does not make sense. Frequently when students fail to use meaning cues, they also fail to use structure cues.

Responding to Students' Oral Reading Miscues (Errors)

Proficient readers use cues or sources of information when they read. Teachers can help students use all cueing systems when they know how to assess students' oral reading. Teachers can analyze students' errors to inform instruction.

Teachers should provide an immediate prompt when students make a miscue. The prompt should encourage students to self-correct by using visual, meaning, and structure cues. Students improve with an effective prompt. The teacher should listen to one student read aloud while other students read silently during guided or small-group reading instruction.

Guidelines for Responding to Miscues/Oral Reading Errors

- **Students may make miscues because they are hurrying.** They may think fast reading is better, and teachers should encourage them to read with expression at an appropriate pace.

  Respond with a prompt that helps the student gain independence in reading. Students will confront unknown words as they read, including in state exams as well as texts they read outside of school. If students use the first letter sound(s) of a word and the rest of the words in the sentence (context—i.e., clues), they can decode most unknown words and continue reading.

- **Do not ask students to "sound it out."** This approach is unreliable because many English words do not follow phonics generalizations and cannot be "sounded out." For example, *said* does not follow the rule for *ai* as does *wait* and *sail* and *come* does not follow the rule for the long *o* sound as does *home.*

- **Do not immediately tell students the unknown word.** This leads to overreliance upon the teacher and thinking that someone must supply unknown words.

- **Encourage students to read to the end of the sentence before providing a prompt.** When students make a miscue, they may self-correct at the end of the sentence. If students do not know a word, encourage them to read to the end of the sentence before providing a prompt. Students then can use the full context of the sentence to identify the word.

- **Use the same wording for a prompt so that students can internalize the wording over time to monitor their reading.** If teachers use the same wording, students will self-correct and try to figure unknown words rather than give up.

- **If the student's miscue makes sense, the teacher should encourage the child to discuss troubleshooting strategies while also encouraging the student to use all visual cues.** A simple prompt can help students identify the meaning of the unknown word while also internalizing wording: "That makes sense, but look more carefully at the word."

- **If the student's miscue does not make sense, the teacher can encourage using all cues and comprehension monitoring:** "Does that make sense?"

- **If a student still does not know a word, determine whether the word can be identified by using initial consonant sounds and the context of the sentence.** Then point this out to the student: "This word starts with *w.* Think about what word could start with *w* that would make sense in this sentence."

- **Some words need to be identified by also using visual cues at the middle or end of the word,** such as in this situation:

Text:	Where did he go?
Student:	When did he go?
Teacher Prompt:	"That makes sense, but look more carefully at the end of this word."

- **When students do not recognize multisyllabic words, the teacher can use structural analysis to help them break the word into parts.** This includes pointing out the prefix, suffix, and/or endings (such as -s, -es, -ies for plurals and -s, -ed, -ing for inflectional endings) for the base word. Teachers also may ask students to read one word of a compound word and then the next.

- **Teachers may be unable to listen to all students read each day, but they can be systematic in listening to students read aloud during guided reading or small-group instruction.** The teacher's prompts serve as instruction because students internalize the questions and self-correct. To have time to listen to individual students read aloud while the other students read silently, teachers can tell students they can read the section again or read ahead to the next chapter of a longer work.

- **Notes can be useful. Jot down what you observe when hearing a student read aloud.** Then provide instruction based upon the students' miscues.

Running Records

Running Records is an assessment tool in which teachers listen to students read aloud to learn how to meet their needs. The teacher records what students say via shorthand. The notations represent what the students did or said for each word they read, whether they (1) correctly read a word, (2) made an oral reading error or miscue, (3) repeated a word or series of words, (4) self-corrected, or (5) were unable to try to read a word.

At the beginning of a year, running records can help assign students to a guided reading or small instructional group. A group must be homogenous so that students in a group have similar needs. **Similarly, running records can help find the best level of book for students.** If students read a text that is too hard, they cannot use all sources of information or understand what they are reading. Teachers can use benchmark books or selections that correspond to different reading levels.

Teachers can use running records throughout the year to make sure students are progressing in the books they have read once or twice during their guided reading instruction. Teachers can assess progress when they listen to a student read aloud while other students read silently during guided reading. They can assess at other times as well.

Teachers also can analyze a student's miscues shown in running records to determine which instruction a student needs. Running records can document a student's progress over time.

Running Records provide insights into students' oral reading. Comprehension of a text can be determined by asking students to retell what was read or by asking them about the text. If students are proficient in word identification, teachers will rely on assessing students' comprehension in determining the level of text and how to meet students' needs.

Taking a Running Record

- Select the text to use for assessment. If forming reading groups, different levels may be needed. If the assessment is for reading instruction in guided reading groups, the text should be current or one recently finished.

- Students need not read an entire story or book. Students should read enough for the teacher to assess each student's reading ability, which can be 100 to 200 words.

- Use a blank sheet of notebook paper or Running Record form. Make notes on the paper, not on copies of the reading.

- Write the student's name, the title of the selection, the date on the sheet or form.

- Sit next to the student to see each word as the students reads.

- Use the notation system and mark the sheet or form for each word in the text to show what the student did.

- Arrange the marks to match how the words on the page are arranged. Move from the left, starting a new line when the text does. Show page numbers so that you will know what the student said.

- Use a horizontal line to show new page numbers.

- Use a check mark to show each word read correctly. The following example shows the words in the text, what the student read, and what the running record would be.

Text:	After school, we are going to my friend's house.
Student:	After school, we are going to my friend's house.
Running Record:	✓ ✓ ✓ ✓ ✓ ✓ ✓ ✓ ✓

- Use other marks to show errors. What the student says goes above a line, and what the text says or the teacher says goes below the line. Do not include punctuation.

Text:	After school, we are going to my friend's house.
Student:	After stool, we are going to my friend's house.
Running Record:	✓ stool ✓ ✓ ✓ ✓ ✓ ✓
	school

Students' Reading, Notation, and Error Count

- **Accurate Reading**—The student reads the word correctly.

    ✓

Types of Miscues Counted as an Error:

- **Substitution**—The student says a word different from the word in the text. The teacher's substitution is counted as an error unless the student self-corrects. Names are counted wrong one time in the text.

Student	depended
Text	decided

- **Omission**—The student leaves out the word in the text.

Student	__
Text	a

- **Insertion**—The student adds or inserts a word not in the text.

Student	the
Text	__

Not Counted as an Error:

- **Repetition**—A repetition takes place when a student repeats a word or section of words. A repetition is not counted as an error because the student knows the words, but this behavior is noted because the student may be unable to recognize a word automatically. A line is drawn over the word or words repeated.

  ⌐————————————R
  ✓ ✓ ✓ ✓ ✓ ✓ ✓

- **Self-Correction**—The student substitutes a word but then corrects the error. This is not counted as an error, but it is noted.

Student	depended | SC
Text	decided |

Intervention—One Error:

- **Appeal (asks for help)/Told**—Each word told is counted as an error. During assessment, the teacher strives not to tell a student a word or give prompts for word identification to obtain an accurate assessment of what the student can do. Teachers provide prompts when listening to students read aloud individually during guided reading or small-group work because this is instruction. When assessing by administering a running record, the teacher wants to determine how to meet students' needs. However, when a student does not make an attempt, the teacher tells the word after waiting 5 to 10 seconds for the student to figure it out.

Student	d- | A
Text	decided | T

Scoring a Running Record

Scoring a running record is based upon the total of correctly read words. Running words (RW) are the total number of words the student reads. Errors (E) represent the number of miscues counted as an error.

The accuracy rate is found by determining the percentage of words read correctly out of the total number of words read: RW – E/RW × 100

Example: RW = 100
Errors = 2

Accuracy Rate Formula

Step 1. Running Words – Total Errors

$$\boxed{100} - \boxed{2} = \boxed{98}$$

Step 2. Score ÷ Running Words × 100 = % Accuracy

$$\boxed{98} \div \boxed{100} \times 100 = \boxed{98}\%$$

The accuracy rate can help determine whether a text is at the independent, instructional, or frustration level.

95%–100%	Independent Level (easy)
90%–94%	Instructional Level (can be read with support/instruction)
below 90%	Frustration Level (too difficult)

Analyzing Miscues

By analyzing the miscues of a running record, the teacher can determine the sources of information a student is using. A student using **visual cues** is using what is printed in the book to identify words.

Students use their knowledge of (language) **structure cues** when they use what they know about how words combine in the language to figure an unknown word, such as in the following:

We will ride to school on the _____.

Although the student may not know terms, the student would know the words that could fit for the unknown word (i.e., the blank), such as knowing intuitively that the word *the* signals a certain kind of word to follow (a noun). Knowing how words can combine is using **knowledge of syntax,** or language structure.

Students use their knowledge of **meaning** when they consider what would make sense given the context of a reading selection and a particular sentence, such as in the following: We will ride to school on the _____. Because the student knows about ways to go to school and that it would not make sense to ride *on* a car, the student knows that the unknown word will fit these criteria. Using meaning is using **knowledge of semantics.**

If a student fails to use **visual cues**, the student may have a problem in word identification. Instruction in phonics, structural analysis (or morphemic analysis), and sight words help students improve in using **visual cues.**

If a student fails to use **structure cues**, the student may need help in using context clues or may need more oral language development to gain expertise in English syntax. Similarly, if a student fails to use **meaning cues**, the student may need help in using context clues or may need more oral language development to gain expertise in English. The student also may need to monitor comprehension.

Example of Analysis of a Miscue in a Running Record

Student: *I have a bag dog.*
Text: *I have a big dog.*

✓ ✓ ✓ bag ✓
      big

  A. Meaning cues: No, the miscue does not make sense or does not show that the student is using knowledge of semantics.

  B. Structure cues: No, the miscue does not show using knowledge of syntax.

  C. Visual cues: Yes, the miscue indicates the reader has used visual cues because of using initial and final consonant letters.

  D. Needed instruction: The student used short *a* and did not know short *i*. Short *i* thus must be taught.

Student: *This vase is under because it is broken.*
Text: *This vase is unacceptable because it is broken.*

✓ ✓ ✓   under   ✓ ✓ ✓ ✓
      unacceptable

  A. Meaning cues: No, the miscue does not make sense or show that the student is using knowledge of semantics.

  B. Structure cues: No, the miscue does not show using knowledge of syntax.

C. Visual cues: Yes, the reader used *un* when trying to identify the word.

D. Needed instruction: The student must be taught how to identify multisyllabic words by examining the prefix and base word. The student also may not know the base word, *acceptable*.

Informal Assessments

Such informal assessment as **running records** provides data to inform instruction daily. Other informal assessments also are beneficial. Because they provide specific feedback about a student. The assessments can help revise instruction, determine abilities at designated times of the year, monitor progress, and share progress with parents.

Letter Identification—Students get a sheet with uppercase and lowercase letters arranged from left to right. The letters are not presented alphabetically. The teacher points to the letters and the student identifies them. Students also can be assessed to determine whether they can write the letter. The teacher keeps a record sheet for each student.

Sight Words—Students are asked to read leveled lists of high-frequency sight words. Students also can be assessed to determine whether they can spell the words. The teacher keeps a record sheet for each student.

Phonics Generalization Word Lists—Students are asked to read lists of words that feature phonics generalizations. For example, if students can read the word *tape,* they show they can read long *a* words with the vowel, consonant, silent *e* pattern. Reading *chop* shows understanding the sound of *ch.* Students also can be assessed to determine whether they can spell the words. The teacher keeps a record sheet for each student.

Reading Logs—Students write the title, author, and illustrator of each book they read during independent reading. This assessment documents independent reading and the literature the student is reading.

Anecdotal Notes—Teachers jot down comments or write longer entries to remember what a student did and said. For example, a student is asked to read individually during guided reading or to document what happened during a writing conference.

Writing Samples and Written Checklists—Teachers maintain a cumulative folder for students. Checklists correspond to the students' ability (1) to compose and (2) to use spelling, punctuation, and usage. Students' writing samples are dated and can include rough drafts stapled to the final draft.

Formal Assessments

Formal assessments can be used by schools to get data to assess students' progress in literacy as well as for other purposes.

Criterion-referenced tests are developed to assess a specific set of skills or concepts or criteria at a designated level of difficulty. These exams can determine how much a student knows before and after instruction. Each skill or concept is measured by enough items to obtain an adequate sample of students' knowledge while controlling guessing.

Norm-referenced tests are standardized tests that compare a student's test performance with a sample of similar students (e.g., of the same grade level) who took the test at the same time of the school year. The administration and scoring of the test are standardized by using the same procedures for giving the exam and scoring it. Norms are obtained from the standardization sample. The scores provide information about how the student's achievement compares to other students nationally. A percentile score can range from 1 to 99. A score of the 60th percentile means that 60% of the norm group performed at the same level or below the student's score.

CHAPTER 5

Competency 003: Word Identification Skills and Reading Fluency

COMPETENCY 003 (WORD IDENTIFICATION SKILLS AND READING FLUENCY)

The teacher understands the importance of word-identification skills (including decoding, blending, structural analysis and sight-word vocabulary) and reading fluency and provides many opportunities for students to practice and improve word-identification skills and reading fluency.

A. Understands that many students develop word-analysis skills and reading fluency in a predictable sequence and recognizes that individual variations occur.

B. Understands differences in students' development of word-identification skills and reading fluency and knows instructional practices for meeting students' individual needs in these areas.

C. Understands the connection of word-identification skills and reading fluency to reading comprehension.

D. Knows the continuum of word-analysis skills in the statewide curriculum and grade-level expectations for attainment of these skills.

E. Knows how students develop fluency in oral and silent reading.

F. Understands that fluency involves rate, accuracy, and intonation and knows the norms for reading fluency that have been established in the Texas Essential Knowledge and Skills (TEKS) for various age and grade levels.

G. Knows factors affecting students' word-identification skills and reading fluency (e.g., home language, vocabulary development, learning disability).

H. Understands important phonetic elements and conventions of the English language.

I. Knows a variety of informal and formal procedures for assessing students' word-identification skills and reading fluency on an ongoing basis and uses appropriate assessments to monitor students' performance in these areas and to plan instruction for individual students, including English-language learners.

J. Analyzes students' errors in word analysis and uses the results of this analysis to inform future instruction.

K. Applies norms and expectations for word-identification skills and reading fluency, as specified in the Texas Essential Knowledge and Skills (TEKS), to evaluate students' reading performance.

L. Knows how to use ongoing assessment of word-identification skills and reading fluency to determine when a student needs additional help or intervention to bring the student's performance to grade level, based on state content and performance standards for reading in the Texas Essential Knowledge and Skills (TEKS).

M. Knows strategies for decoding increasingly complex words, including using the alphabetic principle, structural cues (e.g., prefixes, suffixes, roots) and syllables and for using syntax and semantics to support word identification and confirm word meaning.

N. Selects and uses instructional strategies, materials, activities, and models to teach students to recognize high-frequency irregular words, to promote students' ability to decode increasingly complex words and to enhance word-identification skills for students reading at different levels.

O. Selects and uses appropriate instructional strategies, materials, activities, and models to improve reading fluency for students reading at different levels (e.g., having students read independent-level texts, engage in repeated reading activities, use self-correction).

Word Identification

Instruction in identifying words provides students with the ability to analyze unknown words or recognize words when reading. Students also must comprehend what they read. Early literacy instruction must help students decode print, but students from the outset must see word identification as a means to understanding what they read.

Proficiency and Rationale for Instruction

By fourth grade, many students will be proficient in pronouncing the words they encounter while reading at their grade level. With words they know, students can decode new words. However, many students are still unable to recognize words at their grade level. In an eighth-grade classroom, for example, students can be reading on a first- or second-grade level.

The ability to identify words immediately is critical in reading. If students must focus attention on figuring out a word, a bottleneck occurs with short-term memory, and students can lose track in comprehending. Students also can read every word in a passage correctly and still not comprehend it.

Some educators maintain that up to third grade students' literacy development focuses more on learning how to read. After third grade, development focuses more on reading to learn. However, many students will need specific instruction on learning to identify words after third grade. Many students read below grade level—even far below it. These students need a teacher who knows how to help them.

How Readers Identify Words

Readers use four major ways to identify/recognize words: (1) **sight words**, (2) **phonics**, (3) **structural analysis**, and (4) **context clues** (in which they use surrounding words of a sentence and/ or pictures to identify an unknown word).

Since readers can use all four ways to identify words, instruction should include assessing what students know and then teaching with their needs in mind.

Sight Words: Assessment and Instruction

Students can recognize sight words instantly. Students first must know high-frequency sight words they will encounter when they read and use when they write. Students must know how to read and write 20 to 30 sight words before engaging in guided reading lessons so that they do not struggle with fluency. When students are not ready for guided reading, they can do choral reading with the teacher and point to the words to make a voice-print match.

Educators have developed a number of sight-word lists. Dr. Edward Dolch developed a list by studying the most common words students would encounter when reading. The Dolch list includes about 300 words organized in groups of 100 or by grade levels, ranging from Pre-K through Grade 3.

Dr. Edward Fry expanded the Dolch list. The Fry list contains 1,000 words based on the most common words in reading materials. These words represent approximately 90% of those found in a typical book, website, or news article. This list can be used with students in Pre-K through high school. The Fry words are listed by their frequency and are often broken into groups of 100. The first 100 Fry words are thus the 100 most frequently used words in the English language.

Sight-word lists are presented by levels. Students can be assessed by reading a list of words. When a student can read the words, a higher level of words can be assessed.

Students also must spell high-frequency words because they will use these often to write. A student who can read a word may be unable to spell it even if the student is reading on grade level. Spelling tests can determine which words students do not know and must learn to spell.

Phonics: Assessment and Instruction

Phonics pertains to the relationship of sounds and letters. Many words in English have irregular spellings and thus cannot be "sounded out." However, some patterns exist in English, and knowing the major phonics generalizations can help students with reading and spelling. The phonics generalizations presented here occur often enough to make it useful for teachers to help students discern the generalizations.

To assess students, ask them to write/spell one-syllable words that have the generalization. Have students learn to spell words that have the generalization so that they see the pattern, as in learning short *a* words, such as *cap, had, bat.* Students can learn word families from words they learn to read/spell. When students know how to read/spell, *bat,* for example, they can use an analogic approach and learn *cat, fat, hat, mat, sat.* With an analogic approach, students learn to detect patterns. In a synthetic approach, students blend individual sounds. Effective instruction can include both approaches and provide practice in reading and spelling words so that students master phonics generalizations.

Major Phonics Generalizations

Effective phonics instruction should help students apply phonics generalizations as part of word identification. However, instruction should avoid asking students to memorize many rules. Effective instruction provides practice in reading words that have a generalization so that students internalize the pattern.

Consonants

The English alphabet is composed of vowels and consonants. The vowels are *a, e, i, o, and u.* Sometimes *y* is a vowel in a word (e.g., *play*), and sometimes *w* is a vowel *(*e.g., *snow*). When *y* sounds like it does in words such as *yellow* and *yes*, it functions as a consonant. When *w* sounds like it does in *water* or *went*, it functions as a consonant. Consonants are the other letters.

- **initial consonant sounds:** When a single consonant is at the beginning of a word, it is considered an initial consonant. The consonants *y* and *w* are consonants in the initial position of a word, such as *yellow* and *with.*

- **final consonant sounds:** When students know final consonant sounds, they usually can identify sounds of the letters in a final position, but the letters can be vowels when combined with another vowel to create a sound, such as in *play, cow,* and *snow.*

- **consonant blends:** Consonant blends are two or three blended consonant sounds. Adults may not see these combinations as different from single initial consonant sounds because they know how to read, however, children can perceive differences, such that the initial sound of *brown* sounds different from the initial sound of *boat*. Three categories of consonant blends are as follows:

  l-blends (such as *bl, cl, fl, pl*)

  r-blends (such as *br, cr, dr, fr, pr, tr*)

  s-blends (such as *st, sp, str, spr*)

- **consonant digraphs:** In consonant digraphs, the sounds do not blend. Two consonants together create a new sound: *ch, sh, wh, th.*

Vowels

Vowel sounds are not as consistent as consonants. A vowel sound depends on orthographic patterns, or the letters that surround the vowel. Students need not know whether the vowel is "long" or "short" to read words with vowels. They must discern the pattern by seeing many examples of that pattern. For example, students will discern the pattern of short *a* by seeing short *a* words in a spelling list when first learning these words rather than having short *a* words combined with other short vowel words. They then can be shown how the sound changes, depending on what surrounds the *a* (such as *can* versus *car* or *can* versus *cane*).

- **short vowels:** Consonant-Vowel-Consonant (CVC) pattern:

a	cap	man	had
e	bed	pet	test
i	sit	fish	ship
o	dog	hot	mop
u	cut	rug	must

- **long vowels:** The vowel "says" its name, and this takes place in three major patterns:

  1. **Two vowels together**—The first one "says" its name, and the second one is silent.

long a	ai (wait)	ay (play)
long e	ea (seat)	ee (green)
long i	ie (lie)	
long o	oa (boat)	ow (snow—but not long in *cow*)
long u	ui (fruit)	

2. **VCe-Vowel-Consonant-silent *e***

long *a*	name
long *e*	Pete
long *i*	kite
long *u*	flute

3. **Single vowel after a consonant**

   Students learn these words as sight words and are usually taught that way, such as *me*, or *so*.

- *r*-controlled vowels: The vowel appears as a CVC pattern, but it is not a short vowel because the *r* changes the sound of the vowel.

   car

   fern

   stir

   corn

   turn

- **vowel digraphs:** Two vowels come together to create a new sound that is not long, short, or r-controlled.

   au, aw—haul or saw

   oo—look, book and soon or pool

- **dipthongs:** Diphthongs entail the slurring of two letters and are a special case of digraphs.

   oy, oi—boy or boil

   ou, ow—house or cow

Structural Analysis or Word-Parts Instruction: Assessment and Instruction

Readers use structural analysis or word parts by examining parts of a word. Students develop this ability in the early grades when they know sight words. As they progress, students use structural analysis as they encounter words with more than one syllable and when they examine word roots as part of vocabulary development.

- **forming plurals:**

    -s: cat, cats   rake, rakes

    -ies (y-drop): puppy, puppies

    adding -es when the word ends in x, s, sh, ch:

    box, boxes   bus, buses   dish, dishes   church, churches

    special cases of forming plurals:

    wolf, wolves

    foot, feet

    deer, deer or sheep, sheep

    potato, potatoes

    child, children

- **inflectional endings—adding -s, -ed, -ing:**

    walk, walks, walked, walking

- **possession:**

    singular versus plural

    dog's bone versus the two dogs' bone

- **compound words:** Two words can come together, such as *hotdog* or *something* (but not in the word *mother*.)

- **contractions:** The apostrophe is used to show where one or more letters have been omitted. Students should be shown this because it is easier to learn to spell contractions when they see the logic of where the apostrophe is placed.

    it is   did not

    it's   didn't

- **prefixes:** A prefix is an affix at the beginning of a word.

    un—not or opposite of   unhappy, unaware

    dis—not or opposite of   disappear, discover

    trans—across   transportation, transmit

    sub—under   submarine, subway

- **suffixes:** A suffix is an affix at the end of a word.

ful — full of	helpful, playful
less — without	homeless, worthless
ly — manner of	sadly, badly
able, ible — can be	capable, audible

- **syllables of words:** A syllable is a unit containing one vowel sound, which may form a complete word or part of a word.

walk ing	se nile	cheer ful ly

In **open syllables**, the syllable contains one vowel at the end of the combination of letters, such as *me* in *meteor*. Even one vowel can form a syllable, such as *e* in *enough* and *a* in *able*.

In an **open syllable**, the vowel can "say" its name, which is a long vowel sound. At times, the pronunciation is "uh" as the *me* in me-tic-u-lous, but the *u* makes the long sound.

In a **closed syllable**, the vowel has a consonant next to it or is "closed" by a consonant, such as *bag* in *baggage*. In a **closed syllable**, the vowel will make a short vowel sound, as in *mat* in *matter* or *ac* in *accurate*.

Morphemic analysis is related to **structural analysis**. This facet of vocabulary development takes place when students use prefixes, suffixes, and roots or base words to determine or remember the meanings of words.

- A **morpheme** is a word or part of a word that has meaning.

- A **morpheme** is not necessarily a word.

- A **bound morpheme** is not a word on its own and cannot stand on its own. A bound morpheme appears with a root. Bound morphemes include affixes, which are prefixes and suffixes, such as *dis* in *disappear* and *-s* as in *dogs*.

- A **free morpheme**, such as *appear*, can stand on its own.

- A **compound word** (e.g., *football*) consists of two free morphemes.

Through **structural** or **morphemic analysis**, students analyze parts of words to identify or understand words. Structural analysis begins when students learn to apply plurals, such as in *cat, cats, or* when adding an inflectional ending such as *s, ed, ing* to a verb, as in *walks, walked, walking*.

Structural and morphemic analysis becomes more complicated as students learn to read and spell such plurals as *puppies* for *puppy*. Structural and morphemic analysis also becomes more complicated as students learn to identify multisyllabic words and break words into syllables.

Learning **Latin and Greek roots and derivations** can help students increase their vocabulary and more readily understand new words, especially when they also use context clues.

Examples of Greek Roots and Derivations:

auto — self   autobiography, automobile

bio — life   biography, biohazard

homo — same   homogenous, homophones

hyde — water   hydration, dehydrated

logy — study of   biology, geology

Examples of Latin Roots and Derivations:

cord, cor, cardi — heart   cordial, discord, cardiogram

duc, duct — to lead   conduct, reduction

fract, frag — break   fraction, fragment

loc — place   location, relocate

port — to carry   export, transportation

Cognates are words in two languages and share a similar meaning, spelling, and pronunciation. When shown these similarities, English learners benefit.

Cognates in English and Spanish can be found in words with common Greek and Latin roots, such as the following examples:

Greek Root	English	Spanish
astir — star	astrology	astrología
bio — life	biology	biología
phon — sound	microphone	micrófono
Latin Root	**English**	**Spanish**
aud — to hear	auditorium	auditorio
dict — to tell, speak	dictate	dictar
mit, mis — send	mission	misión

Context Clues

When they use context clues, readers identify an unknown word by using the known words that surround it. Context clues also can illustrate a page and show what the text is about or what the setting is.

Knowing how to combine words uses **knowledge of syntax**, or **language structure**. When students use context, they are using their knowledge of syntax. They know which words can be combined. In the following sentence, for example, the blank or unknown word would be a thing, not a verb or preposition:

I want to eat the _____.

Students who know English intuitively know the term is a *noun*. They do not need to know the parts of speech to identify the unknown word. Even children intuitively know this because they discern principles of language as they acquire language.

In using context clues, students also use their knowledge of **meaning** because they know what would make sense, such as in the example: I like to eat _____. Because they know English and know what people can eat, they know the unknown word (the blank) will be a food.

Students, especially beginning readers, also can use illustrations or pictures in using context. A student can look at the illustration on the page to decide that in this sentence the unknown word is *cake*, if the illustration shows a child eating a piece of cake: I want to eat the _____.

To use context clues, students must know sight words because they must be able to read at least some of the words in the sentence.

Readers also often use context clues, phonics and/or structural analysis as they try to identify a word. A reader can use the first consonant sound, which is phonics, with context clues, such as in this example:

I will ride to school on the b_____.

Initial consonant sounds, and context clues especially, can help readers identify unknown words.

In this example, the student may use structural analysis and break the word *instead* into syllables. The student then uses context clues to determine what makes sense:

I want to eat this dessert _____ (instead).

If students can speak English, they can use context more readily. They come to know semantics (meaning) and syntax (language structure) of English in the course of learning how to speak the language.

Context clues provide the fastest way for students to identify words, and students can use them before they know all of the phonics and structural analysis generalizations. Oral language development is thus important in learning how to recognize English words.

In the **cloze procedure**, students are asked to supply missing words. This requires them to use context clues. The cloze procedure has been used to assess comprehension, but it also can be used to encourage students to use context clues.

Effective Word-Analysis Development

Spelling

Spelling is among the best ways for students to learn word analysis or identification skills. Spelling helps students focus on each letter of a word. As students learn to spell words, they learn to read them. Students can master phonics, sight words, and structural analysis if they learn to spell words that feature phonics generalizations, sight words, and structural/morphemic analysis. By focusing upon a designated list of sight words and either phonics or structural analysis generalizations, teachers can ensure that students learn what they need to know.

After students master word analysis, teachers can focus on systematic study of Latin and Greek derivations to help students see patterns in roots.

Word Games

To strengthen students' learning of words, teachers can provide small-group learning stations where students play such word games as high-frequency word bingo. When students are shown how to work together to play the game, they can do so while the teacher works with other students. As students learn new words, the teacher can add those words to the game.

Demonstrations Using Context and Cloze Procedure

Teachers also can **demonstrate** the use of context clues by showing students how to use surrounding words in a sentence to identify an unknown word. This can take place through listening to students read aloud individually or as part of group instruction, including guided reading groups. Using sentences from the reading section, the teacher can model how to discern an unknown word by reading before and after the word in the sentence to determine what makes sense. **Cloze** passages leave blanks at designated points to determine whether students can read and understand the texts with the missing words. When asked to supply the missing words, students show their ability to use context clues. Students must be able to read the surrounding words to be able to supply the missing word, or teachers must read the sentences for them. Cloze activities also can help students review words they are learning by providing a word bank. Students then can complete the sentences with a choice from the word bank.

Independent Reading

Daily reading helps students in word identification. Gains in reading are linked to how much time students devote to reading. Although students need specific instruction in spelling and skills, competent readers apply skills individually and in combination as they read. This takes place during sustained reading. Daily instruction should provide opportunities for students to **read books of their own choice independently**. If they choose books that are easy to read, the students still benefit. Reading easy books enables progress in fluency. If teachers read aloud daily, students will also be more likely to read because they see what books offer. They often will select the same book the teacher read aloud or a book by the same author.

Guided Reading

Guided reading enables the teacher to help students progress in reading by providing texts at the students' instructional level. Instructional-level texts are slightly more difficult than the independent-level texts the students can read on their own. Students can read instructional-level texts after the teacher provides support by introducing new words and activating/building background for reading. The teacher also supports growth by fostering comprehension. Through **multiple readings** of a text, students can improve their recognition of the words, which supports fluent reading.

Shared Reading

Shared reading can take place daily when the teacher and students read together. This enables students to learn words and then read on their own that day or after subsequent readings with the teacher. Poems that students enjoy are ideal. Shared reading can also occur when students must read a text in content areas. These texts may have so many unknown words that students cannot understand the content on their own.

Students also can read **with a partner** or read along **with an audio recording** during small group work while the teacher works with a group for guided reading. These learning experiences work especially well for students who are unable to engage in sustained silent reading.

Guided Reading Groups and Small-Group Instruction

Guided reading is small-group instruction in which the teacher works with students who read at about the same level. Although students profit from heterogeneous groups for the independent work, guided reading groups work best with homogeneous grouping in which they read a text at their instructional level. Students can be overwhelmed when texts are too hard and contain too many unknown words. Students can read the texts for guided reading with some support from the teacher, and the students thus can progress. Small-group instruction lets the teacher provide more individual attention. A guided reading lesson combines three parts that work together: before, during, and after reading.

Before reading, the teacher builds or activates **background knowledge** to help students understand the text. The teacher also helps students prepare for reading unfamiliar components of the text, including **unknown words**, speech bubbles, charts, or bold print.

During reading, the students **read** the story or designated segment **silently,** or softly if they are children or beginning readers. Students who finish before others can read the text again to help fluency. The teacher **listens to individual students read** aloud to assess the ability to recognize words.

The teacher then provides prompts to help students identify unknown words. Although teachers usually cannot listen to all students read in the same day, they can listen to some students one day and the rest the next.

During reading is a critical time for the teacher to assess informally. The teacher can determine what needs to be addressed during word study, including words students do not know. The teacher can also discern whether students read fluently or know how to use multiple cues for word analysis. Teachers should create brief anecdotal notes to address the students' needs. Teachers should also respond to a student's miscues to show students how to use all sources of information or cueing systems.

After reading, the teacher and students discuss the story. Teachers ask students to recall what happened to ensure students understand the plot while helping students remember and compose what happened. After **retelling**, students **discuss** the story to engage in higher levels of comprehension; they make inferences and form connections among texts (**text-to-text connections**) as well as to their lives (**text-to-self connections**). Student also can discuss big ideas or lessons that emerge from the text. After the sharing of their personal responses to the fiction and poetry, subsequent discussion can focus on literary elements and writers' strategies. When students know the story and make connections to it, the students and teacher can discuss plot, setting, characterization, and/or themes.

When reading informational texts, discussions can include aspects of how to read and remember the information, such as learning how to take notes with headings to remember details.

After reading also focuses on word study. The teacher can show students how to spell a few words and address meanings of words to build vocabularies. Teachers also can model reading unfamiliar strategies, such as how to use context, read with expression, or read charts.

Round-robin reading, when students take turns reading segments aloud, should be avoided. Reading experts agree it hampers progress in word identification. Students read at different rates, and a student who reads slower will have trouble following faster readers. The students who read faster must slow their rate to accommodate slower readers, which hampers their fluency. Students also can be embarrassed and dread reading if they see themselves as less capable than others. Students also may not follow when others read, and they may read only when it is their turn.

Teachers should instead show students how to read softly or silently thorough guided reading/small-group instruction. Teachers can teach students in small groups while the rest of the class reads independently.

Guided reading/small-group reading can occur during language arts blocks. It also can take place during science and social studies when students must read more difficult textbooks. If students cannot read the textbook, teachers can use shared reading, with students following as the teacher reads. Students will gain in sight vocabulary so that they can read a text.

Fluency

Fluency in reading is essential for comprehension. Fluency entails reading a text smoothly, accurately, and expressively. When reading fluently, a reader can pay more attention to the meaning of a text because attention is not needed for identifying words. Creating meaning is not disrupted by a slow rate or word-by-word reading, and readers can connect ideas within the text itself and to their background knowledge.

Screening and diagnosing as well as monitoring progress will support students' growth in fluency. Teachers determine fluency by listening to students read.

Guidelines for Fluency Assessment

- Fluency is not speed reading. With rate and accuracy, fluent reading includes adding appropriate intonation.

- If a student fails to read a text fluently, the student may need more instruction in word identification or may need practice in reading the text smoothly and expressively.

- Using an easier text may help the student read fluently.

- If the student can identify words, the teacher may need to model how to read fluently, showing how to pay attention to punctuation as well as reading expressively.

- When students have difficulty identifying words, they may need support in oral language development, phonemic awareness, sight vocabulary, phonics, structural analysis, and using context clues.

- If the text used for fluency assessment is too difficult, a text at a lower reading level should be used. When students cannot identify at least 90% of the words in a text, they are reading at their frustration level.

- Students gain fluency when they can read at least 95% of the words so that they need not devote attention to word analysis. It is best when the student can read 98%–100% of the words.

- If students identify all words when reading a text, they may be "word calling" rather than comprehending. Fluency assessment is essential because fluency bridges word identification and comprehension.

- Teachers can detect fluency, and formal screening can provide specific data.

- Research studies have recommended reading rates, or how many words a student reads per minute. These rates are established for the beginning as well as later in the school year to determine whether students are progressing.

- Teachers can compare a student's reading rates to average rates.

- Hasbrouck and Tindal (2017) have provided guidance for grades 4–8. For middle-school students, the words correct per minute (WCPM) at the 50th percentile at the beginning of the year when screening would start are as follows:

Grade 4	94 WCPM
Grade 5	110 WCPM
Grade 6	127 WCPM
Grade 7	128 WCPM
Grade 8	133 WCPM

Instructional Support for Fluency

- **Reading Materials**

Students develop fluency through multiple readings of materials that let them succeed. When students must devote attention to identifying words, they cannot read fluently.

- **Rereading**

Reading texts again for instruction can help students reach the independent reading level, which is when they can recognize 95%-100% of the words in a text. Rereading a text on a subsequent day after a guided reading lesson thus can be a valuable activity.

Multiple readings are feasible when students read shorter texts again, and poetry is ideal, especially when teachers do shared reading of a poem daily. If the teacher selects quality poetry for young people, students will enjoy reading.

- **Choral Reading and Shared Reading**

Choral reading occurs when the teacher and students read a text together. Choral reading can take place by displaying an enlarged text or when the teacher and student each have a book on hand.

In shared reading, the teacher reads first to model, and students follow. Students read with the teacher until they can read on their own. Choral reading and shared reading begin with the teacher reading the selection aloud . The teacher models fluent reading, and students can enjoy the story or poem and consider its meaning.

Teachers often present a poem for daily shared reading. When students can read the poem, the teacher introduces a new poem. Shared reading provides differentiated instruction. Students will gain what they need, whether it is new words or reading with expression. Multiple poetry readings can include showing students how to pay attention to punctuation and expression. Students also can learn not to pause when reading until they see a comma, period, or question mark in the poem, even when coming to the end of the line. Students also learn how to consider the "voice" or speaker of the poem in reading expressively.

TExES ELAR 4–8

- **Showing Fluent Reading**

  Teachers can model how to read fluently. This can take place daily with reading aloud. Teachers also can model fluent reading at the end of a guided reading lesson or when working with students individually. The teacher also can provide a short lesson for students by reading a segment to model. Students first read with the teacher and then on their own.

- **Audio-Assisted Reading**

  Students can read with the person reading on the audio recording of a text. If the reading material is easy, the student can focus on reading smoothly and expressively. Audio-assisted reading can be a learning station or an independent activity. Students can participate while the teacher works with a small group for guided reading or for small-group work. Students should enjoy the reading if the teacher selects relevant poetry, picture books, or short stories that are relevant to students.

  Audio-assisted reading especially helps English learners and other students who need support.

- **Readers' Theatre**

  Readers' theatre is a drama in which the presentation takes place by reading a script. Readers' theatre does not require memorizing lines. The presentation comes alive through the readers' voices.

  Readers' theatre can be a rewarding way for students to revisit a story or the content in a textbook. The reading can foster comprehension and vocabulary development as students review content. The rereading also helps with word recognition when students strive to read fluently while practicing the reading for the presentation. Fluency also is enhanced as students try to become the character and speak how the character would, observing punctuation and using correct intonation.

  Reader's theatre does not require costumes and is thus an easy drama to incorporate while fostering fluency, vocabulary, and comprehension as well as oral language development. Oral language development takes place when students talk and listen during the presentation.

  Reader's theatre is ideal for developing oral and written language because students use language for actual reasons. Different literature can provide the script, but it must be at students' independent-reading level to develop fluency. By reading the script with the teacher or other students, students can practice a script at their instructional level of 90%–94% word identification. Through practice, students can reach 100% of the words in the script.

- **Partner Reading**

  Students can be shown how to read in pairs to practice reading a poem they may have read during shared reading with the teacher. This can help them progress in fluency. Students also can reread a story from their guided reading instruction with the teacher. When students are shown how to read together, partner reading can be a beneficial literacy station* or independent activity while the teacher meets with small groups for guided reading or other instruction.

---

* An area in the classroom where students work solo or in teams, using instructional materials to build their literacy.

DOMAIN II: Language Arts, Part II

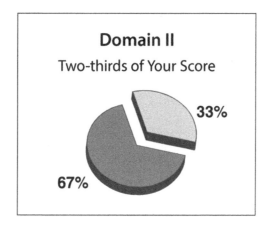

Domain II
Two-thirds of Your Score

33%

67%

Domain II covers the following competencies, which together account for 67% of your score on the TExES ELAR 4–8 test:

- **Competency 004:** Reading Comprehension and Assessment

- **Competency 005:** Reading Applications

- **Competency 006:** Written Language – Writing Conventions

- **Competency 007:** Written Language – Composition

- **Competency 008:** Viewing and Representing

- **Competency 009:** Study and Inquiry Skills

Domain II covers the following standards:

- **Standard IV.** Reading Comprehension: Teachers understand the importance of reading for understanding, know the components of comprehension, and teach students strategies for improving their comprehension.

- **Standard V.** Written Language: Teachers understand that writing is a developmental process and provide instruction that helps students develop competence in written communication.

- **Standard VI.** Study and Inquiry Skills: Teachers understand the importance of study and inquiry skills as tools for learning and promote students' development in applying study and inquiry skills.

- **Standard VII.** Viewing and Representing: Teachers understand how to interpret, analyze, evaluate, and produce visual images and messages in various media and to provide students with opportunities to develop skills in this area.

CHAPTER 6

Competency 004: Reading Comprehension and Assessment

COMPETENCY 004 (READING COMPREHENSION AND ASSESSMENT)

The teacher understands the importance of reading for understanding, knows components and processes of reading comprehension and teaches students strategies for improving their comprehension.

A. Understands reading comprehension as an active process of constructing meaning.

B. Understands the continuum of reading comprehension skills in the statewide curriculum and grade-level expectations for these skills.

C. Understands factors affecting students' reading comprehension (e.g., oral language development, word analysis skills, prior knowledge, language background, previous reading experiences, fluency, vocabulary development, ability to monitor understanding, characteristics of specific texts).

D. Knows characteristics of informal and formal reading comprehension assessments (e.g., criterion-referenced state tests, curriculum-based reading assessments, informal reading inventories, norm-referenced tests).

E. Selects and uses appropriate informal and formal assessments to monitor and evaluate students' reading comprehension.

F. Analyzes student errors and provides focused instruction in reading comprehension based on the strengths and needs of individual students, including English-language learners.

G. Knows how to use ongoing assessment to determine when a student needs additional help or intervention to bring the student's performance to grade level, based on state content and performance standards for reading in the Texas Essential Knowledge and Skills (TEKS).

H. Understands metacognitive skills, including self-evaluation and self-monitoring skills and teaches students to use these skills to enhance their own reading comprehension.

I. Knows how to determine students' independent, instructional, and frustration reading levels and uses this information to select and adapt reading materials for individual students, as well as to guide their selection of independent reading materials.

J. Uses various instructional strategies to enhance students' reading comprehension (e.g., linking text content to students' lives and prior knowledge, connecting related ideas across different texts, engaging students in guided and independent reading, guiding students to generate questions and apply knowledge of text topics).

K. Knows how to provide students with direct, explicit instruction in the use of strategies to improve their reading comprehension (e.g., previewing, self-monitoring, visualizing, retelling).

L. Uses various communication modes (e.g., written, oral) to promote students' reading comprehension.

M. Understands levels of reading comprehension and how to model and teach literal, inferential and evaluative comprehension skills.

N. Knows how to provide instruction to help students increase their reading vocabulary.

O. Understands reading comprehension issues for students with different needs and knows effective reading strategies for those students.

P. Knows the difference between guided and independent practice in reading and provides students with frequent opportunities for both.

Q. Knows how to promote students' development of an extensive reading and writing vocabulary by providing them with many opportunities to read and write.

Defining Success in Reading

Reading requires comprehension. When students reach the middle and upper grades, many can pronounce the words but struggle with understanding what they have read. Accurate word identification is important to comprehension but is not the only component of understanding a text. Instruction and assessment in reading comprehension should begin when students learn to read and continue throughout their education.

Dyslexia and Comprehension Assessment

Students can have high levels of listening comprehension and adequate levels of intelligence, indicating they can comprehend what they read. However, these students may struggle when processing print. The inability to read words accurately may result from the lack of effective instruction, but it also can signal the need for assessment to determine whether the student has dyslexia or another learning disability. Primary difficulties of students with dyslexia include single-word recognition, reading fluency, and spelling. Difficulties in comprehension and written expression can be secondary consequences of the difficulties in reading and spelling words. Teachers must seek assessment for students who might have dyslexia or a related disability to get them the instruction they need.

Dimensions of Comprehension

Asking students well-developed questions about a text can help assess comprehension, but instruction should not be limited to providing passages and learning to answer questions. Instruction must help students understand challenging texts. Teachers can model proficient reading and then provide guided practice. Rather than solely assessing comprehension by asking questions, teachers can teach comprehension.

Reading is an active, constructive transaction between the reader and the text. In constructing meaning, readers use knowledge of: (1) **language**, (2) **the world**, and (3) **navigating print**. The created meaning also can depend on the **reader's purpose for reading**. Different texts and **text structures** also make different demands on readers.

Students vary in the experiences that enable them to comprehend a reading, and teachers can help their proficiency. Because readers use knowledge of language to comprehend, teachers can help students increase the use of their knowledge of language to understand texts. Teachers also can activate and build students' background knowledge as they read fiction, poetry and nonfiction. Teachers also can help students learn to adjust how their reading suits their purpose. Additionally, teachers can help students learn to monitor their reading to determine whether they are comprehending as they read. Students then can revise their approach.

Knowledge of Language and Comprehension

Teachers can help students increase their knowledge of language by providing oral language experiences in which students can use language daily in different ways. Teachers also must help students meet the demands of written language. Although students often can communicate through informal talking and listening, they may lack proficiency in written language.

Students use their knowledge of language to understand words in the text, including words rarely or never used in their oral language experiences. Students also must use syntax or how sentences are developed in written language. In oral language, people can rely on gestures or ask questions to construct meaning. Readers must rely upon the text.

Students see how written language works when teachers read aloud and when students themselves read on their own. Students also learn more about how print conveys meaning when they write every day. Reading informs the students' writing, and students also grow as readers when they make the choices other writers make to communicate.

Knowledge of the World and Comprehension

Before students read a selection, teachers can **build or activate background knowledge** to help them comprehend the text. Capable readers draw instinctively on their knowledge, and teachers may assume their students will also do so. Teachers, however, should show students this is a part of reading by activating that background knowledge.

Background knowledge helps when students read a text similar to a previous reading. For example, if students are reading a variant of a folktale they have read, the teacher may remind them of the previous version. If students are reading the second book in a series, the teacher can discuss the connection with the first book. Teachers also can review concepts from a previous section of a textbook to enhance understanding of the next section.

If students lack background knowledge, teachers should provide it. For example, if students are reading historical fiction that took place during the Great Depression, teachers should explain the setting. In a content area, the teacher should teach the necessary concepts to understand a textbook section.

Preparing students to read a text includes helping them with vocabulary. Vocabulary development includes understanding concepts and pronouncing unfamiliar words. Looking up the definition of words in a glossary does not help students understand concepts. Teachers should explain unfamiliar concepts with examples in ways students can understand, keeping in mind the difficulty of the concept and students' varying experiences.

The amount of instruction depends on the demands of the text, the background of the students, and the difficulty of the concept. For example, in reading a story set at a circus, the teacher may have to explain such terms as *trapeze* or explain what *mill* means when the students read a *Little Red Hen*. In informational or expository texts as well as in the plot of a challenging story, concepts and vocabulary may require even more background.

Navigating Textual Space: Knowledge of Text Structure, Purposes for Reading, Monitoring

Besides identifying and understanding words, students must be prepared for differences in **text structure.** Narrative texts make different demands on readers than informational or expository texts. Even children can remember and retell stories they hear because of their having a schema or a cognitive framework for organizing and interpreting narratives. Similarly, older students may readily comprehend fiction but struggle with informational texts.

The text structures of informational texts differ from the text structure of stories. While readers have a schema for stories, they must figure the text structure of informational material. Informational or expository texts often demand more than a single straight-through reading to understand and remember the information.

The text structures of informational texts can vary, depending on how the information is organized in the discipline or is needed for relating the information. For example, when presenting a chapter about rocks, the authors may use such headings as *igneous*, *sedimentary*, and *metamorphic* to signal how the information is organized. Each section describes each rock. If students use *igneous*, *sedimentary*, and *metamorphic* to guide their reading, they can organize the information. Students also can use headings to relate concepts, such as the role of *magma* when considering igneous rocks or what *sediments* are.

When students reach the middle grades, they must read longer informational texts that make greater demands on their memory. Teachers can help students read and remember information by helping them figure how the text is organized.

What follows are **major types of text structures** writers use in informational texts:

- descriptive—The writer describes the topic by listing characteristics.

- sequence—The writer presents a series of steps in a process or a sequence of events.

- compare/contrast—The writer compares or contrasts concepts and events by showing similarities and differences.

- problem/solution—The writer presents a problem followed by a solution.

- cause/effect—The writer presents information that explains a relationship of one or more causes and the effect(s).

Students also must be shown that a text can use more than one structure. For example, a chapter in a history textbook may use sequence to present the chronology of the American Revolution while also using cause and effect as well as description.

Applying the knowledge of text structures is more important than defining them. Knowing text structures provides a tool for learning and reading. Students can be frustrated if they are asked to use text structures without having enough scaffolding from the teacher. As students apply knowledge of text structures while reading in different disciplines, they will gain flexibility and expertise.

Vocabulary Development

Reading proficiency depends on immediate recognition and understanding of words so that readers can devote attention to creating meaning, or comprehension. Students also rely on understanding the meanings of words to succeed in instructional experiences that rely on listening and speaking.

Before entering school, children have gained in their speaking and listening vocabularies through meaningful interactions with others. Even without being taught directly, children acquire and refine their knowledge of words. Education provides opportunities for students to expand their **speaking** and **listening** vocabularies while also expanding their **reading** and **writing** vocabularies.

Although students continue to progress in vocabulary development through their informal interactions with others, instruction plays a decisive role in helping them succeed. Acquiring vocabulary entails the ability to: (1) understand a word when it is used, (2) define a word in one's own words, (3) decode and spell a word, and (4) know multiple meanings as they apply.

Vocabulary Development and Instruction

- **Vocabulary development** entails **connecting a word** (or label) **with concepts**. If students understand a concept, they will remember and use the word. Learning how to use a dictionary is important and can help. However, gains in vocabulary development do not take place optimally when students look up words and memorize definitions. Knowing how to use a word requires more understanding.

Vocabulary development occurs when students expand their understanding of a known concept and learn new words to label it. Students also will relate new concepts to existing labels or known words, such as the *bark* of a dog versus the *bark* of a tree. Students also may need to learn both concept and label, such as in learning about photosynthesis.

Instruction depends on what students need. A brief example may suffice if students understand a concept and are learning a new word for it. However, students will need more experiences if they understand a concept but are learning a word in a non-native language. Understanding a concept while also learning new words is especially challenging.

Concepts in content areas such as science and social studies are often abstract. Instruction thus must build understanding of the concept while also helping students acquire the necessary vocabulary.

When students comprehend a concept at a deeper level, they understand how concepts relate to other concepts. Students gain conceptual development by encountering a concept first-hand and by viewing it through written language and other media. Teachers can provide learning experiences to foster students' vocabulary development.

Types of Instruction for Vocabulary Development

Reading Aloud and Independent Reading

Teachers help students progress in vocabulary development by reading aloud to them and providing time for independent reading. Reading exposes students to words different from their oral language experiences. Students understand and learn new words by using **contextual analysis** in which they use surrounding words and illustrations to determine the meanings of words. Although instructors are not teaching words directly, students gain through their reading. The words that become a part of their reading vocabularies can become part of their speaking, listening, and writing vocabularies. When students encounter different literature, they can progress more. Besides reading fiction and poetry aloud, teachers should do the same with nonfiction/informational books.

Systematic Vocabulary Instruction

Vocabulary development also must include systematic instruction to help students attain strategies for gaining vocabulary. Deciding when to teach or review vocabulary depends on what students need to engage in their task as well as on their oral and written language development.

Vocabulary development can take place **before reading** to help students identify new concepts and words so that they can comprehend the text. Teachers should consider students' background knowledge and how to relate new concepts to previous learning and background. Rather than ask students to look up a word in a glossary, teachers should provide examples, gestures, features, pictures, or visual diagrams. Teachers also should show students how to use any illustrations or diagrams the text provides.

Students can use context clues or surrounding words and illustrations to understand unknown words. When teachers interact with students **during reading**, they help students learn to use the context of the sentence, text, or illustrations to figure what a word means. This can help students learn to identify unfamiliar words when they read on their own.

Vocabulary instruction **after reading** can help students review concepts. Instruction after reading also can help students relate concepts. Instruction can include using sematic maps or diagrams as well as talking about concepts. Writing experiences also can help, but students are unlikely to learn by copying definitions. The following ways can help students gain vocabulary: (1) describe the concept, (2) give examples and analogies, (3) discuss how the concept fits in a category, (4) use actions, illustrations and media, (5) provide additional reading aloud experiences on the topic, and (6) make a conscious effort to use new words on subsequent days to help ensure students' retention.

Systematic instruction can include helping students learn to use **word structure** to understand and remember new words. **Morphemes** are the smallest units of meaning in language, and these can be words that have meaning as they are (e.g., happy). Morphemes also can be word parts that lack meaning on their own but change or expand the meaning of words when added, such as prefixes (e.g., *un-*) and suffixes (e.g., *ment-*). Helping students see spelling–meaning connections also helps. Words can be related in meaning even when the sounds change, such as in *nation* and *national*. Learning Latin and Greek roots and derivations also helps students understand and remember new words, such as understanding the Latin root in *cordial*, *accord*, and *discord*.

Showing students how to use the dictionary also can help with unknown words, but asking students to copy definitions does not help understanding. Students still need to learn to use the **dictionary** and must be shown how to locate a word, which may not be apparent if the word has an inflectional ending (e.g., repairs or repairing). Students thus should be shown that they may need to figure out the base word. Students also should be shown how to decide which definition fits the sentence they are reading by using context.

Teaching Vocabulary for Understanding and Learning in Subject Areas

Teaching all new words of a reading selection often is unnecessary and ineffective. Teachers must decide which words are important. Teachers then must decide whether students can gain enough understanding by the way a selection is used. This varies, depending on students' language development. For example, a word that could be discerned by a native speaker using context clues may not be one that an English learner can understand. Teachers also must decide how much instruction is needed without disrupting the enjoyment and understanding of the reading.

Vocabulary of informational material often requires direct instruction. The concepts are new to students. Students also must be shown how concepts relate to understand individual concepts deeply and understand concepts collectively.

Basic words usually will not require instruction for native speakers, and these are **Tier One words**, such as *puppy* or *house*. Students are apt to encounter these words in their daily oral language experiences, and explicit instruction thus is not often needed.

Although teachers should not assume that English learners have encountered these words in English, these learners may know the concept in their native language, such as *family* or *butterfly,* and these words are more easily taught. However, Tier One instruction can include such expressions or idioms as "give it a shot" or "piece of cake," which can confuse English learners.

Tier Two words require instruction more often because students are unlikely to encounter these words in their daily talking and listening. Examples include *inhibit, adjacent,* or *guarantee.* Students encounter Tier Two words most often in print. Tier Two words also can include such commonly confused words as *fowl* and *foul.* Tier Two words are not directly related to a certain discipline but may appear in technical and literary texts.

Tier Three words are associated with a discipline. Examples are *condensation, diameter,* or *senator.* These words are critical to understanding and learning concepts presented in texts. Instruction is often needed for students to read and understand the text. It is also often needed after the reading so that students can remember, learn, and connect concepts.

Although students can understand some words with brief descriptions and examples, vocabulary associated with new concepts requires more instruction. Research shows that supplying definitions does not help students understand and learn new concepts. When more in-depth vocabulary instruction is needed, teachers should describe or explain the word in language the students can understand. Examples or illustrations help. Students can then be asked to describe the word in their own words or to create a picture or symbolic representation. To help retain the new words, students can develop vocabulary notebooks. Students also can play games that use the vocabulary or talk with a partner about words in their notebooks.

Competency 005: Reading Applications

COMPETENCY 005 (READING APPLICATIONS)

The teacher understands reading skills and strategies appropriate for various types of texts and contexts and teaches students to apply those skills and strategies to enhance their reading proficiency.

A. Understands skills and strategies for understanding, interpreting, and evaluating different types of written materials, including narratives, expository texts, technical writing, and content-area textbooks.

B. Understands different purposes for reading and related reading strategies.

C. Knows and teaches strategies to facilitate comprehension of different types of text before, during, and after reading (e.g., previewing, making predictions, questioning, self-monitoring, rereading, mapping, using reading journals, discussing texts).

D. Provides instruction in comprehension skills that support students' transition from "learning to read" to "reading to learn" (e.g., matching comprehension strategies to different types of text and different purposes for reading).

E. Understands the importance of reading as a skill in all content areas.

F. Understands the value of using dictionaries, glossaries and other sources to determine the meanings, pronunciations, and derivations of unfamiliar words and teaches students to use these sources.

G. Knows how to teach students to interpret information presented in various formats (e.g., maps, tables, graphs) and how to locate, retrieve, and retain information from a range of texts and technologies.

H. Knows how to help students comprehend abstract content and ideas in written materials (e.g., by using manipulatives, examples, diagrams).

I. Knows literary genres (e.g., historical fiction, poetry, myths, fables) and their characteristics.

J. Recognizes a wide range of literature and other texts appropriate for students.

K. Provides multiple opportunities for students to listen and respond to a wide variety of children's and young people's literature, both fiction and nonfiction, and to recognize characteristics of various types of narrative and expository texts.

L. Understands and promotes students' development of literary response and analysis, including teaching students elements of literary analysis (e.g., story elements, features of different literary genres) and providing students with opportunities to apply comprehension skills to literature.

M. Selects and uses a variety of materials to teach students about authors and about different purposes for writing.

N. Provides students with opportunities to engage in silent reading and extended reading of a wide range of materials, including expository texts and various literary genres.

O. Engages students in varied reading experiences and encourages them to interact with others about their reading.

P. Uses strategies to encourage reading for pleasure as well as lifelong learning.

Q. Can teach students strategies for selecting books for independent reading.

R. Uses technology to promote students' literacy and teaches students to use technology to access appropriate narrative and expository texts.

Balanced, Comprehensive Reading Instruction

Through balanced, comprehensive reading instruction, students can become proficient. Teachers should **read aloud to students** to help them understand texts they cannot read on their own and/or expand their experiences with different genres, authors, and texts.

Besides reading to students, teachers should **read with students** through small-group or guided instruction. Competent readers in upper grades may not need this for skill development, but small groups read and discuss books differently from large groups, which can discourage some students from sharing. Teachers also cannot assess comprehension as well in a large group. Reading in disciplines especially can be more effective when students read with the teacher in small groups to learn more about how to navigate informational texts and read to learn. Even students who can comprehend do not always know how to read to learn or use study strategies.

Reading with students includes **shared reading** in which the teacher reads a text and students follow until they can read the text. When students read the text and make a voice-print match, they improve sight vocabulary. The teacher also can model how to pause or use appropriate intonation, depending upon punctuation. Shared reading also works through audio-assisted reading, with students following the words.

Reading by students should take place daily so that they read independently. When students can choose their books, they engage in the authentic reading that readers do beyond school. Owning their reading also motivates them.

Word Study is another component of a comprehensive reading program. Word study includes identifying and understanding words. In the middle grades, students can often identify words easily, but they should increase their knowledge of the meanings of words as well as morphemic analysis.

Role of Quality Literature in Meeting Students' Needs

Students who encounter varied literature will progress more. Besides fiction and poetry, teachers should read nonfiction, including informational books, aloud.

Books written for youth vary in how well they meet students' needs, but teachers can find reading that will engage their students.

Genres of Literature and Multicultural Literature

The content of any book, including picture books, determines its genre. Literature, which includes poetry, falls under two major categories: fiction and nonfiction. Teachers should incorporate a range of literature to meet their students' interests when they plan lessons for reading aloud and for independent reading.

Teachers also can help students understand different perspectives by choosing diverse literature. When teachers use a range of quality books in different genres, their students should find rewards in that range.

Nonfiction

- Nonfiction is literature that emphasizes information, including facts, interpretation, and opinion.
- Nonfiction includes biography, autobiography, memoir, and informational books.
- **Biography** is an account of a person's life.
- **Autobiography** is an author's account of his or her life.
- **Memoir** is autobiographical but focuses upon selected parts of the author's life.

- **Informational books** provide factual information about a topic or event and can include interpretation and opinion.

Fiction

- Fiction can be realistic and believable, but the story conveyed is not entirely factual. The author may be inspired by an actual event or person and even include such events and people in the narrative, but the author also creates characters, episodes, and/or settings.

- **Realistic fiction** offers stories that could have happened in the real world.

- **Historical fiction** offers stories of history based upon facts, although the actual characters and episodes are fictional.

- **Traditional literature** is derived from narratives originally told orally and set in an alternate reality. It includes folktales, fairy tales, legends, and myths.

- **Fantasy and science fiction** offer narratives similar to traditional literature in exploring an alternate reality, but the stories have been written by authors rather than originating as oral tales sharing a culture's beliefs, values, and morals. Science fiction relies upon scientific concepts or technologies.

Poetry

- Poetry does not fit readily under fiction or nonfiction.

- Poetry is often recognized by its form or the way the words are arranged on a page. Poetry can rhyme, but it need not do so, although it is characterized by rhythm. Carefully chosen and arranged words convey its meaning.

Literary Elements

Students must know literary elements to understand how literature works and thus enhance their reading of it. Knowledge of literary elements also can guide their own writing of prose and poetry. To analyze literature, students must be confident that their thoughts are legitimate. Teachers support students by providing instruction that recognizes the role of personal responses in reading. After reading, students should thus first share personal responses before analyzing a work. In sharing their responses, students consider what they like or dislike about the plot as well as the big ideas that emerge from the work and how they connect to them. Through discussions and grand conversations, students hear others, including the teacher, and thus expand their experiences. Students also see that their responses are legitimate, but responses should be consistent with the text, and teachers should encourage students to refer to the text when they respond. By reviewing key sections of a work, teachers and students can focus on literary elements:

- **Plot** is what happens in the story, and it should proceed logically, even in imaginative works. In historical fiction, for example, the plot must be accurate in that its events need to be things that could have happened. When teachers discuss what took place in a story, students learn about plot.

- **Setting** is the time and place of a story. Setting in historical fiction determines what can take place. In fantasy, the setting also should be believable because of the detailed, vivid description.

- **Theme** relates to messages, big ideas, or larger meanings that emerge from a story.

- **Characterization** is how the author reveals characters. Readers learn about characters through what they say, do and/or think. Readers also learn about a character through what other characters say or think about the character. Fictional characters can grow and change, but they must seem real. Their actions must be plausible.

- **Style** is how a writer tells a story and determines the choices and arrangement of words.

- **Point of View** refers to the perspective from which a story is told.

The omniscient view lets readers know what each character thinks, and the author can speak to the readers as the storyteller.

Limited omniscient lets the reader know only what the main character feels, thinks and understands. It thus tells the story from the protagonist's perspective.

First person occurs when a character tells the story.

Formal Comprehension Assessments

Schools can use formal assessments to get data to assess students' progress in literacy. When students reach the middle grades, they must read longer, more complex texts and connect their ideas.

Criterion-referenced tests assess a specific set of skills, concepts or criteria at a designated level of difficulty. These exams can determine what a student knows before and after instruction. Each skill or concept is measured by items to help control for guessing and get an adequate sample of students' knowledge.

Norm-referenced tests are standardized exams that compare a student's performance with a sample of similar students (e.g., of the same grade level) who took the test at the same time of the school year. The administration and scoring of the test uses standardized procedures. Norms are obtained from the standardization sample. The scores provide information about how the student's achievement compares to other students nationally. A percentile score can range from 1 to 99. A score of 60th percentile means that 60% of the norm group performed at or below the student's score.

Strategies and Instruction for Comprehension Development

Visualizing

If students create images of what they read, they are engaged. Visualizing especially helps in comprehending fiction.

If students can identify words when reading a story but cannot retell what they read, then they can benefit from instruction that shows them how to visualize as they read. The teacher can model visualizing by reading a segment of text aloud while the students follow. The teacher then stops and thinks aloud to share a mental picture that can include the action, characters, and setting. When the teacher shares, students also can share. The teacher can then show how readers may have accurate mental pictures even with different images.

Self-Monitoring

Comprehension requires connecting ideas while reading. As they read, proficient readers monitor their understanding. They adjust their rate of reading, according to the purpose of the reading and difficulty of the text. A proficient reader rereads a challenging section and stops to consider its difficult ideas.

To encourage students to monitor their reading, teachers use prompts to help students correct miscues when they read aloud, asking them if what they said makes sense when an error shows the student needs to pay more attention to meaning.

Teachers also can provide opportunities for students to self-monitor by discussing short segments of text rather than waiting until the end. These discussions can encourage students to pay attention to meaning and recognize that texts require considering ideas, not just a superficial read-through.

Story Maps

Story maps can help students learn elements of fiction. A visual representation can foster a discussion of plot, conflict, setting, characters and theme(s). In using story maps, teachers should model and work with students to complete the map. After the first reading and discussion of a narrative, story maps can be used to help students recognize how elements of fiction work. Teachers should remember that story maps are a tool to enhance understanding of how literature works. They should avoid emphasizing how to complete a story map. If students are shown how literature works, they will become more proficient readers and writers, but this instruction should not hinder motivation to read.

Previewing and Text Features

Previewing can help students anticipate what they will read. When students read expository text, they can overlook features important to learning and comprehension.

Proficient reading recognizes features of text and how to use them to understand. Features include the following: illustrations, images, diagrams, labels, captions, graphs, charts, timetables, bold print, italics, headings and subheadings, glossary, table of contents, and index. Students will best learn about text features when teachers show them how to use a relevant text feature in something they are reading.

Discerning Text Structure and Using Strategies

Students have a schema for the narrative structure of fiction. With expository text, especially in such disciplines as social studies and the sciences, the topics often have their own structure, which is determined by how a subject is inherently organized. The author of an expository text uses the inherent organization in presenting and connecting ideas. Successful reading and learning requires understanding the major ideas and their support, as well as connecting these ideas to understand the broader topic.

Students cannot always remember the new information presented in expository prose, but teachers can help them learn how to read and study such material. Students must be shown that proficient readers change their approach when they read to learn. Through modeling and guidance, teachers can help students understand the major ideas of headings and the supporting details, and how major ideas connect in presenting information about a topic as indicated in the title of the reading. Authors do not always use headings, but students also can be shown how to infer what the implied headings are.

Strategies can help students understand and remember. Teachers must provide enough modeling and guided practice to show how to use strategies. A gradual release of responsibility helps students use a strategy effectively, as follows: (1) The teacher models while students observe. (2) The teacher and students do the task together. (3) The students work together, and the teacher monitors to make sure they understand what to do. (4) The students work on their own.

Students vary in how soon they can apply a strategy. Guided practice is valuable because students can learn in their current subjects and be prepared for their coming grade levels. Teachers must devote enough time to modeling and guidance because students will use strategy throughout their education.

Showing students how to read short chunks at a time also helps. Students can be asked to read shorter segments before a discussion, with the length of the segment determined by balancing the students' abilities with the difficulty of the material.

Question-Answer Relationships (QAR)

QAR is a strategy used after reading to help students understand that questions about a passage can vary in what they require of a reader. Students often assume they must search a passage to answer a question, but answers to some questions can be found by connecting information in the text with their experience and knowledge. The QAR strategy categorizes questions by the question-answer relationship:

- **Right There**—The answer to these questions can be found in the text. These are literal questions that often have the same words as those in the text.

- **Think and Search**—The answer to these questions is also in the text but is found by searching parts of the text to connect information.

- **Author and You**—These questions require students to relate information in the text to their experience and knowledge.

- **On My Own**—These questions require students to use their experience and knowledge, but they must draw solely on their experience and background knowledge, not the text, for the answers.

Students should practice answering all four types. The teacher should read a short passage aloud while students follow. The teacher then can present questions about the passage and think aloud to model how to answer them. With practice, students gain in thinking about a text and answering questions they can expect on exams.

Directed Reading Thinking Activity (DRTA)

DRTA is a comprehension strategy that encourages students to activate their knowledge, make predictions, and monitor their understanding. Teachers should provide modeling and other support as students engage in DRTA. The procedures are as follows:

- **Direct**—Teachers point students' attention to the title, chapter heading(s), illustrations, captions, and other related text features. Teachers ask a general question based on the title and heading(s) of material to be read (e.g., "What do you think we will learn, based on this title? "Look at this heading. What do you think we will learn?") As with any strategy, teachers *must think aloud when introducing the strategy*. Teachers also should provide prompts and add to what students say to provide differentiated instruction for English learners and less capable readers as well as students with a learning disability.

- **Reading**—The teacher plans on a good point to stop students when they read, because students often should read in segments rather than an entire section. The size of the segment is determined by balancing the difficulty of the material with the ability of the students. After students read, the teacher asks them what they learned and how it matched their predictions. The students continue until they have read the entire section under a heading or even the whole textbook.

- **Think**—When students finish reading a section, the teacher guides them in thinking about their predictions and what they read. Students can think about what they learned and whether they should modify predictions.

Teachers can write students' predictions and what they say they learned to provide a record of their thinking as well as their later review of the passage or chapter. This modeling can show how to take notes. This helps students to read.

Reciprocal Teaching

Reciprocal teaching encourages students to monitor their reading. Reciprocal teaching entails four strategies to read and understand text: summarizing, asking questions, clarifying, and predicting. Teachers model and provide students with ample practice to learn each strategy of reciprocal teaching. After teachers observe that students know what to do, they have students work in four-person groups to discuss the reading and teach each other.

The teacher should first show students how to use the strategies. This can be done with the whole group or via small-group work before students use reciprocal teaching. Students must know what to do before they work with each other in a small group. The time devoted to reciprocal teaching strategies is merited. Students learn content through the guidance. The payoff is large when students can work on their own to use all four strategies.

The strategies are as follows:

Summarizing—Students read a segment in a section of the text, and then a **summarizer** condenses the key ideas and tells them to the group.

Question Generating—After the summarizer shares, the questioner asks about any unclear parts and/or how ideas connect to other ideas or concepts.

Clarifying—The clarifier answers the questions presented by the questioner.

Predicting—The predictor anticipates what the author will present next.

The procedure for conducting these strategies works as follows:

- The teacher places students in groups of four and assigns each student a role written on an index card.

- Students read up to the stopping point determined by the teacher so that the students read appropriate segments of a section.

- Students assume their roles in leading the dialogue and teaching each other.

- Students can change roles, passing the card to the right, and repeat the process (if the teacher knows all the students are able to perform the role).

- The teacher guides and monitors to ensure students succeed. The teacher's participation decreases as students become more proficient.

Think-Pair-Share (TPS)

Think-Pair-Share (TPS) is a strategy to encourage students to consider their own response to a question the teacher provides and then share their thoughts with another student. TPS provides scaffolding for students as they share with a classmate, helping them learn concepts and develop oral language abilities. The procedures are as follows:

- The teacher determines when and what to ask. The question can be general: "What did you learn from what you just read?" "What did the author tell us?"

- The teacher shows how to use each part of TPS by working with a small group or the whole class. The teacher models and then gradually lets students participate with the teacher's guidance while making sure they know what to do before they apply TPS.

The procedure for applying TPS works as follows:

Think—After reading or viewing, students think about the question the teacher asks.

Pair—Students join a partner or small group for sharing what they have been thinking.

Share—Students share what they have been thinking with the partner or small group. Students then can share with the whole group. Teachers can use this for a whole-group discussion.

Concept Maps

Concept Maps provide a visual organizing display to enhance understanding and retention. Through the visual organizer, students can see main ideas as well as how they relate. The organizer presents a concept with lines connecting it to other concepts. The visual organizer can be a web, timeline, or Venn diagram.

Concept maps also can show a process via terms associated with the process. For example, the visual organizer for photosynthesis might include photos or illustrations, such as a plant with its parts explained.

Concept mapping also can be **semantic maps** for vocabulary development as well as representing concepts. The word for the concept is placed at the center of a web. Each concept then gets at least three important associations: class, property, and example. Class is the class of things the concept is part of. For example, hurricanes are in the class of types of storms. Property refers to attributes or properties of the concept, such as defining characteristics, which can be captured in examplars.

Concept and semantic maps can be used before, during, and after reading a unit of study:

Before—Students tell what comes to mind when they think of the topic/concept/word. The teacher adds students' thoughts to the map. Activating students' experience and knowledge can help them relate new information.

During—As students read, they discuss what they are learning to add to the map.

After—Students can review the map after different points in the unit of study have been completed.

SQ3R

SQ3R is a comprehension and study strategy that helps students navigate expository text. The steps of the strategy are as follows:

- **Survey**—Students skim the chapter title, headings, illustrations, and bold text to get an idea of the topic as well as the framework for how information is presented.

- **Question**—When they start a section, students turn a heading into the question(s) they anticipate the section will answer.

- **Read**—Students read to gain answers, and a stopping point can be determined based on the section's difficulty.

- **Recite**—After reading a section, students say what they learned in their own words. In guiding students, teachers ask them to speak. When they speak, the teacher writes notes that students can study later. This writing also models for students how to take notes. The students do not copy the notes so that they can devote attention to ideas they are reading and then recalling.

- **Review**—Reviews can occur after reading each section as well as after reading all of the sections by reviewing the notes that were developed.

K-W-L

K-W-L is a strategy in which students discuss and complete three columns of a chart while reading expository text: **What I Know, What I Want to Learn, and What I Learned**. This strategy helps students consider their knowledge and experience, set purposes for reading, and monitor their comprehension.

Before reading, students discuss what they know about the topic while the teacher or students list those ideas to help them use their background knowledge (What I Know). Students then discuss and list questions they think the text could answer. This helps them set a purpose for reading as well as consider what they are reading (What I Want to Learn).

After reading the text or a segment of it, students discuss and write what they learned in that last column. Answers can be written next to the questions. Because students phrase ideas in their own words, they process the information better. Students also can see for themselves which ideas they know from the reading and which ideas they need to study further.

This strategy works when teachers model for students and guide the development of the chart.

Questioning the Author

Through Questioning the Author, students read a segment and then collaborate with the teacher to understand it and learn to solve comprehension problems as they read. Students use this strategy while reading a text, not after, and it helps them read actively and recognize that an author creates the text.

When planning, the teacher should first decide what major understandings students should build while reading as well as what could be difficult for them. The teacher then determines the best way to segment the text.

The teacher also develops questions to help foster understanding. The questions should be queries, not comprehension questions. The latter assess comprehension, while queries try to foster discussion and encourage students to use their own words to build meaning.

Initial queries let students describe what the text says in their own words. It can help prepare them for the next segment as they build meaning: What is the author saying here? Do I understand the author?

Follow-up prompts can help students consider what a text means, not just what it says: How does this connect with what the author said in the last chapter? Does the author explain the idea so that it makes sense?

The teacher and students collaborate. The teacher participates to foster discussion by helping students develop and share their thoughts.

Competency 006: Written Language— Writing Conventions

COMPETENCY 006 (WRITTEN LANGUAGE— WRITING CONVENTIONS)

The teacher understands the conventions of writing in English and provides instruction that helps students develop proficiency in applying writing conventions.

A. Knows predictable stages in the development of writing conventions (including the physical and cognitive processes involved in letter formation, word writing, sentence construction, spelling, punctuation, and grammatical expression), and recognizes that individual variations occur.

B. Knows and applies appropriate instructional strategies and sequences to teach writing conventions and their applications to all students, including English-language learners.

C. Knows informal and formal procedures for assessing students' use of writing conventions and uses multiple, ongoing assessments to monitor and evaluate students' development in this area.

D. Uses ongoing assessment of writing conventions to determine when a student needs additional help or intervention to bring the student's performance to grade level, based on state content and performance standards for writing in the Texas Essential Knowledge and Skills (TEKS).

E. Analyzes students' errors in applying writing conventions and uses the results of this analysis as a basis for future instruction.

F. Knows writing conventions and appropriate grammar and usage and provides students with direct instruction and guided practice in these areas.

G. Understands the contribution of conventional spelling toward success in reading and writing.

H. Understands stages of spelling development (prephonetic, phonetic, transitional and conventional) and how and when to support students' development from one stage to the next.

I. Provides systematic spelling instruction and gives students opportunities to use and develop spelling skills in the context of meaningful written expression.

Role and Importance of Writing Conventions

Writing conventions make reading easier, and the conventions thus let writers be "polite" to their readers. Creating content may be the writer's biggest challenge, but teachers still should devote time to writing conventions: handwriting, capitalization, punctuation, usage, and spelling. Instruction must help students develop and apply writing conventions.

Handwriting instruction must help students use manuscript as well cursive writing. Because students constantly use keyboards, some may question the usefulness of handwriting instruction. However, legal documents often require a signature, and some documents also require printing with a signature. Some writers also prefer to use cursive and then type the final draft. People also use writing in other ways, such as signing a greeting card as well as adding a personal note to it.

Handwriting instruction should help students write legibly and efficiently. Guides for forming letters are available to help teachers show students how to write legible cursive efficiently while writing from left in English.

When students can identify and write letters, they learn to spell. The first words they learn to spell should be the high-frequency words they encounter while reading as well as writing. Spelling is important to their education.

When students have a corpus of sight words, they have a basis for learning to spell words that have phonics generalizations. Students also should learn to spell words that have different aspects of morphemic/structural analysis, including multisyllabic words. As students progress in spelling, they can learn commonly confused and misspelled words.

Students also need regular skill lessons on capitalization, punctuation, and usage. English handbooks provide guidance to help teachers provide instruction. By developing checklists and using anecdotal records, teachers can help students master skills. Skill instruction is best provided for no more than 10–20 minutes at a time. It should focus on one skill or a few words to spell. More time leads to diminishing returns and detracts from other instruction. However, a lesson can be reviewed and built upon. Students retain what they learn over time.

Role of Proofreading and Publishing Conferences

Besides systematic skills instruction, students also must apply skills for real reasons. During the publishing conference, the teacher meets with a small group to guide students as they proofread their draft to create a final draft or "publish" their work. Students should learn that just as professional writers proofread a draft, they too should polish writing. Students may write a final draft to display on the bulletin board. They also might develop a book to be added to the class library or given as a gift. Students also might add to a classroom document. When they write for a broader audience beyond the teacher, students are more likely to invest time in proofreading.

To prepare for the conference, the teacher reads each student's draft and decides on two skills for each student to learn.

During the conference, the teacher shows students how to use an editing checklist for spelling, capitalization, and punctuation. Students use one ink color for marking. The checklists become more sophisticated as students learn more about spelling, capitalization, punctuation, and usage.

The teacher provides short lessons on one or two writing conventions to each student while the others listen. The teacher first tells the student what the student did well before showing what to revise via the one or two writing conventions. The teacher focuses on one or two conventions to avoid overwhelming students. The final draft will not contain errors because the teacher uses a different ink color to make changes for typing a final draft.

Stages of Spelling Development

Researchers who have studied children's writing describe stages of spelling development. The movement to different stages is gradual, and a speller can be in more than one stage.

The assigned age levels are approximate and depend on a child's experiences with print as well as spelling instruction. Some researchers recommend that teachers avoid considering grade levels and instead view each student as an individual. They then should provide instruction based upon what the student can do.

Precommunicative stage (typically ages 3–5)

The child uses letters, but the letters and words do not correspond when the child reads what's written. The child thus knows that letters are used in writing, but the writing looks like a random array of letters. The child has a message in mind, but a reader would be unable to read it. The child also may not know that writing moves from left.

M E M M S (I am with my dog.)

Semiphonetic stage (typically ages 4–6)

The child knows that letters represent sounds in words and uses the name of a letter to represent sounds, words, and syllables. Spelling is abbreviated. This stage begins "invented spelling" in which the child accounts for the sounds heard in words.

> R (are)   U (you)   B (be)

The child understands letter-sound correspondence—that sounds are assigned to letters. The child often applies rudimentary logic and uses single letters, for example, to represent words, sounds and syllables (e.g., U for *you*).

Phonetic stage (typically ages 5–7)

The child represents all major speech sounds heard in a word. The words may not be spelled conventionally, but the spellings are systematic and can be understood.

> TAK (take)   CHRAN (train)   CHRUK (truck)

Transitional stage (typically ages 6–11)

The child does not only rely on representing sounds to spell but also uses visual and morphological information. The child knows many common words and may use such common letter strings as *igh*. The use of visual information may include reversing letters in words: siad (said).

Correct stage (typically ages 10–11+)

The speller knows nearly all the sound-symbol principles and has learned generalizations as well as irregular spellings of words. The speller can use prefixes and suffixes as well as silent consonants. Commonly misspelled words and some individual words may create difficulty.

CHAPTER 9

Competency 007: Written Language— Composition

COMPETENCY 007 (WRITTEN LANGUAGE—COMPOSITION)

The teacher understands that writing to communicate is a developmental process and provides instruction that promotes students' competence in written communication.

A. Knows predictable stages in the development of written language and recognizes that individual variations occur.

B. Promotes student recognition of the practical uses of writing, creates an environment in which students are motivated to express ideas in writing, and models writing as an enjoyable activity and a tool for lifelong learning.

C. Knows and applies appropriate instructional strategies and sequences to develop students' writing skills.

D. Knows characteristics and uses of informal and formal written language assessments and uses multiple, ongoing assessments to monitor and evaluate students' writing development.

E. Uses assessment results to plan focused instruction to address the writing strengths, needs and interests of all individuals and groups, including English-language learners.

F. Uses ongoing assessment of written language to determine when a student needs additional help or intervention to bring the student's performance to grade level, based on state content and performance standards for writing in the Texas Essential Knowledge and Skills (TEKS).

G. Understands the use of self-assessment in writing and provides opportunities for students to self-assess their writings (e.g., for clarity, interest to audience, comprehensiveness) and their development as writers.

H. Understands differences between first-draft writing and writing for publication and provides instruction in various stages of writing, including prewriting, drafting, editing, and revising.

I. Understands the development of writing in relation to the other language arts and uses instructional strategies that connect these various aspects of language.

J. Understands similarities and differences between language (e.g., syntax, vocabulary) used in spoken and written English and helps students use knowledge of these similarities and differences to enhance their own writing.

K. Understands writing for a variety of audiences, purposes, and settings and provides students with opportunities to write for various audiences, purposes, and settings.

L. Knows how to write using voices and styles appropriate for different audiences and purposes, and provides students with opportunities to write using various voices and styles.

M. Understands the benefits of technology for teaching writing and writing for publication and provides instruction in the use of technology to facilitate written communication.

Process and Product in Writing

Writing instruction should help students learn the strategies and techniques of successful writers, and the conditions for writing should foster growth in writing proficiency. Much traditional writing instruction focuses on the end product. Students get a writing assignment and work on their own to complete it. The teacher then grades the finished assignment. The grade may depend on how well the writing established and presented ideas. The grade also could be based upon how well the student applied correct spelling, punctuation, capitalization, and usage. This focus on the final product fails to keep in mind the process of writing—what occurs when people write. Focusing on a finished product provides feedback only at the end. It offers no support during the writing process.

Current theory and research emphasize that effective writing instruction should support students during the process to help them learn to develop a better product and become proficient writers. During the process, attention first focuses on establishing content, but instruction should not dismiss the application of writing conventions when writing is going to be "published" or shared. Students thus should be shown how to proofread.

By writing rough drafts, students learn to establish content and share their writing so that others can understand it. By paying attention to the final product, students then further learn to apply conventions of spelling, punctuation, capitalization, and usage.

Writing instruction should recognize that students can vary where they are in the process. Some students may finish a piece on the second day, while others may be working on a piece for several days. Students just need to know that when they finish a piece, they should begin another. Over a few weeks, teachers can ask students to select one piece for "publishing" and sharing the final draft.

They then learn further proofreading so that what they share adheres to conventions of spelling, punctuation, capitalization, and usage.

Daily Writing Instruction and Structure of Writing Workshop

With a writing workshop approach, teachers can provide conditions akin to how writers write in the real world. In a writing workshop, students write daily to gain fluency through practice, as they do with reading. Students cannot progress with occasional writing or writing only for assessments.

A writing workshop is structured to help students gain proficiency. Each part plays a role, and the combined parts support students' development. The workshop helps students learn strategies and techniques, and it provides authentic writing experiences, thereby providing conditions for learning. The simple, predictable structure of a workshop helps students because they then know what to expect each day. Students who know they will write each day think about topics when they are outside of school. A predictable structure also helps teachers. Teachers know what they will do rather than choreographing something each day or week. Structure is not regimentation, but it avoids chaos.

Through **mini-lessons**, teachers help students based on their abilities and the writing they need to learn. At the start of each day, students meet as a group. Mini-lessons are usually brief, but they have the same focus for more than one day, depending on students' needs. The teacher first must devote attention to procedures of the writing workshop. Procedures include how to get writing folders as well as paper and pencils. Procedures also include writing names and dates on drafts and starting another writing when a draft is finished. Mini-lessons focus mostly on the craft of writing, such as strategies and techniques that writers use. Instead of lecturing, teachers think aloud and show students the writing process. For example, the teacher can model how to select a topic by brainstorming and listing what the teacher knows and cares about. The teacher also might show revising by sharing a draft and then add needed details to it. Literature previously read aloud also can be reviewed as a **mentor text** to show students how a professional writer used a strategy or technique.

Small-group work can build upon mini-lessons. For additional scaffolding, teachers can provide small-group instruction while other students write. Each student should meet the teacher during the week according to a daily schedule created for each group.

During **writing** and **conferences**, the teacher and students write. After about 10 minutes, the teacher should move about the room for **rough-draft conferences** with students. These conferences should be one to three minutes and focus solely on establishing content, with later proofreading reserved for addressing conventions. As most writers do, the student or the teacher reads the piece aloud. The teacher then "receives" the work by telling the student what the teacher heard or learned, using the student's exact words. Next, the teacher asks genuine questions about anything that needs clarifying. This structure lets students know what works and what needs to be clearer. The conference also lets the teacher help students with problems, such as selecting a topic. Teachers should not assign a topic so that students maintain ownership. Teachers can help students pick a topic they know and care about so that students are more able to express ideas.

Whole-class sharing can occur daily. A few students can share each day, and students can sign up to do so. All who want to share should have that opportunity, but sharing should not be not required of students who do not wish to share. Students learn from each other in whole-group conferences, which should be structured like the rough-draft conferences with the teacher. The student reads the piece aloud. The students then "receive" the work by telling the student what they heard or learned. Next, the students ask genuine questions that can show what needs clarification.

The structure of a writing workshop can remain the same with any writing. The content to be learned changes according to what students need to learn. The structure provides opportunities for growth while managing the class. The structure also provides differentiated instruction. Students participate according to their abilities while getting support from the teacher as well as their classmates.

Publishing Conferences

Publishing conferences can occur while students write. Kindergartners and early first grade-students do not proofread, and their invented spelling should be recognized as positive, not as errors. Invented spelling contributes to phonemic awareness, an important ability in learning to read and write. When students master conventional spelling, however, teachers should have publishing conferences. After two or three weeks, students should select one piece to be published from their folders. Students can move at their own pace in writing, but they should write daily. During those two or three weeks, students should put a piece for "publishing" in an editing tray. When enough students do this, the teacher conducts a publishing conference at the table. For rough-draft conferences, the teacher moves among students, but publishing conferences take place in small groups at a table.

The teacher prepares for publishing conferences by reading each draft to determine what the student can do and where the student needs help. The teacher records this on an anecdotal record sheet kept for each student to document skill development. When focusing on writing to capture their thoughts, students focus on establishing content. First drafts thus may have errors in such writing conventions as spelling, punctuation, capitalization, and usage even when students can otherwise spell a word or use another convention correctly. As students gain proficiency, they will apply the skill more often with drafts.

During the publishing conference with a small group, the teacher shows how to use an editing checklist for spelling, capitalization, punctuation, and usage. Students use one ink color for marking. Students' checklists become more sophisticated as they learn about spelling, capitalization, punctuation, and usage.

The teacher conducts short lessons on one or two writing conventions with each student while the others listen. The teacher starts by telling the student what works and then suggests what should be revised according to one or two conventions. By limiting the focus of revision, the teacher avoids overwhelming the student. The goal will still be a final draft without errors.

The teacher corrects errors in a different ink color to distinguish the teacher's corrections from the student's. This is done before a final draft is typed or written and not during the conference. The teacher or the student then types or writes the piece without errors. If the students can do it well, the teacher lets them type the final draft, but reluctant and less capable writers may rely on the teacher to type a final draft.

Strategies and Techniques of Effective Writing

The most difficult part of writing is establishing content that will be understood by the reader as the author intended. For the reader to get the intended meaning, the writer must first form the thoughts while writing to express what is intended. The writer then must determine how to write it so that the audience understands the intended meaning, which requires the writer to have audience awareness. Writers must develop more than one draft, even if the initial drafts are solely thought about and not written. Like most adults, students must write more than one draft to establish content.

In trying to help students meet the demands of writing a draft, teachers act as a coach to show students strategies and techniques that writers use. Rather than just "telling" someone what to do, the writing coach also "shows" what to do and provides support while the student tries to apply the strategy or technique.

Depending on the students' needs and the writing taught, the teacher shows strategies and techniques that writers use, including how to:

- select a topic
- write rough drafts that focus on establishing content rather than disrupt the process by devoting attention to writing conventions
- add or delete a word, sentence, or set of sentences
- spell a word the best you can rather than use a less effective word that is easy to spell
- elaborate by adding details
- select a title
- add dialogue
- create a picture with words to convey what happened

- use strong verbs rather than adverbs

- locate and organize information for writing reports

- use resources for reports without plagiarizing

Mini-Lessons Continued through Small-Group Work

To provide more scaffolding, teachers can provide small-group instruction during the writing workshop while other students write. It is important to make sure each student meets with the teacher to provide support as needed, and creating a schedule for each group can help.

Voice and Types of Writing

The teacher first helps students write stories about themselves because personal narratives are meaningful. Students also know what has happened, making it easier to use details and dialogue to create a picture with words. Students also may select topics they know and care about (e.g., soccer, motorcycles, pets) for informal reports that let them share information they have. When students select the topic, they are more likely to be invested in their writing. Professional writers often write what they know and care about, and it is reasonable to assume that beginning writers will progress more when they share their own experiences and ideas.

State exams and school reports assign topics, but when students get experience at forming their thoughts when writing, they have developed abilities that will help them respond to assigned topics. By writing about what they know and care about, students learn they have something to say when they write. Exams and assigned reports also often provide a choice of topics or focus through the prompts.

As the school year progresses, students can learn about writing reports, essays, fiction, and poetry. The structure of the writing workshop stays the same, with teachers adapting mini-lessons and group work to the writing to be learned.

Teachers consider the strategies and techniques required to develop writing. They plan mini-lessons to show them to students. They then let the students practice the strategies and techniques. For example, in teaching students how to take notes for a report, the students and teacher can read the information together. The students then write notes to put the ideas in their own words.

Competency 008: Viewing and Representing

10

COMPETENCY 008 (VIEWING AND REPRESENTING)

The teacher understands skills for interpreting, analyzing, evaluating, and producing visual images and messages in various media and provides students with opportunities to develop skills in this area.

A. Knows grade-level expectations in the Texas Essential Knowledge and Skills (TEKS) and procedures for assessing students' skills in interpreting, analyzing, evaluating, and producing visual images, messages, and meanings.

B. Uses ongoing assessment and knowledge of grade-level expectations in the Texas Essential Knowledge and Skills (TEKS) to identify students' needs regarding the interpretation, analysis, evaluation, and production of visual images, messages, and meanings and to plan instruction.

C. Understands characteristics and functions of different types of media (e.g., film, print) and knows how different types of media influence and inform.

D. Compares and contrasts print, visual, and electronic media (e.g., films and written stories).

E. Evaluates how visual image makers (e.g., illustrators, documentary filmmakers, political cartoonists, news photographers) represent messages and meanings and provides students with varied opportunities to interpret and evaluate visual images in various media.

F. Knows how to teach students to analyze visual image makers' choices (e.g., style, elements, media) and evaluate how these choices help to represent or extend meaning.

G. Provides students with opportunities to interpret events and ideas based on information from maps, charts, graphics, video segments, and technology presentations and to use media to compare ideas and points of view.

H. Knows steps and procedures for producing visual images, messages, and meanings to communicate with others.

I. Teaches students how to select, organize, and produce visuals to complement and extend meanings.

J. Provides students with opportunities to use technology to produce various types of communications (e.g., class newspapers, multimedia reports, video reports) and helps students analyze how language, medium, and presentation contribute to the message.

Visual Literacy

Developing literacy is not limited to spoken and written language. Students also must understand and produce visual images as well as learn and solve problems in visual spheres. Just as they engage in authentic use and get scaffolding from the teacher to gain oral and written literacy, students will progress in visual literacy when they engage in it while supported by effective instruction.

Visual literacy includes photographs, illustrations, paintings, graphic art, films, videos, maps, charts, and graphs. Visual literacy is used in a variety of disciplines, and it can be developed as part of students' learning in reading/language arts as well as other subject areas.

Students must first observe well enough to identify details accurately. Higher-level abilities include understanding what is seen, including comprehending visual relationships. Some contexts require students to create meaning by integrating images they receive or produce with language they read or write. To facilitate progress in comprehending and producing visual images, teachers must help students learn vocabulary and concepts as well as strategies and techniques to create images.

Multimodal Literacy

Leaders in reading/language arts education provide guidance for fostering multimodal literacy, including art, text, speech, drama, and physical movement as well as digital literacy.

- Developing students' learning in different modes of expression should be among their curricular goals. Ample time and resources also should be allocated.

- Electronic environments should provide students with quick access to a range of information platforms to meet the expanded ways of acquiring information and understanding concepts. However, students also must be shown techniques for locating, selecting, organizing, and evaluating information.

- Multimodal projects are complex, and students will vary in the abilities they bring to the projects. This will require much collaboration and team work. When students work together, the process should foster increased learning as well as better outcomes when they create such products as brochures, magazines, books, videos, or greeting cards.

- An exclusive emphasis on digital literacies can limit students' access to other modes of communication.

Competency 009: Study and Inquiry Skills

11

COMPETENCY 009 (STUDY AND INQUIRY SKILLS)

The teacher understands the importance of study and inquiry skills as tools for learning in the content areas and promotes students' development in applying study and inquiry skills.

A. Understands study and inquiry skills (e.g., using text organizers; taking notes; outlining; drawing conclusions; applying test-taking strategies; previewing; setting purposes for reading; locating, organizing, evaluating, and communicating information; summarizing information; using multiple sources of information; interpreting and using graphic sources of information) and knows the significance of these skills for student learning and achievement.

B. Knows grade-level expectations for study and inquiry skills in the Texas Essential Knowledge and Skills (TEKS) and procedures for assessing students' development and use of these skills.

C. Knows and applies instructional practices that promote the acquisition and use of study and inquiry skills across the curriculum by all students, including English-language learners.

D. Knows how to provide students with varied and meaningful opportunities to learn and apply study and inquiry skills to enhance their achievement across the curriculum.

E. Uses ongoing assessment and knowledge of grade-level expectations in the Texas Essential Knowledge and Skills (TEKS) to identify students' needs regarding study and inquiry skills, to determine when a student requires additional help or intervention, and to plan instruction.

F. Responds to students' needs by providing direct, explicit instruction to promote the acquisition and use of study and inquiry skills.

Challenges of Reading and Writing to Learn

Students' learning in subject areas entails comprehending what they read. Textbooks and other informational documents present challenges. Students often assume that content-area texts can be read as they would read a story. However, even students who read fiction easily can be challenged by content-area texts. Students must read these texts to learn, and they thus must know how to study.

A major challenge in content-area texts is an academic vocabulary that often consists of words used only in that discipline. Acquiring the vocabulary is essential to relating concepts that require in-depth understanding. Such understanding does not come from memorizing a glossary definition.

Another challenge of informational texts is using their text structure to relate concepts and ideas. Readers have a schema for stories, and they can retell stories and comprehend them as they read. Unlike the structure of narratives, the text structures of informational texts are based on how information is organized in a given field. The text structure in a chapter also can differ depending on how ideas relate. For example, the nature of a battle could be described, thus using the descriptive text structure. Alternatively, however, the description of the battle could be part of a cause-and-effect text structure the author uses to present a major event in history. Expository texts typically demand more than a single straight-through reading to understand and remember the information.

Even when students can comprehend a content-area text, their education depends on learning and retaining new information, and can require them to write about it.

With new information, students typically must study it to learn it. Some information can be grasped readily when students have a lot of background information or prior learning. However, even capable readers face challenges when reading and writing to learn. Students rely on instruction to help them comprehend the texts. They also must be shown how to take notes and prepare for tests.

Writing in different disciplines also can challenge students, who must learn strategies associated with writing in each discipline. Students also must be shown how to locate information, take notes, synthesize ideas, and organize information in writing a report. The writing should be demonstrated by teachers and then used by students as they learn the subject.

Guidelines for Instruction in Reading and Writing to Learn

- Remember that strategies are a means to an end. Rather than focus on teaching an array of strategies, teachers should think of how to help their students before, during, and after reading. They should be selective in what they incorporate.

- Learning how to read to learn is a complex process. Students need time to master the procedures as they monitor how long it will take to learn the content.

- Small-group instruction provides differentiated instruction and guided practice. Other students can work independently or with a partner while the teacher meets with a group.

- Less capable readers can learn how to read content-area texts. They will need more scaffolding, and this may be needed before, during, and after reading. If students cannot read the text, teachers can try shared reading in which the teacher reads and students follow, joining in when they can.

- Students should read segments rather than an entire section because of the demands of content-area texts. The length depends on the complexity of the text and the students' background and ability. If students read in small groups, they can reread a section while others finish.

- Instruction must address not only understanding what is read but also connecting ideas. Students get confused when they try to remember content-area ideas as they do when reading a story. Instruction must include showing how the ideas of a content-area text connect in a section and how ideas of a passage or chapter relate.

- Understanding vocabulary and concept development is integral to learning in subject areas.

- Teachers should think aloud and demonstrate as part of instruction. Guided practice also is needed, and students should not work on their own before they are ready.

- With guided practice, students not only can learn the content but also gain in learning how to learn.

PRACTICE TEST 1

TExES ELAR 4–8

Also available at the REA Study Center (www.rea.com/studycenter)

This practice test is also offered online at the REA Study Center. We recommend that you take the online version of the test to simulate test-day conditions and to receive these added benefits:

- **Timed testing conditions**—helps you gauge how much time you can spend on each question

- **Automatic scoring**—find out how you did on the test, instantly

- **On-screen detailed explanations of answers**—gives you the correct answer and explains why the other answer choices are wrong

- **Diagnostic score reports**—pinpoint where you're strongest and where you need to focus your study

Practice Test 1 Answer Sheet

1. Ⓐ Ⓑ Ⓒ Ⓓ
2. Ⓐ Ⓑ Ⓒ Ⓓ
3. Ⓐ Ⓑ Ⓒ Ⓓ
4. Ⓐ Ⓑ Ⓒ Ⓓ
5. Ⓐ Ⓑ Ⓒ Ⓓ
6. Ⓐ Ⓑ Ⓒ Ⓓ
7. Ⓐ Ⓑ Ⓒ Ⓓ
8. Ⓐ Ⓑ Ⓒ Ⓓ
9. Ⓐ Ⓑ Ⓒ Ⓓ
10. Ⓐ Ⓑ Ⓒ Ⓓ
11. Ⓐ Ⓑ Ⓒ Ⓓ
12. Ⓐ Ⓑ Ⓒ Ⓓ
13. Ⓐ Ⓑ Ⓒ Ⓓ
14. Ⓐ Ⓑ Ⓒ Ⓓ
15. Ⓐ Ⓑ Ⓒ Ⓓ
16. Ⓐ Ⓑ Ⓒ Ⓓ
17. Ⓐ Ⓑ Ⓒ Ⓓ
18. Ⓐ Ⓑ Ⓒ Ⓓ
19. Ⓐ Ⓑ Ⓒ Ⓓ
20. Ⓐ Ⓑ Ⓒ Ⓓ
21. Ⓐ Ⓑ Ⓒ Ⓓ
22. Ⓐ Ⓑ Ⓒ Ⓓ
23. Ⓐ Ⓑ Ⓒ Ⓓ
24. Ⓐ Ⓑ Ⓒ Ⓓ
25. Ⓐ Ⓑ Ⓒ Ⓓ

26. Ⓐ Ⓑ Ⓒ Ⓓ
27. Ⓐ Ⓑ Ⓒ Ⓓ
28. Ⓐ Ⓑ Ⓒ Ⓓ
29. Ⓐ Ⓑ Ⓒ Ⓓ
30. Ⓐ Ⓑ Ⓒ Ⓓ
31. Ⓐ Ⓑ Ⓒ Ⓓ
32. Ⓐ Ⓑ Ⓒ Ⓓ
33. Ⓐ Ⓑ Ⓒ Ⓓ
34. Ⓐ Ⓑ Ⓒ Ⓓ
35. Ⓐ Ⓑ Ⓒ Ⓓ
36. Ⓐ Ⓑ Ⓒ Ⓓ
37. Ⓐ Ⓑ Ⓒ Ⓓ
38. Ⓐ Ⓑ Ⓒ Ⓓ
39. Ⓐ Ⓑ Ⓒ Ⓓ
40. Ⓐ Ⓑ Ⓒ Ⓓ
41. Ⓐ Ⓑ Ⓒ Ⓓ
42. Ⓐ Ⓑ Ⓒ Ⓓ
43. Ⓐ Ⓑ Ⓒ Ⓓ
44. Ⓐ Ⓑ Ⓒ Ⓓ
45. Ⓐ Ⓑ Ⓒ Ⓓ
46. Ⓐ Ⓑ Ⓒ Ⓓ
47. Ⓐ Ⓑ Ⓒ Ⓓ
48. Ⓐ Ⓑ Ⓒ Ⓓ
49. Ⓐ Ⓑ Ⓒ Ⓓ
50. Ⓐ Ⓑ Ⓒ Ⓓ

51. Ⓐ Ⓑ Ⓒ Ⓓ
52. Ⓐ Ⓑ Ⓒ Ⓓ
53. Ⓐ Ⓑ Ⓒ Ⓓ
54. Ⓐ Ⓑ Ⓒ Ⓓ
55. Ⓐ Ⓑ Ⓒ Ⓓ
56. Ⓐ Ⓑ Ⓒ Ⓓ
57. Ⓐ Ⓑ Ⓒ Ⓓ
58. Ⓐ Ⓑ Ⓒ Ⓓ
59. Ⓐ Ⓑ Ⓒ Ⓓ
60. Ⓐ Ⓑ Ⓒ Ⓓ
61. Ⓐ Ⓑ Ⓒ Ⓓ
62. Ⓐ Ⓑ Ⓒ Ⓓ
63. Ⓐ Ⓑ Ⓒ Ⓓ
64. Ⓐ Ⓑ Ⓒ Ⓓ
65. Ⓐ Ⓑ Ⓒ Ⓓ
66. Ⓐ Ⓑ Ⓒ Ⓓ
67. Ⓐ Ⓑ Ⓒ Ⓓ
68. Ⓐ Ⓑ Ⓒ Ⓓ
69. Ⓐ Ⓑ Ⓒ Ⓓ
70. Ⓐ Ⓑ Ⓒ Ⓓ
71. Ⓐ Ⓑ Ⓒ Ⓓ
72. Ⓐ Ⓑ Ⓒ Ⓓ
73. Ⓐ Ⓑ Ⓒ Ⓓ
74. Ⓐ Ⓑ Ⓒ Ⓓ
75. Ⓐ Ⓑ Ⓒ Ⓓ

76. Ⓐ Ⓑ Ⓒ Ⓓ
77. Ⓐ Ⓑ Ⓒ Ⓓ
78. Ⓐ Ⓑ Ⓒ Ⓓ
79. Ⓐ Ⓑ Ⓒ Ⓓ
80. Ⓐ Ⓑ Ⓒ Ⓓ
81. Ⓐ Ⓑ Ⓒ Ⓓ
82. Ⓐ Ⓑ Ⓒ Ⓓ
83. Ⓐ Ⓑ Ⓒ Ⓓ
84. Ⓐ Ⓑ Ⓒ Ⓓ
85. Ⓐ Ⓑ Ⓒ Ⓓ
86. Ⓐ Ⓑ Ⓒ Ⓓ
87. Ⓐ Ⓑ Ⓒ Ⓓ
88. Ⓐ Ⓑ Ⓒ Ⓓ
89. Ⓐ Ⓑ Ⓒ Ⓓ
90. Ⓐ Ⓑ Ⓒ Ⓓ
91. Ⓐ Ⓑ Ⓒ Ⓓ
92. Ⓐ Ⓑ Ⓒ Ⓓ
93. Ⓐ Ⓑ Ⓒ Ⓓ
94. Ⓐ Ⓑ Ⓒ Ⓓ
95. Ⓐ Ⓑ Ⓒ Ⓓ
96. Ⓐ Ⓑ Ⓒ Ⓓ
97. Ⓐ Ⓑ Ⓒ Ⓓ
98. Ⓐ Ⓑ Ⓒ Ⓓ
99. Ⓐ Ⓑ Ⓒ Ⓓ
100. Ⓐ Ⓑ Ⓒ Ⓓ

Practice Test 1

TIME: 4 hours and 45 minutes
        100 questions

> **Directions:** Read each item and select the best answer(s). Most items on this test require you to provide the one best answer. However, some questions require you to select all the options that apply.

1. Students in sixth grade started the school year by writing personal narratives and informal reports drawing upon their experiences. Subsequently, the students learned how to write reports. Now, the students are going to learn to write fiction by focusing upon creating a folktale. What instruction does the teacher need to provide to make the transition to learning a new form of writing?

   A. The teacher needs to make sure each student knows how to spell words they are likely to use in writing a folktale.

   B. The teacher needs to make sure English learners create an oral version of a tale to provide instruction that meets their needs.

   C. The teacher needs to develop a checklist of features of folktales that students use to begin writing.

   D. The teacher needs to provide mini-lessons that help ensure students are aware of features of folktales and must demonstrate techniques as she writes.

Use the information below to answer questions 2 through 9.

Ms. Johnson teaches language arts, and she is providing instruction for students as they read and learn content about types of rocks to help them learn how to read and learn from informational texts. Parts of the unit of study are presented below.

Part 1. Before students begin to read the chapter, Ms. Johnson directs students' attention to the title of the chapter, "Types of Rocks." Then she guides students to notice the headings: Sedimentary, Metamorphic, and Igneous.

Part 2. Ms. Johnson displays the word *sedimentary*, and she shows an illustration of sediment while briefly discussing the word *sediment*.

Part 3. Ms. Johnson points out the first heading, Sedimentary Rock. Ms. Johnson tells the students that this part of the textbook will present information about sedimentary rock and reminds students that it can be helpful to use a heading to think about questions the information might answer. Thinking aloud, Ms. Johnson says: "We know that types of rock are formed in different ways.

How are sedimentary rocks formed?" Next, Ms. Johnson asks students to share questions they think might be answered in this section.

Part 4. Ms. Johnson asks students to read the first paragraph to see what they learn about sedimentary rocks.

Part 5. Ms. Johnson asks the students to share with a classmate sitting next to them what they learned. Then the students share with the whole class.

Part 6. Ms. Johnson displays a table (see below) that the students complete with her guidance as they learn about each type of rocks in the unit of study:

Type of Rock	Sedimentary	Metamorphic	Igneous
Formation			
Key Characteristics			
Examples			

2. What is a major rationale for Part 1?

   A. Ms. Johnson is providing shared reading to help students acquire new information.

   B. Ms. Johnson is helping students preview the chapter to gain an understanding of how the overall topic is organized.

   C. Ms. Johnson is helping students acquire visual literacy by helping them pay attention to bold print.

   D. Ms. Johnson is helping students understand academic vocabulary.

3. In Part 2, Ms. Johnson draws students' attention to the word *sediment*. How does this play a primary role in students' reading and learning about the topic of the chapter?

   A. Understanding a root word can help students understand an unfamiliar concept, as well as build vocabulary.

   B. Ms. Johnson is helping students apply phonics as they read the short vowels of each syllable.

   C. Ms. Johnson is helping students learn a multisyllabic word.

   D. Ms. Johnson is pronouncing the word, and this helps students learn the meaning by looking up the word in their glossary for vocabulary development.

4. In Part 3, Ms. Johnson shares a question she thinks will be answered in the text by turning the heading into a question. Then students share questions they think could be answered in that section of the textbook. Which of the following statements indicates why this approach is effective?

   A. The teacher is helping students be able to complete the table.

   B. The teacher is building background knowledge.

   C. The teacher provides modeling to help students understand what to do in reading to learn from expository text.

   D. The teacher is activating students' prior knowledge.

5. In Part 4, Ms. Johnson asks students to read the first paragraph. What is a primary purpose for this approach?

   A. Students can learn the concept of paragraph.

   B. More students have the opportunity to read aloud if they read one paragraph at a time.

   C. The students will be able to understand content by reading and thinking about smaller chunks as compared to reading an entire section for text.

   D. Teachers should help students preview the text.

6. Which of the following statements is a rationale for the teacher's instruction in Part 5? Select *all* that apply.

   A. English learners and other students can make gains in oral language development from "turn and talk," when they talk to a classmate.

   B. Talking to a classmate can help students learn content.

   C. The students are given opportunities to talk in small-group and whole-group situations.

   D. Students can talk about information to learn it, and not read.

7. In Part 6, Ms. Johnson displays a table the students complete with her guidance as they learn about each type of rock in the unit of study. After reading about sedimentary rocks and viewing a video, Ms. Johnson asks the students to describe how sedimentary rocks are formed based upon information they had encountered in the textbook and video. Ms. Johnson adds the information to the table. In the next lesson, the students continue in this way after encountering information about key characteristics for identifying sedimentary rocks. Which of the following best explains how this approach helps students remember new information?

   A. The categories of the table help students organize individual facts in memory.

   B. Building background knowledge helps students relate the new to the known.

   C. The academic vocabulary in bold print should be discussed so students understand concepts.

   D. Previewing headings can help students before reading a text.

8. Which of the following would represent an effective way to incorporate viewing the video as part of the unit of study?

   A. The students could be given a test to make sure they gained insight from the video.

   B. Students can add information to the appropriate part of the table after viewing the video. They can then discuss how the textbook and video provided the same information or additional information.

   C. The students could be asked to find a video online to view to learn about digital resources.

   D. The teacher should provide the video for English learners instead of having them read the text.

9. In Part 6, the teacher displays a table the students complete with her guidance as they learn about sedimentary, metamorphic, and igneous rocks. For each type of rock, they learn how the rock is formed, key characteristics for identifying rocks, and examples of the type of rock. How does this approach help students as they subsequently learn to conduct research and write reports?

   A. The students are learning how to proofread for writing a final draft.

   B. The students are learning academic vocabulary.

   C. The students learn how to organize individual units of information they encounter according to categories, a skill also required in writing a report.

   D. The students are learning how to develop an effective lead-in for a report.

10. When writing rough drafts, students should do their best in spelling and using punctuation, but they should not be overly concerned about writing conventions. Which of the following identifies the rationale for this approach?

   A. Teachers need to provide differentiated instruction in teaching writing, so some students should not be overwhelmed by learning about writing conventions.

   B. Students are likely to not want to write if they have to care about spelling and punctuation.

   C. Writers need to establish content first, and students need to focus on that while writing drafts. Proofreading can come before a final draft.

   D. Establishing meaning in communication is what is most important, so spelling and punctuation do not need to be taught.

11. As part of vocabulary instruction throughout the year, the teacher has shown students the connections among words, such as *cordial*, *discord*, and *accord*. What is the rationale for this instruction?

    A. Students can learn that a root word always needs an affix.

    B. Students need to be shown how root words need a suffix.

    C. Students can be shown how the Latin root that means *heart* (*cor*) is a basis of the words and relates to their meanings.

    D. Students need to learn how to read multisyllabic words.

Use the information below to answer questions 12 and 13.

A teacher wants her students to make gains in fluency, and she provides opportunities for students to engage in readers' theatre.

Part 1. The teacher writes a readers' theatre script based upon a reading selection the students enjoyed and read previously as part of their instruction. The teacher makes copies of the script so that each character has one.

Part 2. The teacher works with a group and demonstrates how to read a script and how to work together in practicing the script.

Part 3. Students work in a small group and practice a readers' theatre script while the teacher works with a small group for reading instruction over a series of days; the students ask the teacher if they can present to the class.

12. In Part 1, which of the following identifies the rationale for the teacher's decision?

    A. The teacher makes it possible for students to use a mentor text.

    B. The teacher is making sure students know the story well so they can answer questions about it.

    C. The teacher is sure the students can read the words and understand the story before they gain further practice through readers' theatre.

    D. The teacher is introducing drama to students.

13. Regarding Part 2, which of the following states why the activities described make for effective teaching?

    A. The teacher should provide instruction because students can rely upon mentor texts they have read.

    B. The teacher needs to provide mini-lessons where she demonstrates and students practice the strategies and techniques of writing fiction.

    C. The teacher is introducing a type of text the students have not read, and she needs to make sure students know how to engage in a task and work together in productive ways before they work independently.

    D. The teacher needs to make sure students can read words of a script before asking them to read independently.

14. A student wrote the following:

    Last year I went to the zoo. Because my class went on a field trip.

    Which statement accurately describes the student's mastery of writing conventions?

    A. The student has difficulty with subject-verb agreement.

    B. The student does not know that a clause that begins with a subordinating conjunction is not an independent clause.

    C. The student does not know about capitalization.

    D. The student has difficulty spelling high-frequency words.

15. A teacher is listening to a student read a story that is the basis of instruction, and the student hesitates in reading the last word of the sentence, *payment*. During word study, the teacher shows these words to students in the reading group: *payment, statement, pavement, placement*. Which of the following indicates the rationale for this instruction?

    A. Students need to learn how to read with prefixes.

    B. Students need to be shown how root words need a suffix.

    C. Teachers should make sure students know how phonics generalizations can be applied.

    D. The teacher is reinforcing a suffix that is used in words.

16. Which of the following statements provides an accurate description of what teachers should know to support students as they read to learn from expository texts?

    A. Students have a schema for the text structure of expository texts, but they can struggle with the narrative structure of fiction because it is unfamiliar.

    B. Expository text is too hard for students to grasp, so it is best to use discussion.

    C. Topics in expository text have a structure that is based upon how the subject is organized, so students need to uncover the text structure as they read expository texts.

    D. If students read fiction, they will be prepared for the text structure of expository texts.

17. A teacher shows students how to use *its* (the possessive) as compared to *it's* (the contraction). In so doing, which of the following is the teacher focusing upon?

    A. The teacher is showing students that *its* is an incorrect spelling.

    B. The teacher is focusing upon the difference between the possessive and the contraction in spelling the words.

    C. The teacher is showing how to use plurals.

    D. The teacher is helping the student apply phonics generalizations.

18. If a student cannot read the word *mother*, what is the best way the teacher can provide effective support?

    A. The teacher should ask the student to read to the end of the sentence to determine what the word is, based upon the initial sound of the word.

    B. The teacher should ask the student to "sound it out" to determine the word.

    C. The teacher should ask the student to "look for the little word" in the word.

    D. The teacher should ignore the miscue to motivate, rather than discourage, the student.

19. Which of the following is a rationale for using running records?

    A. The teacher can keep a record of books the student has read for independent reading.

    B. The teacher can keep a record of whether the student can spell high-frequency words.

    C. The teacher can determine how well the student reads as compared to other students in the state at the end of the school year.

    D. The teacher can use the running record to help determine the correct text for students' reading instruction and to analyze students' oral reading errors.

20. Which of the following represents a way that a teacher could use a visual organizer to help students understand information they encounter in learning about the branches of Texas government?

    A. Concept Maps

    B. Think-Pair-Share

    C. Reciprocal Teaching

    D. DRTA

21. Mrs. Monahan writes the following pair of sentences on the board:

    The ball was caught by the pitcher.
    The pitcher caught the ball.

    What aspect of writing does this instruction feature?

    A. Subject-verb agreement

    B. Dangling modifiers

    C. Verb tense

    D. Passive and active voice

22. The teacher listens to a student read a text. The student makes a miscue when reading, as shown below. What type of prompt should the teacher say to help the student become more effective in identifying words?

    Child: The girl almost stored as she walked on rocks.

    Text: The girl almost stumbled as she walked on rocks.

    A. The teacher should ask the student, "Does that make sense?" to help the student self-correct.

    B. The teacher should tell the child to "sound out" the word the child missed.

    C. The teacher should not say anything because this could discourage an English learner.

    D. The teacher should tell the child the word he did not know so the child knows the correct word.

23. A teacher is planning to provide vocabulary instruction for students who are English learners on the following group of words: *also, and, however, but,* and *although.* Why is this beneficial?

    A. These words are easy for the students to pronounce.

    B. These transitional words represent cohesive devices that show types of connections between ideas.

C. These words can provide a basis for morphemic analysis.

D. These words are ideal for showing phonics generalizations.

24. Which of the following statements describes "invented spelling" used by students as they learn to write in English?

    A. When learning to spell, students will try to account for sounds of a word which can demonstrate growth in phonemic awareness.

    B. Students should not write unless they can spell words correctly.

    C. "Invented spelling" could be an indicator of a learning disability.

    D. "Invented spelling" is an indicator of difficulty in phonological awareness.

25. A teacher is providing a mini-lesson to help students learn about how to write informal reports. The teacher tells the students she is going to write an informal report about her cat. The teacher writes *Missy* in the center of the web, and then adds lines extending from the center as she talks briefly about the following: finding Missy, feeding Missy, Missy's favorite things to do. Which of the following best explains why the teacher would provide this mini-lesson?

    A. The teacher is encouraging students to write about a pet they have or had.

    B. The teacher is showing students how to take a topic they know about, and then create a web to see possible ways to develop the topic through paragraphs, chapters, or a series of stories.

    C. The teacher is showing students how to revise their writing by demonstrating.

    D. The teacher is teaching a unit of study on pets.

26. A teacher incorporates sustained silent reading each day in which students select books they read. Which of the following is a main rationale for this practice?

    A. Students are able to apply phonics generalizations.

    B. The teacher can give tests to make sure students do read.

    C. The teacher can make sure students read required books.

    D. To make gains in reading, students need to read connected text and see that they can find books that are rewarding to read.

Use the information below to answer questions 27, 28, and 29.

A student wrote the following rough draft during writing workshop:

> Last Summer my family went to see my grandmother in florida. My grandmother made pancakes for me for breakfast, because I love her pancakes. We went to the beech one day. My cousins live in florida. I also have cousins in texas. We went to Six Flags two times.

27. During a rough-draft conference, what should the teacher address to help the student establish content for the personal narrative?

    A. The student uses correct subject-verb agreement, so the teacher should praise the student for that.

    B. The student should use the internet and find information about beaches in Florida.

    C. The student needs to focus in on a topic.

    D. The student spells well, so the teacher can praise the child for that.

28. What is an accurate assessment of the student's abilities in using writing conventions?

    A. The student needs instruction on comma usage.

    B. The student needs instruction on misplaced modifiers.

    C. The student has not developed one narrative.

    D. The student needs to learn when to use a semicolon instead of a comma.

29. What type of instruction in capitalization should the teacher focus upon in meeting the student's needs?

    A. The student needs instruction in capitalization of states.

    B. The student needs instruction in capitalization of seasons and states.

    C. The student needs instruction in capitalization of seasons, states, and family members.

    D. The student needs instruction in capitalization of family members and states.

30. Traditional literature includes *all but* which of the following?

    A. Myths

    B. Fables

    C. Legends

    D. Poetry

Use the information below to answer questions 31 and 32.

As a regular facet of the reading workshop in an eighth-grade classroom, students volunteer to talk to the whole class about a book they have been reading during independent reading time.

31. Which of the following shows how a teacher may directly foster oral language development?

    A.   The student sharing is able to use language in talking before a whole group.

    B.   The teacher can grade the student to provide feedback.

    C.   The student is expanding other students' awareness of books to read.

    D.   The student will reflect further on the book as part of the process of sharing a book.

32. Which of the following statements best describes how the teacher is developing readers through this facet of the reading workshop?

    A.   Students make text-to-text connections.

    B.   Students learn about books they can read and enjoy.

    C.   These experiences help students write book reports.

    D.   The teacher is helping the students make gains in morphemic analysis.

33. How do teachers contribute to students' oral language development when they read aloud quality literature that meets students' needs?

    A.   Students make gains in word identification.

    B.   Students make gains in fluency.

    C.   Students can make gains in vocabulary.

    D.   Students learn how to preview a text.

34. A student receives a score of 70th percentile on a norm-referenced test. Which of the following best explains what this score means?

    A.   The score indicates that the student answered 70% of the questions correctly.

    B.   The score means that 70% of the norm group performed at the same level or above the student's score.

    C.   The score means that 70% of the norm group performed at the same level or below the student's score.

    D.   The student is probably failing in reading.

35. A school district wants to monitor each student's abilities in terms of learning to read and spell high-frequency words. Which of the following assessments should be used?

    A.   Criterion-referenced

    B.   Norm-referenced

    C.   Running records

    D.   Cloze procedure

36. A teacher shows students how to identify an unknown word by reading the rest of the sentence and thinking about what word would make sense, as well as by giving the students the first letter of the word. Which of the following abilities is the teacher developing?

    A.   How authors use foreshadowing

    B.   How to use visualization

    C.   How to use cause and effect

    D.   How to use context clues and phonics

37. When listening to a student read a story, the teacher observes that the student can read 85% of the words in the text. Which of the following statements indicates what this observation reveals to the teacher?

    A.   The text is at the instructional level for the student.

    B.   The text is at the independent level for the student.

C. The student could read the text if the teacher provides some instruction.

D. The text is too difficult for the student to read.

Use the information below to answer questions 38 through 42.

Part 1. Students read a designated chapter of a novel independently and then meet to have grand conversations with the teacher and others in their small group.

Part 2. Once the novel has been read and discussed, the teacher focuses upon a literary element for instruction. The teacher gives the students a list of five page numbers from the novel. For each page, students read to determine what they learn about one of the characters. Then the students decide whether the author helps readers know the character through (1) what the character says, (2) what the character does, (3) what the character thinks, (4) how the character looks, or (5) what others say or think about the character.

Part 3. For the first page, the teacher reads and thinks aloud in sharing what he learned about the character from the excerpt on that page. Then the teacher tells how the author revealed the character. The teacher and students work together on the next two page numbers. For the last two pages on the list, the students work with a partner, and the teacher listens in to monitor and help as needed.

38. How is the teacher directly fostering oral language development in Part 1?

A. The teacher asks questions, and students listen to tell the answer.

B. The students have the opportunity to formulate and exchange ideas in authentic ways.

C. Students read aloud their answers to packet questions, and others can tell if they agree with the answer.

D. The students assume a role of either summarizing, asking questions, clarifying, or predicting.

39. How is the teacher fostering comprehension development in Part 1?

A. Students examine text structure.

B. Students develop concept maps.

C. Students can engage in critical thinking about what they have read.

D. Students share their completed packet activities and learn from each other.

40. What would be a primary rationale for examining a literary element after students have been able to share their thoughts and feelings through grand conversations?

A. Students become comfortable talking with others through the grand conversations, so they will do better when learning the literary element.

B. The teacher can ask questions in the grand conversations to encourage students to start thinking about the literary element they will examine.

C. Students are able to engage in reading literature as an aesthetic experience and share their personal responses in grand conversations first. This fosters connections to the text which are basic to analysis of literature.

D. Students can create a story map that helps with understanding literary elements.

41. In Part 3, why would the teacher do the first page for students?

A. The teacher is modeling for the students what procedures they need to follow to complete the task and understand characterization.

B. The teacher knows the students do not have time to complete all of the work.

C. Students need to be shown how to monitor their comprehension.

D. The teacher is demonstrating making predictions.

42. In Part 3, the teacher models the process of the task, and then the students and the teacher work together. The students work on the task and the teacher provides assistance, as needed. Which of the following states the rationale for this approach?

    A. The teacher is making sure students monitor their comprehension.

    B. The teacher is developing the students' ability to retell.

    C. The teacher is developing the students' ability to visualize.

    D. The teacher is providing scaffolding for students through a gradual release of responsibility that supports students' learning.

43. A teacher "publishes" each sixth-grade students' work in a book after they write personal narratives during writing workshop. The students then read and give their books to their first-grade reading buddies. How does this experience support the sixth-grade students' writing development?

    A. The students gain practice in topic selection.

    B. Students gain practice in developing a title for their writing.

    C. The students experience having authentic reasons for writing, including reasons for proofreading a final draft.

    D. Students learn about text structure of informational texts.

44. The teacher notices that a student seems to overlook periods and question marks when the student reads. The teacher asks the student to follow along as he reads the sentence to model reading in a way that acknowledges a period and in a way that acknowledges a question mark. Which of the following statements indicates how this instruction could foster fluency?

    A. Fluency involves rate of reading.

    B. Fluency involves accuracy.

    C. Fluency involves phonemic awareness.

    D. Fluency involves intonation.

45. A teacher presents these pairs of sentences and asks students to select the one in each pair that is correct:

    The box of pencils is on the shelf.
    The box of pencils are on the shelf.

    The group of kittens likes to play.
    The group of kittens like to play.

    Which of the following aspects of writing does this instructional activity feature?

    A. Dangling modifiers

    B. Subject-verb agreement

    C. Verb tense

    D. Passive and active voice

46. Examine the student's writing sample that follows.

    My friend likes to play soccer with me,
    she is on my soccer teem.

    Which of the following is an accurate assessment of the student's abilities in using writing conventions?

    A. The student does not use correct subject-verb agreement.

    B. The student knows how to use a period and a comma correctly.

    C. The student has a comma splice.

    D. The student is not using correct verb tense.

47. As fourth-grade students silently read a story in their reading group, the teacher tells them to stop after reading the first two paragraphs and to talk with their partner about what they read. How can this foster the students' growth in reading comprehension?

    A. Students gain practice in monitoring their comprehension as they stop to think and talk about what they are reading.

    B. Students are learning to preview text features.

    C. Students are learning how to use structural analysis.

    D. Students are making text-to-text connections.

48. Which of the following statements best describes how to foster fluency?

   A. Encourage students to recognize the purpose of headings.

   B. Provide students challenging materials with high-frequency words they need to learn.

   C. Make sure students can recognize text structure.

   D. Provide opportunities for students to reread texts.

49. The teacher plans to present the following words as a basis of instruction:

   wolf–wolves, wife–wives, half–halves.

   Which of the following describes the type of instruction the teacher is providing to help students learn writing conventions?

   A. The teacher will ask students to look up words in a dictionary.

   B. The teacher is showing a common error in writing a plural form of a noun.

   C. The teacher is showing how to apply phonics generalizations.

   D. The teacher is showing how to form the plural of words in a way that is different from how plurals are often formed.

Use the information below to answer questions 50 through 54.

   Part 1. A teacher reads aloud versions of Cinderella stories: Chinese, Native American, and Caribbean.

   Part 2. After the teacher reads aloud a version, the teacher and students share their thoughts about the story.

   Part 3. The teacher displays a map of the world so students can locate the geographical areas where the stories are based.

   Part 4. Students examine the illustrations of the versions again.

   Part 5. The teacher and students complete a chart that shows differences and similarities of the versions.

50. Which type of literature is the teacher featuring in this instruction?

   A. Historical fiction

   B. Traditional literature

   C. Realistic fiction

   D. Nonfiction

51. What is a rationale for Part 2?

   A. The students are able to share their connections to each story, which enhances their experiences with the book and helps them prepare to make comparisons in subsequent lessons.

   B. The students are learning about previewing a text which can enhance comprehension.

   C. Through retelling the story, students will be able to remember the plot.

   D. Through asking students to retell the story, the teacher can ensure that all students understand what took place.

52. In Part 3, the teacher displays a map of the world. Which of the following statements best describes how this instruction could enhance students' understanding of traditional literature?

   A. The teacher can help students learn about geographical locations.

   B. The teacher is helping students gain in using maps.

   C. The teacher is helping students be able to read the names of geographical regions where tales have been based.

   D. The teacher is helping students see that even though people have been separated by time and space, they have developed oral tales that are similar.

53. In Part 4, the illustrations of picture books provide the basis of the learning experiences. How could this instruction enhance students' understanding of folktales?

   A. Students can be asked to draw their own illustrations to review events of each tale.

   B. The students can gain information about cultural markers that complement words of the text and that show differences among variants of the Cinderella stories.

   C. The students can learn about elements of art, such as line and light.

   D. Students gain in previewing abilities.

54. In Part 5, the teacher and students complete a chart that shows differences and similarities among the versions of Cinderella. Which of the following is *not* a way that this learning experience fosters understanding of folktales?

   A. Students can compare differences in characters among variants of the story.

   B. Students can compare differences in setting and plot among variants of the story.

   C. Students can compare common aspects of plot and conflict resolution.

   D. Students compare their personal responses to the tales.

55. The teacher projects a copy of the first draft of a personal narrative he is writing. The teacher reads the piece aloud and tells students he notices that he left out something. The teacher then writes the needed information in the margin and uses an arrow to show where it needs to be added.

   Which of the following best illustrates why this is an effective teaching practice?

   A. The teacher is demonstrating topic selection.

   B. The students are learning about conventions of writing.

   C. The teacher is helping students expand their vocabulary.

   D. The teacher is showing students that writing rough drafts can entail making revisions to make their writing clearer. He is also showing them how to make revisions.

56. In teaching students how to write a persuasive essay, Mrs. Romero develops categories of wording and models how to use these when writing. She writes the following on the board:

   The first reason…
   In the first place,…
   Another reason…
   Additionally,…
   Furthermore,…
   Finally,…
   In conclusion,…

   This instructional experience supports students' writing development in which of the following ways?

   A. Expanding students' spelling abilities

   B. Fostering vivid word choice

   C. Showing ways to make transitions and connections

   D. Promoting the understanding of propaganda techniques

Look at the following miscue made by a student and then answer the question that follows.

   Student: The boy could play on the slid.

   Text: The boy could play on the slide.

57. Which of the following represents an accurate analysis of the miscue?

   A. The miscue shows the need for instruction in phonemic awareness.

   B. The student is not using any visual cues.

   C. The student needs instruction in high-frequency sight words.

   D. It indicates that the student is not paying attention to meaning and needs phonics instruction.

58. Nonfiction includes *all but* which of the following?

    A. Memoir

    B. Biography

    C. Historical fiction

    D. Informational texts

59. Which of the following factors does *not* apply when determining whether to use a website?

    A. Accurate, understandable content

    B. Large amounts of information on each page

    C. Multimedia and visual materials

    D. Easy navigation and understandable structure

60. Which of the following strategies can be used to activate students' thinking and prompt them to make predictions before they read, then read up to a selected point, and then review what they have read to confirm their predictions?

    A. Reciprocal Teaching

    B. DRTA

    C. Think-Pair-Share

    D. Concept Maps

61. Which of the following shows how the internet can be used to provide support for English learners and other students who find reading challenging as they learn research skills?

    A. Students do not need to monitor their reading comprehension.

    B. Large amounts of information can provide various ways to obtain information.

    C. Multimedia and visual materials can provide information.

    D. Students do not need to set a purpose for reading.

62. Which of the following does *not* represent academic language?

    A. Vocabulary used in a discipline

    B. Text messages exchanged by students to confirm when an assignment is due

    C. Writing a persuasive essay

    D. Summarizing a paragraph of informational text

63. As part of writing a report on Texas, the teacher helped students select a topic by showing various potential topics found in resources online as well as in books in the library. In which of the following scenarios can such instruction contribute to students' writing development?

    A. The teacher can assign topics to students.

    B. Students need to learn to be self-reliant when they write.

    C. Professional writers write what they know and care about, so our students also will be most apt to write well when they select the focus of their writing.

    D. The teacher can provide differentiated instruction by not requiring English learners to select a topic.

Below is what a student said in reading a story versus what the text presented. Find the miscue and then answer the question that follows.

Student: Henry walks to school each day.

Text: Henry walked to school each day.

64. Which of the following represents an accurate analysis of the miscue?

    A. The miscue shows the need for instruction in sight words.

    B. The student is not using any visual cues.

    C. The student needs instruction in structural analysis.

    D. The student's miscue indicates that the student is not using meaning cues.

65. Which of the following does **not** provide conditions for learning that would support English learners' acquisition of language and content?

A. Asking students to look up definitions of words in a dictionary

B. Letting students talk to a classmate about what they learned after reading a small chunk of information in a chapter

C. Using gestures or pantomime to explain the definitions of words

D. Explaining a new concept by building upon background knowledge of the students

66. The teacher plans to present the following words as a basis of instruction:

moose-moose, sheep-sheep.

Which of the following best describes why the teacher would use these words in teaching writing conventions?

A. The teacher is showing words that do and do not have a silent *e* in teaching phonics.

B. By writing a word two times, students can learn to spell it.

C. These pairs of words show irregular plural nouns.

D. These pairs of words show a common error in writing a plural form of a noun.

67. Which of the following statements accurately describes best practices in reading fluency development for English learners?

A. English learners can enjoy making gains in fluency through reading games where they read quickly.

B. Shared reading and audio-assisted reading can support English learners' gains in reading fluency.

C. Fluency instruction should not be addressed when working with English learners because they could become overwhelmed.

D. Fluency development takes place best when texts present a challenge for English learners.

68. Which of the following takes place during the revision of rough-draft writing?

A. Checking for spelling errors

B. Correcting punctuation errors

C. Elaborating by adding details

D. Selecting a topic

69. Which of the following does **not** represent a rationale for including blogging as part of students' learning?

A. Students are provided authentic writing experiences.

B. Students can be tested on what other students write.

C. Students of various proficiency levels can participate.

D. Students can learn from each other.

70. Which of the following is a visual organizer that can enhance students' understanding of how important ideas relate in expository texts/subject-matter learning through a visual organizer?

A. DRTA

B. Think-Pair-Share

C. Concept Maps

D. Reciprocal Teaching

71. Which of the following literary elements pertains to the time and place of the work?

A. Characterization

B. Plot

C. Point of view

D. Setting

Examine the sample of a student's writing and answer the question that follows.

> We learned about why the Stars look so small and why the moon looks like it changes shape even though it does not really change.

72. What is an accurate assessment of the student's abilities in using writing conventions?

   A. The student has not used capitalization correctly.

   B. The student knows how to use capitalization and periods correctly.

   C. The student does not know how to use consistent verb tense.

   D. The student does not know when a comma is needed.

73. Which of the following strategies can be used so that students talk with a classmate to share thoughts before whole-group sharing?

   A. Reciprocal Teaching

   B. Think-Pair-Share

   C. Concept Maps

   D. DRTA

74. The teacher presents the word *biography*. The teacher points out to the students that *bio-,* a Greek root, means life. The teacher adds that *-ology*, another Greek root, means study. The teacher also points out how the word *geology* is related. Which of the following indicates why this instruction would help students?

   A. The teacher is helping the students gain in phonemic awareness.

   B. The teacher is helping students gain in applying phonics.

   C. The teacher is using knowledge of syntax to help students identify words.

   D. Morphemic analysis can help students learn about word structure and meaning.

75. Which of the following is an informal assessment? Select *all* that apply.

   A. Norm-referenced tests

   B. Running records

   C. Anecdotal accounts of writing conferences

   D. High-frequency word identification assessment

76. To help teach a phonics generalization, a teacher is listing words the students know.

   Which of the following pairs represents words that clearly show a long vowel pattern?

   A. *play–stay*

   B. *jar–car*

   C. *bag–hat*

   D. *toy–boy*

Use the information below to answer questions 77 through 79.

> A student wrote the following in a rough draft:

> My sister helped me wash the dishs one day.
> I droped a plate and it broke.

77. Which of the following would be an effective way to address errors in writing conventions?

   A. The teacher should tell the student how to correct the errors so the student learns.

   B. The teacher should use a different color of ink to make corrections on the paper, so the student learns as soon as possible.

   C. The teacher should focus upon helping the student establish content as the student writes a rough draft, but the teacher can also teach needed skills during a proofreading conference.

   D. The teacher should use the student's paper to teach the class common errors.

78. Which of the following would *not* be an accurate assessment of the student's abilities in using writing conventions?

    A. The student does not know how to write many of the words most frequently used in writing.

    B. The student needs to learn more about using a consistent tense.

    C. The student understands how to write about one topic.

    D. The student needs to be shown more about how to spell plurals.

79. What would be an accurate assessment of the student's abilities in using punctuation?

    A. The student's writing sample does not indicate a need for instruction in using punctuation.

    B. The student needs to learn how to add a comma when using a coordinating conjunction to join two independent clauses, or write a compound sentence.

    C. The student has written a complex sentence so a comma is not needed.

    D. The student needs to be shown how to use quotation marks.

80. After students have silently read a story during guided reading, the teacher asks the students to retell the story before discussing it. What type of data can teachers obtain from using retelling as an informal assessment?

    A. The teacher can determine whether the student can make inferences.

    B. The teacher can determine whether the student understands at a literal level what was read.

    C. The teacher can determine whether the student is making text-to-self connections.

    D. The teacher can determine whether the student can make evaluations.

Use the following information to answer the question that follows.

A student wrote the following:

I hop mi mom makes macroni and chez for dinr.

81. What stage of writing development is indicated by this writing sample?

    A. Precommunicative

    B. Semiphonetic

    C. Phonetic

    D. Transitional

82. At what stage in the writing workshop can the teacher show procedures of the workshop, such as how to get materials and how to apply strategies and techniques writers use, such as selecting a topic?

    A. Mini-lessons and small-group work

    B. Writing

    C. Author's chair/whole-class conferences

    D. Proofreading/publishing conference

83. A teacher is listing words the students know to teach a phonics generalization.

Which of the following pairs represents words that clearly show a consonant digraph?

    A. *ship–share*

    B. *star–stick*

    C. *brown–bring*

    D. *blue–black*

84. Students are going to read to find information as part of writing a report. Before they begin, the teacher asks the students to preview a resource by looking at the headings of the passage.

    Which of the following pinpoints how the teacher is developing students' research skills at this point?

    A. The teacher is helping students understand new vocabulary.

    B. The teacher is building background knowledge.

    C. The teacher is modeling to help students understand text features in gathering information from expository text.

    D. The teacher is activating students' prior knowledge.

85. Which of the following best defines the omniscient point of view?

    A. The events that take place in the story

    B. Signals readers what each character feels, thinks, says, and does

    C. When the story is told by a narrator from one character's viewpoint

    D. When a character tells the story

86. A teacher and his students have grand conversations in which they share their thoughts and feelings about what happened in the book. How do these experiences contribute to students' development?

    A. The students are able to rest and engage later in other tasks.

    B. Sharing personal responses to literature helps students make gains in comprehension as important ideas are brought up for discussion.

    C. These learning experiences foster development in study skills.

    D. The teacher is helping the students make gains in word identification.

87. Which of the following could be used to organize students' discussions to compare a work of nonfiction with a work of fiction that features the same topic?

    A. Visualization

    B. SQ3R

    C. Venn diagram

    D. Previewing

88. Which of the following statements does ***not*** describe how teachers can provide students opportunities to speak in various types of audience situations to reinforce oral language development?

    A. Students should recite poetry in front of the class.

    B. Students should be given regular opportunities to speak and listen with partners as well as in small-group and whole-class situations.

    C. Students can engage in speaking and listening with guest speakers.

    D. Students can read books with kindergarten reading buddies.

89. Which of the following is a rationale for author's chair/whole-class conferences to reinforce students' writing abilities?

    A. Students learn to use a proofreading sheet for their writing and for checking the writing of others in the class.

    B. Students see a real reason to write when they have an audience, and they can learn as they hear what others have written and what others say in offering feedback.

    C. Students are able to receive feedback from the teacher, who tells them what needs to be improved.

    D. Students are motivated to finish a piece so they can share it with others.

90. The teacher shows the following words:

    child–children

    foot–feet

    tooth–teeth

    goose–geese

    What is the teacher focusing upon for instruction?

    A. These pairs of words show a common error in writing a plural form of a noun.

    B. The teacher is teaching subject-verb agreement.

    C. These pairs of words show irregular plural nouns.

    D. The teacher is addressing phonemic awareness.

Below is what a student said in reading a story versus what the text presented. Identify the miscue that is revealed and answer the question that follows.

Student: Maria depended to go to the mall.

Text: Maria decided to go to the mall.

91. Which of the following represents an accurate analysis of the miscue?

    A. The student is not using language structure cues and meaning cues.

    B. The student is not using any visual cues.

    C. The student is not using an inflectional ending for past tense.

    D. The student is using meaning cues, but not language structure cues.

92. Which of the following statements does **not** describe the role of prior knowledge in comprehension?

    A. Reading entails relating the information in the text to what the reader knows.

    B. Teachers activate prior knowledge by reminding students of what they know that relates to new information they will encounter in the text.

    C. Students can build background knowledge needed for understanding content by writing definitions of words in bold print.

    D. The extent to which teachers need to build background knowledge before students read can depend upon students' prior knowledge and whether the text provides new information that students can understand.

93. Which of the following shows the correct use of a hyphen?

    A. Very-beautiful bracelet

    B. Six-year old student

    C. Family owned business

    D. Fifty-four dollars

94. Which of the following is **not** a coordinating conjunction?

    A. Because

    B. And

    C. Or

    D. But

95. Which of the following is a strategy in which students work in small groups and teach each other by reading up to a stopping point assigned by the teacher; then they assume roles the teacher has modeled, such as summarizer, questioner, clarifier, and predictor?

   A. Concept Maps

   B. Reciprocal Teaching

   C. Think-Pair-Share

   D. DRTA

96. After the teacher administers a running record, he determines that the student can read the words accurately, but the student ignores punctuation and reads slowly without expression. Which of the following types of instruction does the student need?

   A. High-frequency words

   B. Fluency

   C. Visualization

   D. Phonics

97. Which of the following is *not* a rationale for proofreading/publishing conferences as part of the writing workshop?

   A. In a proofreading/publishing conference, students learn about spelling, punctuation, capitalization, and usage through worksheets.

   B. Students focus on content during rough drafts, and they proofread for spelling, punctuation, capitalization, and usage when writing a final draft.

   C. Students need to learn how to apply spelling, punctuation, capitalization, and usage as part of the process of writing.

   D. If students apply writing conventions as they proofread their writing, they gain more than by learning skills only in isolation.

98. In the course of introducing how to write a persuasive essay, Mrs. Watson and her students write an essay together. Which of the following is *not* an aspect Mrs. Watson would model to show how to develop a persuasive essay?

   A. Focusing only on the stated position

   B. Doing research to locate compelling evidence

   C. Using an effective lead-in, or "hook," in the opening paragraph.

   D. Making transitions from one paragraph to the next

Below is what a student said in reading a story versus what the text presented. Identify the miscue and answer the question that follows.

   Child: The students will go to the park today.

   Text: The students will come to the park today.

99. Which of the following represents an accurate analysis of the miscue?

   A. The student's miscue indicates the need for instruction in structural analysis.

   B. The student's miscue indicates the need for instruction in phonics.

   C. The student is not paying attention to meaning.

   D. The student's miscue indicates the need for instruction in sight words because *come* is a sight word.

100. In which of the following strategies would the teacher point students' attention to the title and then ask them a general question (such as "What do you think we will learn, based on this title?"), after which they would read and discuss a segment of the text, and think about predictions?

   A. Reciprocal Teaching

   B. Concept Maps

   C. Think-Pair-Share

   D. DRTA

Practice Test 1 Answer Key

Test Item	Answer	Competency
1.	D.	007
2.	B.	005
3.	A.	004
4.	C.	009
5.	C.	005
6.	A., B., C.	001
7.	A.	008
8.	B.	008
9.	C.	009
10.	C.	007
11.	C.	004
12.	C.	003
13.	C.	005
14.	B.	006
15.	D.	003
16.	C.	009
17.	B.	003
18.	A.	003
19.	D.	005
20.	A.	004
21.	D.	006
22.	A.	005
23.	B.	004
24.	A.	002
25.	B.	008
26.	D.	005
27.	C.	007
28.	A.	006
29.	B.	006
30.	D.	005
31.	A	001
32.	B.	005
33.	C.	001
34.	C.	004

Test Item	Answer	Competency
35.	A.	004
36.	D.	003
37.	D.	004
38.	B.	001
39.	C.	005
40.	C.	005
41.	A.	005
42.	D.	005
43.	C.	007
44.	D.	003
45.	B.	006
46.	C.	006
47.	A.	004
48.	D.	003
49.	D.	006
50.	B.	005
51.	A.	005
52.	D.	008
53.	B.	008
54.	D.	008
55.	D.	007
56.	C.	007
57.	D.	002
58.	C.	005
59.	B.	008
60.	B.	004
61.	C.	008
62.	B.	004
63.	C.	007
64.	C.	002
65.	A.	001
66.	C.	006
67.	B.	003
68.	C.	007

Test Item	Answer	Competency
69.	B.	008
70.	C.	004
71.	D.	005
72.	A.	006
73.	B.	004
74.	D.	003
75.	B., C., D.	004
76.	A.	003
77.	C.	006
78.	D.	006
79.	B.	006
80.	B.	004
81.	C.	006
82.	A.	007
83.	A.	003
84.	C.	009
85.	B.	005
86.	B.	001
87.	C.	004
88.	A.	001
89.	B.	007
90.	C.	006
91.	A.	002
92.	C.	004
93.	D.	006
94.	A.	006
95.	B.	004
96.	B.	004
97.	A.	007
98.	A.	007
99.	D.	003
100.	D.	004

Practice Test 1 Detailed Answers

1.   D.

Option D is correct because students need support in learning the strategies and techniques of any type of writing. The teacher should model thinking about features of folktales and demonstrate incorporating those features in writing. If the teacher simply tells students what to do, students will not have a clear understanding of how to engage in writing a folktale, so reminding is not sufficient. **Option A is incorrect** because when writing rough drafts, the focus is on creating content. Students can learn how to spell words during the proofreading conference before writing a final draft. **Option B is incorrect.** Making it possible for students to talk about what they want to write is helpful for all students because it provides scaffolding, but English learners also can participate in writing to grow as writers through sheltered instruction. **Option C is incorrect** because students need to be shown what to do, not solely told to follow a checklist. **(Competency 007 Written Language–Composition)**

2.   B.

Option B is correct because students often overlook text features, such as headings. Students will be better able to organize in their memory individual facts if they understand the text structure and how the topic is organized. **Option A is incorrect** because Ms. Johnson does not provide shared reading, where the teacher and students read a text together to help students be able to read a text they cannot read on their own. **Option C is incorrect** because the teacher is directing students' attention to the title and heading, not images. **Option D is incorrect** because the teacher is not focusing upon unfamiliar concepts or terms at this point in the lesson. **(Competency 005 Reading Applications)**

3.   A.

Option A is correct because academic vocabulary can present a challenge to students because they do not use the words in everyday talking, yet they need to understand words and their significance when reading to learn. Understanding a root word can help students understand connections to related words. **Option B is incorrect** because applying phonics, though an important ability, is not the primary focus in this scenario, which concentrates on reading to understand and learn academic content. **Option C is incorrect** because, although students are learning how to read a multisyllabic word, just that by itself is not going to help students read and learn about a topic since students need to understand. **Option D is incorrect** because looking up a definition in a glossary by itself will not help students understand the topic of the chapter. **(Competency 004 Reading Comprehension and Assessment)**

4.   C.

Option C is correct because teachers can support students' learning by thinking aloud and demonstrating before asking students to engage in a strategy for reading expository text. **Option A is incorrect** because the students are learning how to focus on headings of expository text at this point in the lesson, not how to complete a table. **Option B is incorrect** because the teacher is not building background needed to understand the text. **Option D is incorrect** because the teacher is not activating prior knowledge so students can relate the new information to what they already know. **(Competency 009 Study and Inquiry Skills)**

5. C.

Option C is correct because students can comprehend content-area text better when they read small chunks for discussion. Then they are less likely to be overwhelmed by new information and can better connect important ideas. **Option A is incorrect** because the primary purpose is to encourage the students to read chunks of information, not to understand the concept of paragraph writing and organization. **Option B is incorrect** because the point is for students to learn to read in chunks, not to gain experience reading aloud. At this point, it is best if students read silently. **Option D is incorrect** because students are not previewing the text by reading just the first paragraph. Students preview the text when they examine text features such as the title, headings, illustrations, charts, and captions before reading. **(Competency 005 Reading Applications)**

6. A., B., C.

Options A, B, and C are all correct because they present ways the teacher's instruction is effective for helping students use talking to help them learn, while also fostering oral language development. **Option D is incorrect** because students do need to engage in reading texts, as well as have opportunities to talk about what they are learning. **(Competency 001 Oral Language)**

7. A.

Option A is correct because students need to understand and remember important details and how those details relate to each other. **Option B is incorrect** because the teacher is not building background as the students complete the table, but is helping students record information in a table. **Option C is incorrect** because the teacher is not focusing upon bold print. **Option D is incorrect** because previewing headings takes place before reading to help students understand how a topic is organized. **(Competency 008 Viewing and Representing)**

8. B.

Option B is correct because this activity helps students learn techniques for selecting, organizing, and evaluating information from an electronic environment. **Option A is incorrect** because students need guidance to learn from the video and ample time for learning new information before taking a test. **Option C is incorrect** because the teacher needs to ensure that the students view a quality video for this part of the unit of study where the students synthesize information, and students need guidance in locating quality electronic sources. **Option D is incorrect** because all students need to participate in reading the textbook to gain in proficiency, and teachers can provide scaffolding to support English learners so they participate in reading a text. **(Competency 008 Viewing and Representing)**

9. C.

Option C is correct because students need to learn how to organize notes they take in writing a report. **Option A is incorrect** because the students are not being shown how to proofread for errors. **Option B is incorrect.** Learning academic vocabulary is important, but the main focus in this activity is organizing information encountered to understand and remember the concepts. **Option D is incorrect** because the students are not focusing upon effective lead-ins of texts they have encountered. **(Competency 009 Study and Inquiry Skills)**

10. C.

Option C is correct, because the first concern in a rough draft is content, and students will not be able to devote attention to establishing content if their attention is diverted toward a concern for spelling and punctuation they have not mastered. **Option A is incorrect** because students do need to learn about writing conventions like spelling and punctuation, which help students communicate clearly and make it easier for someone to read what they have written. **Option B is incorrect** because students can be supported as they write through proofreading conferences when producing a final draft. **Option D is incorrect** because students do need to learn how to apply writing conventions, and teachers can provide systematic instruction in view of students' needs. **(Competency 007 Written Language–Composition)**

11. C.

Option C is correct because Latin and Greek root words are the basis of many words in English and can help students understand the meanings of words. **Option A is incorrect** because some root words can stand alone. **Option B is incorrect** because neither a suffix nor a prefix (which are affixes) is needed for all root words. **Option D is incorrect** because the primary focus of the teacher is vocabulary development, not word identification of multisyllabic words. **(Competency 004 Reading Comprehension and Assessment)**

12. C.

Option C is correct because students gain in fluency when they reread a text that is at their independent reading level because the words are easier to recognize, making it possible to focus on understanding the content. Using readers' theatre scripts provides a rewarding way for students to read smoothly and with expression. **Option A is incorrect** because the students would use a mentor text when they write, but that is not the focus of instruction. **Option B is incorrect** because students are not answering questions about the story as they engage in readers' theatre. **Option D is incorrect** because the teacher is primarily focusing upon helping her students make gains in fluency, not on introducing principles of drama. **(Competency 003 Word Identification Skills and Reading Fluency)**

13. C.

Option C is correct because the teacher needs to make sure students know how to work together in reading a script when it is a new form of writing for the stu-

dents even though the teacher knows they can pronounce the words. **Option A is incorrect** because the teacher would discuss mentor texts as part of writing instruction. **Option B is incorrect** because writing fiction is not the focus of the lesson. **Option D is incorrect.** The teacher does need to make sure students can read the words, but that should take place during the small-group reading instruction to ensure that the script is at the students' independent reading level. **(Competency 005 Reading Applications)**

14. B.

Option B is correct because while all the clauses in the student's writing have a subject and a verb, the student does not demonstrate knowledge that a subordinating conjunction such as *because* and *although* creates a dependent clause, which must be joined to an independent sentence to avoid being a fragment. **Options A, C, and D are incorrect** because this writing sample does not show difficulties with subject-verb agreement, capitalization, or spelling. **(Competency 006 Written Language–Writing Conventions)**

15. D.

Option D is correct because the teacher noted that a student needed additional instruction identifying a word with a suffix, and the instruction builds upon a word the students have read. **Option A is incorrect** because the words contain a suffix, not a prefix. **Option B is incorrect** because the instruction is focused on how a suffix is used, and not all root words need a suffix. **Option C is incorrect** because phonics generalizations pertain to letter-sound correspondences, not word parts. **(Competency 003 Word Identification Skills and Reading Fluency)**

16. C.

Option C is correct. Students typically can read and remember fiction more easily because they have a schema for stories which makes it easier to remember and retell. When reading expository or informational texts, students need to discern the text structure to be able to connect units of information. **Option A is incorrect** because students have a schema for the narrative structure of fiction. **Option B is incorrect** because students can learn how to read textbooks and other expository texts if teachers provide support through modeling and guided practice. **Option D is incorrect** because reading expository texts makes different demands on readers. Students do make gains in reading fiction that transfer to reading expository texts, but teachers need to teach students how to read and learn from expository texts, not assume that students can. **(Competency 009 Study and Inquiry Skills)**

17. B.

    Option B is correct. The teacher is showing how *its* should be spelled as the possessive, and how adding an apostrophe completely changes the word into a contraction of *it is*. **Option A is incorrect** because *its* can be the correct spelling for the possessive form of *it*, such as in this sentence: *The truck lost **its** wheel.* **Option C is incorrect** because the *s* used in the examples is not used to form a plural. **Option D is incorrect** because the teacher's prompt did not focus upon relating letters and their sounds. **(Competency 003 Word Identification Skills and Reading Fluency)**

18. A.

    Option A is correct because the teacher is showing how to use context and initial letter sounds to identify an unknown word, which is an effective strategy the student also can use in other situations. **Option B is incorrect** because the word represents an irregular spelling as do many words in English so the strategy won't work for students in many situations. **Option C is incorrect** because this strategy of sounding out does not work for this word because *moth* is not a root word nor is it part of a compound word in this instance. **Option D is incorrect** because students can be shown how to identify unknown words, which can help students gain in word identifica-

tion. **(Competency 003 Word Identification Skills and Reading Fluency)**

19. D.

    Option D is correct. Teachers can use running records along with an assessment of the students' comprehension to form reading groups, to monitor students' progress, and teach in view of the miscues. **Option A is incorrect** because a reading log is used by students to record the books they read. **Option B is incorrect** because running records are not a record of words the student can spell. **Option C is incorrect** because running records is an informal assessment the teacher uses, not a standardized test. **(Competency 005 Reading Applications)**

20. A.

    Option A is correct. Concept Maps are visual organizers that can help students understand main ideas and how ideas relate to each other in expository texts. **Option B is incorrect** because Think-Pair-Share is a strategy that lets students think about what they have read and learned and talk with a partner as a way of encouraging students to talk as part of their learning. **Option C is incorrect** because in reciprocal teaching, the teacher models, and then students become teachers and use four strategies to have a dialogue about what they have learned: summarizing, question generating, clarifying, and predicting. **Option D is incorrect** because the Directed Reading Thinking Activity (DRTA) is a comprehension strategy that guides students to ask questions, make predictions, and then read to confirm or refute their predictions. **(Competency 004 Reading Comprehension and Assessment)**

21. D.

    Option D is correct. The example shows how to write a sentence that uses the active voice, where the subject performs the action. In the first sentence, the passive voice is used, having the subject receive the action.

Option A is incorrect because subject-verb agreement is correct in both sentences. **Option B is incorrect** because the sentences do not show placing a word, phrase, or clause in such a way that what is being modified is not clear. **Option C is incorrect** because the verb tense is the same in both sentences. **(Competency 006 Written Language–Writing Conventions)**

22. A.

Option A is correct. The student's miscue shows that the student is not using meaning cues, and the teacher is reinforcing this by asking if the miscue makes sense. **Option B is incorrect** because sounding out does not work for irregular spellings of English words, so this is not a prompt that helps students for all unknown words. **Option C is incorrect**. Teachers should not disregard a miscue because a prompt is an opportunity to help the child learn more about how to identify words. **Option D is incorrect** because the teacher's prompt should help the child learn how to identify words independently, and the teacher should tell the word only when it is apparent the child cannot figure out the unknown word even with a prompt. **(Competency 005 Reading Applications)**

23. B.

Option B is correct. To understand the connections among ideas, students need to understand conjunctions and what they indicate, but the meanings may not be readily apparent for learners. **Option A is incorrect** because vocabulary instruction should be based upon what students need to know, not what is easy to pronounce. **Option C is incorrect** because these words as a group are not ones for examining word parts. **Option D is incorrect** because these words as a group are not ones for phonics instruction, and the teacher is focusing primarily upon meaning in vocabulary instruction. **(Competency 004 Reading Comprehension and Assessment)**

24. A.

Option A is correct. "Invented spelling" takes place when students do not use conventional spelling, but they still show that they are accounting for sounds of a word, so the errors are not random. **Options B and C are incorrect.** Students gain in phonemic awareness when they use "invented spelling" because they are accounting for sounds in a word, which is essential for learning to read, and they eventually will learn conventional spellings through effective instruction. **Option D is incorrect** because invented spelling shows accounting for phonemes of words or phonemic awareness, a dimension of phonological awareness. **(Competency 002 Early Literacy Development)**

25. B.

Option B is correct because developing a web can help students organize their writing by breaking down a topic they know, and the teacher's demonstration makes this process clearer than solely telling students what to do. **Option A is incorrect** because students are not being shown how to write about a pet, but rather how to draw upon their thinking and experiences when they write about any topic. **Option C is incorrect** because revising takes place once students start to establish content. **Option D is incorrect** because how to organize ideas for writing informal reports is the focus of instruction. **(Competency 008 Viewing and Representing)**

26. D.

Option D is correct. Students need to experience authentic reading experiences in which they select books they want to read, and read daily. **Option A is incorrect** because students do apply and orchestrate word identification skills when reading independently, but applying phonics abilities is not the main rationale when they do. **Option B is incorrect** because tests create anxiety about reading rather than motivate, and teachers can assess in other ways, such as through observing and talking with students. **Option C is incorrect** because requiring students to read certain books for independent reading does not let students learn how to select books they like and see how reading can be meaningful for them. **(Competency 005 Reading Applications)**

27. C.

Option C is correct because the student sample presents more than one possible narrative to develop. **Option A is incorrect** because the rough draft conference should focus on establishing content, which pertains to composing, not usage. **Option B is incorrect** because students draw upon their own experiences in developing personal narratives. **Option D is incorrect** because establishing content pertains to composing, not spelling. **(Competency 007 Written Language–Composition)**

28. A.

Option A is correct. The student has used a comma when joining an independent clause and dependent clause, but the comma should not be used. **Option B is incorrect** because the student has not placed a word, phrase, or clause in such a way that what is being modified is not clear. **Option C is incorrect** because developing or establishing content pertains to composing, not writing conventions. **Option D is incorrect** because the student did not use a comma where a semicolon could be used. A semicolon is used for connecting two independent clauses, not for connecting an independent clause and dependent clause. **(Competency 006 Written Language–Writing Conventions)**

29. B.

Option B is correct. The student has capitalized a season, but seasons are not capitalized. The student did not capitalize the names of states, and names of states are capitalized. **Option A is incorrect** because the student needs instruction in more than capitalization of states. **Options C and D are incorrect** because the student used capitalization correctly in using lowercase for *grandmother* because names of family members, such as

grandmother, are not capitalized when the person's name cannot be substituted in the sentence. **(Competency 006 Written Language–Writing Conventions)**

30. D.

Option D is correct. Poetry is a form of literature, not a type of traditional literature. **Options A, B, and C are incorrect.** Myths, fables, and legends are types of traditional literature—tales or stories that have been initially developed orally. **(Competency 005 Reading Applications)**

31. A.

Option A is correct because students gain in oral language when given opportunities to talk for real reasons in various sizes of audience: individual, small-group, and whole-group. The other students gain in listening. **Option B is incorrect** because students would grow in oral language development through mini-lessons and modeling on part of the teacher and other students, not through grading. **Option C is incorrect** because awareness of books to read is not a feature of oral language development. **Option D is incorrect** because reflecting further on a book would lead to gains in reading comprehension, not oral language development, per se. **(Competency 001 Oral Language)**

32. B.

Option B is correct because students can be motivated to read a book that other students have found rewarding. **Option A is incorrect** because text-to-text connections are not necessarily being made when students talk about a book because they should select the content that is salient to them. **Option C is incorrect** because the students' talking about a book is an authentic way for them to reflect upon a book in ways that encourage reading, not as a step in writing a book report. **Option D is incorrect** because examining parts of words is not the focus in the reading workshop. **(Competency 005 Reading Applications)**

33. C.

Option C is correct because teachers can read aloud books that students either cannot or do not read on their own, and the literature that the teachers read aloud uses words that students do not encounter in their daily lives. Option A is incorrect because students are listening, not reading, as they would do to practice word identification. Option B is incorrect because actual gains in fluency pertain to reading development. Option D is incorrect because students are listening to the teacher, not previewing before reading. (Competency 001 Oral Language)

34. C.

Option C is correct because a score of 70th percentile means that 70% of the norm group performed at the same level or below the student's score. Option A is incorrect because the scores of a norm-referenced test provide information about how the student's achievement compares to other students at national levels. Option B is incorrect because a score of 70th percentile means that 70% of the norm group performed at the same level or below the student's score, not above. Option D is incorrect because a norm-referenced score is not based upon a students' performance in the classroom. (Competency 004 Reading Comprehension and Assessment)

35. A.

Option A is correct because criterion-referenced tests can provide information about what students know in regard to a specific set of predetermined outcomes. Option B is incorrect because the scores of a norm-referenced test provide information about a student's ranking or comparison with other students, not specific information of what a student knows and can do. Option C is incorrect because running records provide information about a student's oral reading, but not a specific assessment of a listing of high-frequency words. Option D is incorrect because a cloze procedure is used when students read a text with some words deleted, thereby

measuring a student's ability to comprehend by using context clues. (Competency 004 Reading Comprehension and Assessment)

36. D.

Option D is correct because the students can use the surrounding words as context clues and the initial consonant sound as part of phonics to identify the unknown word. Option A is incorrect because the teacher is not focusing upon words that lead readers to anticipate what is coming later in the narrative. Option B is incorrect because the teacher is not asking students to create a picture in their minds to comprehend as they read. Option C is incorrect because the teacher is not asking students to notice the structure of the text and information presented. (Competency 003 Word Identification Skills and Reading Fluency)

37. D.

Option D is correct because when a student reads below 90% of words the student can have difficulty comprehending, and the text is considered to be at the frustration level. Option A is incorrect because a student needs to read above 90% of words for a text to be at the student's instructional level. Option B is incorrect because students most likely need to read 95%–100% of the words to be able to comprehend a story. Option D is incorrect because a student needs to read above 90% of the words to be able to comprehend a story with support from instruction and for the text to be determined as being at the instructional level. (Competency 004 Reading Comprehension and Assessment)

38. B.

Option B is correct. When having grand conversations, students share their thoughts and feelings in ways akin to the way readers talk about books outside of school settings. Option A and C are incorrect because grand conversations are not directed by a series of questions posed by the teacher. Option D is incorrect because reciprocal teaching is an approach where a small group of students read a segment of the text, and then each individual assumes a role in talking about the text by either summarizing, asking questions, clarifying, or predicting. **(Competency 001 Oral Language)**

39. C.

Option C is correct. Grand conversations make it possible for students to examine their connections to what they have read and engage in an exchange of ideas, which can foster higher-level thinking. **Options A and B are incorrect** because text structure and concept maps are not featured in grand conversations. **Option D is incorrect** because grand conversations are not based upon worksheets or other packet activities. **(Competency 005 Reading Applications)**

40. C.

Option C is correct. Students will find reading literature more rewarding when they can read and share their thoughts in authentic ways. When students see that their thoughts about literature are legitimate, they are more apt to be able to analyze literature. **Options A is incorrect** because students can become more comfortable talking in various situations through being provided opportunities to engage, but the primary reason for analyzing literature subsequently pertains to preserving the aesthetic dimension of the reading. **Options B is incorrect** because grand conversations are based upon students sharing their personal responses, not analyzing literature based upon a literary element. **Option D is incorrect** because grand conversations are not based upon story maps. **(Competency 005 Reading Applications)**

41. A.

Option A is correct. Students are more apt to succeed in a task when the teacher begins instruction by modeling the process necessary for completing that task. **Option B is incorrect** because the modeling is part of a

gradual release of responsibility in teaching. **Options C and D are incorrect** because the instruction is focused upon how an author reveals a character, not comprehension monitoring or predicting. **(Competency 005 Reading Applications)**

42. D.

Option D is correct. Students progressively move from situations in which the teacher takes the majority of responsibility for their success in completing reading tasks, to situations in which the students take on increasingly more responsibility, to the point where all, or nearly all, of the responsibility is shouldered by the students. This progression ensures that students learn how to perform a task. **Option A is incorrect** because the teacher is not working with students to help them comprehend a text. The teacher is focusing upon looking again at the text to determine how the author reveals characters in the novel. **Option B is incorrect** because the teacher is not working with students on retelling, which is where students retell to measure their comprehension of what they read. **Option C is incorrect** because the teacher is not focusing upon using visualization to help students understand what they read. **(Competency 005 Reading Applications)**

43. C.

Option C is correct. Through sharing their writing with others, students have a broader audience, and students see why correct spelling, capitalization, and usage matter in developing a final draft. **Options A and B are incorrect** because, although students should engage in selecting their topics and developing a title, this task focuses on publishing and sharing writing. **Option D is incorrect** because the focus of this experience is not on the structure of a text, and writing personal narratives is not provided to develop students' understanding of informational text structure. **(Competency 007 Written Language–Composition)**

44. D.

Option D is correct. Fluency involves rate, accuracy, and prosody (intonation, stress, pauses), but the teacher is focusing upon intonation in showing how the question mark signals to the reader that this sentence will be read differently from when reading a statement. **Option A is incorrect** because in this situation the fluency instruction does not focus on rate. **Option B is incorrect** because in this situation the fluency instruction does not focus on accuracy. **Option C is incorrect** because phonemic awareness ability is accounting for sounds in words. **(Competency 003 Word Identification Skills and Reading Fluency)**

45. B.

Option B is correct. The teacher's example sentences focus upon an aspect of subject-verb agreement that can be challenging. The subject comes before a phrase that begins with the word *of*, so in these pairs of sentences, the subjects are *box* and *group*, so the verbs need to agree with these words (i.e., *box–is* and *group–likes*). The exception to this rule is when using words that indicate portions such as *percent of, majority of, some of,* or *all of*; in such cases, the noun that follows the word of determines the verb. Thus, the verb in this sentence is singular: *Some of the <u>cake</u> <u>is</u> on the table.* And the verb in this sentence is plural: *Some of the <u>cakes</u> <u>are</u> on the table.* Furthermore, notice in the teacher's second pair of sentences that *group* should be singular because the term is considered as a unit rather than emphasizing individual members within the unit. **Option A is incorrect** because the student has not placed a word, phrase, or clause in such a way that what is being modified is not clear. **Option C is incorrect** because the verb tense is the same in both sentences. **Option D is incorrect** because no contrast is being drawn between active voice and passive voice. **(Competency 006 Written Language–Writing Conventions)**

46. C.

Option C is correct. The student has joined two independent clauses together with a comma, which is incorrect and is a comma splice. **Option A is incorrect** because the student did use correct subject-verb agreement. **Option B is incorrect** because the student has not used a comma correctly. **Option D is incorrect** because the student is using correct verb tense. **(Competency 006 Written Language–Writing Conventions)**

47. A.

Option A is correct because activities such as "turn and talk" help students read actively and be conscious of the message in the text, as compared to word calling alone. **Option B is incorrect** because previewing text features entails examining the title, headings, bold print, and illustrations to create meaning. **Option C is incorrect** because although students could engage in structural analysis when reading to understand a word, the teacher is not focusing upon that type of instruction. **Option D is incorrect** because text-to-text connections are more likely to take place when talking after reading the text, such as when students talk about how a story reminds them of another one, or how two stories are similar or different. **(Competency 004 Reading Comprehension and Assessment)**

48. D.

Option D is correct. Reading fluency develops when students read materials again. This helps them to read smoothly and accurately along with appropriate intonation. They will eventually better comprehend what is being read. **Option A is incorrect** because the purpose of headings pertains to highlighting text features of expository text. **Option B is incorrect** because students do need to learn high-frequency words to read fluently, but fluency is developed when students can read easily the words of the text and devote attention to reading smoothly with expression. **Option C is incorrect** because recognizing text structure is not a prerequisite to building fluency. **(Competency 003 Word Identification Skills and Reading Fluency)**

49. D.

Option D is correct. Rather than adding *s* or *es,* nouns that end in *f* or *fe* form a plural by dropping the *f* or *fe* and adding *ves.* **Option A is incorrect** because students should know the meanings of the words used in teaching writing conventions so that the words represent ones they might use in their writing. **Option B is incorrect** because the plural form of each noun is spelled correctly and does not feature an error. **Option C** is incorrect because singular and plural spellings of words is what is being featured, not phonics. **(Competency 006 Written Language–Writing Conventions)**

50. B.

Option B is correct. Traditional literature includes fairy tales that originally were oral and passed down from one generation to another. **Option A is incorrect** because historical fiction is based upon actual historical events. **Option C is incorrect** because realistic fiction features life as it is, not fantasy. **Option D is incorrect** because nonfiction represents factual information. **(Competency 005 Reading Applications)**

51. A.

Option A is correct. Students are most apt to enjoy literature and be able to analyze it if they first can have authentic conversations where they share their thoughts about a work of literature. **Options B is incorrect** because previewing a text takes place to help students prepare for reading. **Options C and D are incorrect.** Retelling does help students remember the plot and helps ensure all understand what took place, but the teacher is not asking the students to retell the story when students share their thoughts about what took place. **(Competency 005 Reading Applications)**

52. D.

Option D is correct because the students can view the geographical locations as they become familiar with the variants of the tale. **Options A, B, and C are incorrect** because those learning experiences pertain more directly to skills in using maps. **(Competency 008 Viewing and Representing)**

53. B.

Option B is correct because the illustrations reveal aspects of a culture that may not be stated in the words of the tale. **Option A is incorrect** because students would not need to draw the illustrations to remember the tales because students have a schema for stories. **Option C is incorrect** because elements of art pertains more directly to learning about art. **Option D is incorrect** because previewing is a strategy used before reading to encourage students to examine a text to anticipate what they will read. Other text features will help them process information they will read. **(Competency 008 Viewing and Representing)**

54. D.

Option D is correct because the chart categories feature aspects of the various tales, not ways to compare students' comments. **Options A, B, and C are incorrect** because completing a chart could help students discern characteristics of folktales, as indicated in Part 5. **(Competency 008 Viewing and Representing)**

55. D.

Option D is correct. Students are learning that rough draft writing can include the opportunity to revise content. Because of the modeling the teacher provides, the students will better understand how they can apply a revision technique of using arrows. **Option A is incorrect** because the mini-lesson focuses upon revising, not selecting a topic. **Option B is incorrect** because conventions of writing (i.e., spelling, punctuation, capitalization, and usage) are not the focus of this mini-lesson. The students learn about writing conventions primarily in the publishing conference for writing the final draft. **Option C is incorrect** because the mini-lesson is not focusing upon vocabulary development, and it is unclear whether incidental learning takes place. **(Competency 007 Written Language–Composition)**

56. C.

Option C is correct. These groups of words show students how they can make transitions or connections as they move from one paragraph to the next in an essay. **Option A is incorrect** because modeling how to use these words would provide only incidental instruction in how to spell the words. **Option B is incorrect** because the teacher is not showing how to revise the text by using more vivid words. **Option D is incorrect** because the teacher is not focusing upon techniques of propaganda, such as card-stacking, bandwagon, testimonial, glittering generalities, transfer, a plain-folks appeal, or name-calling. **(Competency 007 Written Language–Composition)**

57. D.

Option D is correct. The student's miscue does not make sense, and the student is not aware of the phonics generalization of how the sound of a vowel differs in a CVC pattern (of short vowels) as compared to the VCe pattern of long vowels. **Option A is incorrect** because phonemic awareness assessment is based upon the student hearing and accounting for sounds in words, not reading words. **Option B is incorrect** because the student uses the visual cues of the initial and final sounds of the unknown word. **Option C is incorrect** because the student reads high-frequency sight words correctly. **(Competency 002 Early Literacy Development)**

58. C.

Option C is correct. Historical fiction must be accurate in regard to what could take place during a period in history, but aspects of the work are fictional.

Options A, B, and D are not correct; they are types of nonfiction and consequently not fictional. **(Competency 005 Reading Applications)**

59. B.

Option B is correct because websites should have smaller chunks of information for students to grasp on each page (screen). **Options A, C, and D are incorrect,** because each option has factors that should be characteristic of websites that could be used. **(Competency 008 Viewing and Representing)**

60. B.

Option B is correct. The Directed Reading Thinking Activity (DRTA) is a comprehension strategy where the teacher guides students to ask questions, make predictions, and then read to confirm or refute their predictions. **Option A is incorrect.** Reciprocal Teaching is where students engage in discussions about what they have read and use four strategies to have a dialogue about what they have learned. **Option C is incorrect.** Think-Pair-Share is a strategy that lets students think about what they have read and learned and talk with a partner as a way of encouraging students to talk as part of their learning. **Option D is incorrect.** Concept Maps are visual organizers that can help students understand how ideas relate to other ideas in expository texts. **(Competency 004 Reading Comprehension and Assessment)**

61. C.

Option C is correct because the multimedia and other visual materials make it possible for students to obtain information they could not gain by solely reading text. **Options A and D are incorrect** because students do need to monitor their understanding as they read information and set purposes whether they use traditional literacy or new literacies as they read to gather information. **Option B is incorrect** because large amounts of information can be overwhelming for students as they read to learn about a topic and gather information. (**Competency 008 Viewing and Representing**)

62. B.

Option B is correct because students would be using the language of everyday talking when they text each other. **Options A, C, and D are incorrect,** as these choices feature the types of language students need to use to participate in learning experiences in schools. (**Competency 004 Reading Comprehension and Assessment**)

63. C.

Option C is correct. Even when a type of writing is assigned, students can learn how to focus on and find topics they want to learn more about as they do research for a report. **Option A is incorrect.** Many students are more motivated to write if they select the focus of their writing. **Option B is incorrect.** Students do become self-reliant as writers, but they also can gain from demonstrations from the teacher that provide support as students learn about how to use a new form of writing. **Option D is incorrect.** English learners can be provided with sheltered instruction so that they can participate in language development as they learn content. (**Competency 007 Written Language–Composition**)

64. C.

Option C is correct. The student's miscue shows that the student is not reading the inflectional ending of *-ed*. **Option A is incorrect** because the student is able to read the root word, *walk*. **Option B is incorrect** because the student's miscue does indicate the student used visual cues in saying the root word. **Option D is incorrect** because the student's miscue does make sense. (**Competency 002 Early Literacy Development**)

65. A.

Option A is correct because students are not apt to clearly understand the meanings of unknown words and how such words are used by looking up definitions in dictionaries. **Options B, C, and D are incorrect** because they are ways to develop students' language skills in an effective way while also making it possible for English learners to participate in subject-matter learning. (**Competency 001 Oral Language**)

66. C.

Option C is correct. The nouns featured in the list are irregular in forming the plural. **Option A is incorrect** because the silent *e* in teaching phonics relates to forming a long vowel sound, such as in *cape*, which has a long vowel as compared to *cap*, which is a short vowel sound. **Option B is incorrect** because copying a word two times is not likely to help students learn to spell it. **Option D is incorrect** because the plural forms presented are not incorrectly spelled. (**Competency 006 Written Language–Writing Conventions**)

67. B.

Option B is correct. All readers need to make gains in reading fluently so that they can devote attention to comprehension. English learners as well as other students can profit from audio-assisted reading and shared reading where they can follow print while listening to text read aloud. As English learners hear the sounds and expressions used in reading English text, the English learners can become aware of intonation, pauses, and stress patterns that differ from their native language. If English learners cannot read a text, they can follow the print as they hear the text read aloud. **Option A is incorrect** because, reading fast, per se, is not the goal of fluency instruction. Students need to be able to read accurately and smoothly as well as note punctuation, and use expression. **Option C is incorrect** because English learners will be successful in reading fluently if they practice reading texts, and all students need to be able to read fluently. **Option D is incorrect** because fluency development takes place when students can read a text easily, such as when they reread texts and not when they must devote time to word identification. **(Competency 003 Word Identification Skills and Reading Fluency)**

68. C.

Option C is correct. Revising content pertains to establishing content in writing. **Options A and B are incorrect,** as they pertain to using writing conventions, not revising the content of a rough draft. **Option D is incorrect** because topic selection takes place before starting to write or when a student changes a topic to begin a different piece of writing. **(Competency 007 Written Language–Composition)**

69. B.

Option B is correct because testing students on what others write does not represent an authentic way to foster learning and could work against students' gains in participation. Informal assessments could provide data about students' gains. **Options A, C, and D are incorrect,** as they each represent a rationale that supports blogging. **(Competency 008 Viewing and Representing)**

70. C.

Option C is correct. Concept Maps are visual organizers that can help students understand how ideas relate to other ideas in expository texts. **Option A is incorrect.** The Directed Reading Thinking Activity (DRTA) is a comprehension strategy that guides students to ask questions, make predictions, and then read to confirm or refute their predictions. **Option B is incorrect.** Think-Pair-Share is a strategy that lets students think about what they have read and learned and then talk with a partner as a way of encouraging students to talk as part of their learning. **Option D is incorrect.** Reciprocal Teaching is where the teacher models and then students become teachers as they use four strategies to have a dia-

logue about what they have learned. **(Competency 004 Reading Comprehension and Assessment)**

71. D.

Option D is correct. The setting pertains to where and when the story takes place. **Option A is incorrect** because it pertains to how characters are revealed. **Option B is incorrect** because it pertains to what took place in a story. **Option C is incorrect** because it pertains to who is telling the story (i.e., the narrator) and the way the narrator reveals the story. **(Competency 005 Reading Applications)**

72. A.

Option A is the correct answer. The names of individual stars—and the names of other astronomical terms (e.g., constellations, galaxies, planets), for that matter—are capitalized but not the term *stars*. **Option B is incorrect** because capitalization errors exist. **Option C is incorrect** because the student uses verb tense correctly. **Option D is incorrect** because a comma is not needed in either sentence. The second sentence shows a complex sentence where an independent clause is followed by a dependent clause (where a subordinating conjunction, *even though*, begins the clause), so a comma is not used. **(Competency 006 Written Language–Writing Conventions)**

73. B.

Option B is correct. Think-Pair-Share is a strategy that lets students think about what they have read and learned, and then talk with a partner as a way of encouraging students to talk as part of their learning. **Option A is incorrect.** Reciprocal Teaching is where students engage in discussions about what they have read and use four strategies to have a dialogue about what they have learned. **Option C is incorrect.** Concept Maps are visual organizers that can help students understand how ideas relate to other ideas in expository texts. **Option D is incorrect.** The Directed Reading Thinking Activity

(DRTA) is a comprehension strategy that guides students to ask questions, make predictions, and then read to confirm or refute their predictions. **(Competency 004 Reading Comprehension and Assessment)**

74. D.

Option D is correct because the teacher is showing how a Greek root word is featured in words and how this relates to meaning. **Option B is incorrect** because phonemic awareness is accounting for sounds in words. **Option C is incorrect** because readers use syntax when they use their knowledge of how words can be combined when identifying words when reading. **Option D is incorrect** because phonics is learning about sound-symbol correspondences. **(Competency 003 Word Identification Skills and Reading Fluency)**

75. B., C., D.

Options B, C, and D are correct because informal assessments are used by teachers on a daily basis before, during, or after they teach to inform their teaching. **Option A is incorrect** because it is a formal assessment. **(Competency 004 Reading Comprehension and Assessment)**

76. A.

Option A is correct because the words feature the long vowel sound of *a* through *ay*. **Option B is incorrect** because the words feature an *r*-controlled vowel. **Option C is incorrect** because the words feature the short vowel pattern of consonant-vowel-consonant. **Option C is incorrect** because the words feature the diphthong *oy*. **(Competency 003 Word Identification Skills and Reading Fluency)**

77. C.

Option C is correct. The student needs to focus upon establishing content in the personal narrative, and addressing writing conventions could take place before writing a final draft. **Options A and B are incorrect** because establishing content is the priority in writing a rough draft, and teachers should help students recognize this even as students do their best to properly use capitalization, punctuation, and spelling in rough drafts. **Option D is incorrect** because a student is apt to use only easy words and not take risks if the student knows the teacher will point out errors. Teachers can informally assess students' writing and use data in ways that are effective and foster students' development. **(Competency 006 Written Language–Writing Conventions)**

78. D.

Option D is correct. The student needs to be shown that -*es* is added to a word to form a plural when the word ends in *s*, *x*, *ch*, or *sh*. **Option A is incorrect** because the student can spell high-frequency words correctly. **Option B is incorrect** because the student uses past tense consistently. **Option C is incorrect** because writing about one topic is a facet of establishing content in composing, not writing conventions, which pertains to spelling, punctuation, and usage. **(Competency 006 Written Language–Writing Conventions)**

79. B.

Option B is correct. The student's second sentence features two independent clauses joined by a coordinating conjunction, which requires the use of a comma. **Option A is incorrect** because the student does demonstrate a need for instruction on how to use a comma when writing a compound sentence. **Option C is incorrect** because the student has not written a complex sentence. The first sentence is a simple sentence (with one independent clause). The second sentence is a compound sentence, not a complex sentence. A complex sentence is where an independent and dependent clause are joined together. The student wrote two independent clauses in the second sentence, thus creating a compound sentence. **Option D is incorrect** because the writing sample does not include a sentence that requires a quotation mark, so this cannot be determined. **(Competency 006 Written Language–Writing Conventions)**

80. B.

Option B is correct. When students retell a story, they tell what happened in the story, which is literal-level comprehension, and higher-level thinking about the text can take place through authentic discussion. **Options A, C, and D are incorrect** because retelling does not primarily encourage the student to think at higher levels, as a group discussion could. **(Competency 004 Reading Comprehension and Assessment)**

81. C.

Option C is correct. The student has represented all the major speech sounds of a word. **Option A is incorrect** because in the precommunicative stage, the student uses letters, but there is no correspondence between letters and words. **Option B is incorrect** because in the semiphonetic stage, the student uses abbreviated spelling where a word is represented by a letter, such as *u* for *you*. **Option D is incorrect** because the student is not showing the ability to use visual and morphological information, such as *ight*, but rather still relies upon representing sounds to spell. **(Competency 006 Written Language–Writing Conventions)**

82. A.

Option A is correct. Mini-lessons take place with the whole class and are brief demonstrations based upon what students need to know. Teachers can meet with students in small groups to provide further support. **Option B is incorrect** because during the writing part of the workshop, students and the teacher write, and the teacher also has conferences with students. **Option C is incorrect.** Through author's chair or whole-class sharing, students experience a whole-class conference when they read aloud what they have written. **Option D is incorrect.** In proofreading/publishing conferences, students learn to proofread to develop a final draft that

would be read by others. **(Competency 007 Written Language–Composition)**

83. A.

Option A is correct because *sh* is a consonant digraph, where two consonants create a new sound such as in *sh, ch, th, wh, ph*. **Options B, C, and D are incorrect** because the pairs feature consonant blends *st, br,* and *bl*. **(Competency 003 Word Identification Skills and Reading Fluency)**

84. C.

Option C is correct because if students understand the way a topic is organized in the text, or understand the text structure, they are better able to understand and locate the information for a report. **Option A is incorrect** because the students are learning how to focus on headings of expository text at this point in the lesson, not understanding new vocabulary. **Option B is incorrect** because the teacher is not building background needed to understand the text. **Option D is incorrect** because the teacher is not activating prior knowledge so students can relate the new information to what they already know. **(Competency 009 Study and Inquiry Skills)**

85. B.

Option B is correct because the omniscient point of view embraces complete, all-encompassing awareness. **Option A is incorrect** because it pertains to the plot of the story. **Option C is incorrect** because it pertains to limited third-person point of view. **Option D** pertains to first-person narrative point of view. **(Competency 005 Reading Applications)**

86. B.

Option B is correct because the teacher can expand students' comprehension as important ideas are brought up and discussed. **Option A is incorrect** because resting is not a primary benefit of reading aloud. **Option C is**

incorrect because students are making gains in listening comprehension, but they are not engaging in study skills. **Option D is incorrect** because the students are listening and speaking, not identifying words. **(Competency 001 Oral Language)**

87. C.

Option C is correct. A Venn diagram can be used when comparing two or more items. **Option A is incorrect** because visualization is a strategy for reading comprehension that is used during reading. **Option B is incorrect** because SQ3R is a strategy for reading to learn. **Option D is incorrect** because previewing is a strategy used before reading to anticipate content to be encountered. **(Competency 004 Reading Comprehension and Assessment)**

88. A.

Option A is correct. Reciting poetry in front of the class could work against oral language development and interest in poetry because many students might not succeed, and this does not represent an authentic use of language. **Options B, C, and D are incorrect** because they represent effective ways to provide audience situations that vary in regard to size, age, and familiarity to foster oral language development. **(Competency 001 Oral Language)**

89. B.

Option B is correct. Students are motivated to write when they share their writing with an audience. They can grow as writers by hearing what other students write and what others say in offering feedback about what they liked or learned and by posing questions. **Option A is incorrect** because students were engaged in whole-class sharing and were focused on what each student was reading aloud, not on writing conventions. **Option C is incorrect.** Through author's chair or whole-class sharing, students experience a whole-class conference when they read aloud what they have written, and

other students offer feedback. The teacher can model and offer feedback, but students learn about what is not effective primarily by questions posed by their audience, not by the teacher telling them what needs to be changed. **Option D is incorrect** because students can share initial drafts in this author's chair/whole-class conferences, not just finished pieces. **(Competency 007 Written Language–Composition)**

90. C.

Option C is correct. The words are presented to show that irregular plurals do not follow the standard rules that require adding a letter to the end of the singular form. **Option A is incorrect** because the plural form shown is correct. **Option B is incorrect** because using the correct verb for a subject is not being featured. **Option D is incorrect** because phonemic awareness pertains to hearing words and accounting for sounds of a word. **(Competency 006 Written Language–Writing Conventions)**

91. A.

Option A is correct. The student's miscue indicates not using language structure because the words as spoken do not fit together in a meaningful way. The result is a sentence that does not make sense. **Option B is incorrect** because the student is using letters of the word in the miscue. **Option C is incorrect** because the student has recognized the *ed* of the verb. **Option D is incorrect** because what the student said is incoherent, indicating that the student lacks meaning cues. **(Competency 002 Early Literacy Development)**

92. C.

Option C is correct. Students may be able to state definitions but not understand concepts, so teachers should not rely upon glossary or dictionary definitions to help students understand academic vocabulary. **Options A, B, and D are incorrect** in describing factors teachers should know when helping students understand what they read. (**Competency 004 Reading Comprehension and Assessment**)

93. D.

Option D is correct because hyphens are used for compound numbers from twenty-one to ninety-nine. **Option A is incorrect** because *very* does not require a hyphen after it. **Option B is incorrect** because a hyphen is also needed after *year* because all the words *six*, *year*, and *old* combine to modify the word *student*. The hyphenated words together create a compound noun. **Option C is incorrect** because a hyphen is generally used when two or more words together modify a noun. (**Competency 006 Written Language–Writing Conventions**)

94. A.

Option A is correct because the word *because* is a subordinating conjunction, which creates a dependent clause. Students can use a comma mistakenly when joining an independent clause and dependent clause. **Options B, C, and D are incorrect** because they are coordinating conjunctions that combine two independent clauses using a comma. (**Competency 006 Written Language–Writing Conventions**)

95. B.

Option B is correct. Reciprocal Teaching is where the teacher models and then students become teachers as they use the four strategies to have a dialogue about what they have learned. **Option A is incorrect** because Concept Maps are visual organizers that can help students understand how ideas relate to other ideas in expository texts. **Option C is incorrect** because Think-Pair-Share is a strategy that lets students think about what they have read and learned, setting the stage for them to talk with a partner as a way of encouraging students to talk as part of their learning. **Option D is incorrect** because the Directed Reading Thinking Activity (DRTA) is a comprehension strategy that guides students to ask questions, make predictions, and then read to confirm or refute their

predictions. (**Competency 004 Reading Comprehension and Assessment**)

96. B.

Option B is correct. Fluency entails being able to read smoothly so what is read can be remembered, and prosody is needed because readers understand better when they read with expression and make changes in intonation in response to indicators in the text. **Options A and D are incorrect** because the student does not need word identification instruction. **Option C is incorrect** because the assessment has not focused upon comprehension, and visualization is used to help students create images in their minds to read actively and comprehend. Comprehension can be affected when students do not read fluently, but a comprehension assessment is not described in this situation. (**Competency 004 Reading Comprehension and Assessment**)

97. A.

Option A is correct because students do not engage in worksheets as part of proofreading/publishing conferences. **Options B, C, and D are incorrect** because they do present appropriate rationales for proofreading/publishing conferences where students work with the teacher to check for correct spelling, punctuation, and usage before writing a final draft to be read by others. (**Competency 007 Written Language–Composition**)

98. A.

Option A is correct. The essay should present a viewpoint and provide strong evidence in support of the viewpoint, but the writer should also present opposing points and refute them. **Options B, C, and D are incorrect**, as they all represent aspects of writing a persuasive essay. (**Competency 007 Written Language–Composition**)

99. D.

Option D is correct. The student does not know the sight word *come*, which is irregular in spelling and thus needs to be learned as a sight word. **Option A is incorrect** because *come* is a base word, not a word identified by structural analysis or word parts. **Option B is incorrect** because phonics instruction shows students how to spell words that adhere to phonics generalizations, thereby being regular spellings, not irregular, and *come* is irregular (unlike *home*, for example). **Option C is incorrect** because the miscue does make sense, and therefore there is no reason to suspect student inattention. **(Competency 003 Word Identification Skills and Reading Fluency)**

100. D.

Option D is correct. The Directed Reading Thinking Activity (DRTA) is a comprehension strategy that guides students to ask questions, make predictions, and then read to confirm or refute their predictions. **Option A is incorrect** because Reciprocal Teaching is where students engage in discussions about what they have read and use four strategies to have a dialogue about what they have learned. **Option B is incorrect.** Concept Maps are visual organizers that can help students understand how ideas relate to other ideas in expository texts. **Option C is incorrect** because Think-Pair-Share is a strategy that lets students think about what they have read and learned and talk with a partner as a way of encouraging students to talk as part of their learning. **(Competency 004 Reading Comprehension and Assessment)**

PRACTICE TEST 2

TExES ELAR 4–8

Also available at the REA Study Center (www.rea.com/studycenter)

This practice test is also offered online at the REA Study Center. We recommend that you take the online version of the test to simulate test-day conditions and to receive these added benefits:

- **Timed testing conditions**—helps you gauge how much time you can spend on each question

- **Automatic scoring**—find out how you did on the test, instantly

- **On-screen detailed explanations of answers**—gives you the correct answer and explains why the other answer choices are wrong

- **Diagnostic score reports**—pinpoint where you're strongest and where you need to focus your study

Practice Test 2 Answer Sheet

1. Ⓐ Ⓑ Ⓒ Ⓓ
2. Ⓐ Ⓑ Ⓒ Ⓓ
3. Ⓐ Ⓑ Ⓒ Ⓓ
4. Ⓐ Ⓑ Ⓒ Ⓓ
5. Ⓐ Ⓑ Ⓒ Ⓓ
6. Ⓐ Ⓑ Ⓒ Ⓓ
7. Ⓐ Ⓑ Ⓒ Ⓓ
8. Ⓐ Ⓑ Ⓒ Ⓓ
9. Ⓐ Ⓑ Ⓒ Ⓓ
10. Ⓐ Ⓑ Ⓒ Ⓓ
11. Ⓐ Ⓑ Ⓒ Ⓓ
12. Ⓐ Ⓑ Ⓒ Ⓓ
13. Ⓐ Ⓑ Ⓒ Ⓓ
14. Ⓐ Ⓑ Ⓒ Ⓓ
15. Ⓐ Ⓑ Ⓒ Ⓓ
16. Ⓐ Ⓑ Ⓒ Ⓓ
17. Ⓐ Ⓑ Ⓒ Ⓓ
18. Ⓐ Ⓑ Ⓒ Ⓓ
19. Ⓐ Ⓑ Ⓒ Ⓓ
20. Ⓐ Ⓑ Ⓒ Ⓓ
21. Ⓐ Ⓑ Ⓒ Ⓓ
22. Ⓐ Ⓑ Ⓒ Ⓓ
23. Ⓐ Ⓑ Ⓒ Ⓓ
24. Ⓐ Ⓑ Ⓒ Ⓓ
25. Ⓐ Ⓑ Ⓒ Ⓓ

26. Ⓐ Ⓑ Ⓒ Ⓓ
27. Ⓐ Ⓑ Ⓒ Ⓓ
28. Ⓐ Ⓑ Ⓒ Ⓓ
29. Ⓐ Ⓑ Ⓒ Ⓓ
30. Ⓐ Ⓑ Ⓒ Ⓓ
31. Ⓐ Ⓑ Ⓒ Ⓓ
32. Ⓐ Ⓑ Ⓒ Ⓓ
33. Ⓐ Ⓑ Ⓒ Ⓓ
34. Ⓐ Ⓑ Ⓒ Ⓓ
35. Ⓐ Ⓑ Ⓒ Ⓓ
36. Ⓐ Ⓑ Ⓒ Ⓓ
37. Ⓐ Ⓑ Ⓒ Ⓓ
38. Ⓐ Ⓑ Ⓒ Ⓓ
39. Ⓐ Ⓑ Ⓒ Ⓓ
40. Ⓐ Ⓑ Ⓒ Ⓓ
41. Ⓐ Ⓑ Ⓒ Ⓓ
42. Ⓐ Ⓑ Ⓒ Ⓓ
43. Ⓐ Ⓑ Ⓒ Ⓓ
44. Ⓐ Ⓑ Ⓒ Ⓓ
45. Ⓐ Ⓑ Ⓒ Ⓓ
46. Ⓐ Ⓑ Ⓒ Ⓓ
47. Ⓐ Ⓑ Ⓒ Ⓓ
48. Ⓐ Ⓑ Ⓒ Ⓓ
49. Ⓐ Ⓑ Ⓒ Ⓓ
50. Ⓐ Ⓑ Ⓒ Ⓓ

51. Ⓐ Ⓑ Ⓒ Ⓓ
52. Ⓐ Ⓑ Ⓒ Ⓓ
53. Ⓐ Ⓑ Ⓒ Ⓓ
54. Ⓐ Ⓑ Ⓒ Ⓓ
55. Ⓐ Ⓑ Ⓒ Ⓓ
56. Ⓐ Ⓑ Ⓒ Ⓓ
57. Ⓐ Ⓑ Ⓒ Ⓓ
58. Ⓐ Ⓑ Ⓒ Ⓓ
59. Ⓐ Ⓑ Ⓒ Ⓓ
60. Ⓐ Ⓑ Ⓒ Ⓓ
61. Ⓐ Ⓑ Ⓒ Ⓓ
62. Ⓐ Ⓑ Ⓒ Ⓓ
63. Ⓐ Ⓑ Ⓒ Ⓓ
64. Ⓐ Ⓑ Ⓒ Ⓓ
65. Ⓐ Ⓑ Ⓒ Ⓓ
66. Ⓐ Ⓑ Ⓒ Ⓓ
67. Ⓐ Ⓑ Ⓒ Ⓓ
68. Ⓐ Ⓑ Ⓒ Ⓓ
69. Ⓐ Ⓑ Ⓒ Ⓓ
70. Ⓐ Ⓑ Ⓒ Ⓓ
71. Ⓐ Ⓑ Ⓒ Ⓓ
72. Ⓐ Ⓑ Ⓒ Ⓓ
73. Ⓐ Ⓑ Ⓒ Ⓓ
74. Ⓐ Ⓑ Ⓒ Ⓓ
75. Ⓐ Ⓑ Ⓒ Ⓓ

76. Ⓐ Ⓑ Ⓒ Ⓓ
77. Ⓐ Ⓑ Ⓒ Ⓓ
78. Ⓐ Ⓑ Ⓒ Ⓓ
79. Ⓐ Ⓑ Ⓒ Ⓓ
80. Ⓐ Ⓑ Ⓒ Ⓓ
81. Ⓐ Ⓑ Ⓒ Ⓓ
82. Ⓐ Ⓑ Ⓒ Ⓓ
83. Ⓐ Ⓑ Ⓒ Ⓓ
84. Ⓐ Ⓑ Ⓒ Ⓓ
85. Ⓐ Ⓑ Ⓒ Ⓓ
86. Ⓐ Ⓑ Ⓒ Ⓓ
87. Ⓐ Ⓑ Ⓒ Ⓓ
88. Ⓐ Ⓑ Ⓒ Ⓓ
89. Ⓐ Ⓑ Ⓒ Ⓓ
90. Ⓐ Ⓑ Ⓒ Ⓓ
91. Ⓐ Ⓑ Ⓒ Ⓓ
92. Ⓐ Ⓑ Ⓒ Ⓓ
93. Ⓐ Ⓑ Ⓒ Ⓓ
94. Ⓐ Ⓑ Ⓒ Ⓓ
95. Ⓐ Ⓑ Ⓒ Ⓓ
96. Ⓐ Ⓑ Ⓒ Ⓓ
97. Ⓐ Ⓑ Ⓒ Ⓓ
98. Ⓐ Ⓑ Ⓒ Ⓓ
99. Ⓐ Ⓑ Ⓒ Ⓓ
100. Ⓐ Ⓑ Ⓒ Ⓓ

Practice Test 2

TIME: 4 hours and 45 minutes
100 questions

> **Directions:** Read each item and select the best answer(s). Most items on this test require you to provide the one best answer. However, some questions require you to select all the options that apply.

1. Ms. Grewal, an English teacher, presents the word *destruction*. She points out to the students that *struct,* a Latin root, means "to build." She adds that *de* is a common prefix that means "opposite." Further, Ms. Grewal points out how *construct* and *restructure* are related. Which of the following is a primary rationale why this instruction would help students?

    A. The teacher is helping students gain in applying phonics for word identification.

    B. The teacher is helping students gain in phonemic awareness.

    C. Morphemic analysis can help students learn about word structure and meaning.

    D. Using knowledge of syntax can help students identify words.

Use the information below to answer questions 2 and 3.

Students in fifth grade started the school year by writing personal narratives and informal reports drawing upon their experiences. The students are going to learn how to write a report. The teacher knows that even when students are competent writers, they can find it challenging to demonstrate the skills needed to locate information and write a report.

2. Which of the following is an effective way to support students' initial learning of how to write a report?

    A. The teacher needs to make sure each student knows how to develop an outline.

    B. The teacher should provide differentiated instruction for English learners so they can create an oral version.

    C. Before students independently write a report, the teacher and students could together write a shorter report.

    D. The teacher needs to tell students to make sure they do not copy from a text as they take notes.

3. How can teachers help ensure students use quality online sources that meet their needs as they initially learn about writing a report?

    A. The teacher can locate material and websites that students will find helpful.

    B. The teacher can provide a checklist on how to evaluate a website.

    C. The teacher can show students how to search for a website.

    D. The teacher can let students work in pairs to support each other.

4. The teacher reads aloud over a period of days from an informational book that provides an overview of a topic of research: wolves. The teacher and students work together in deciding questions or aspects of the topic they want to address. The teacher writes each question at the top of a sheet for note-taking. The teacher tells the students they can add other questions or aspects of the topic that they discover as they read further to gain information.

Which of the following best illustrates how this demonstration helps students gain in inquiry skills?

A. The teacher is providing background knowledge students need for reading.

B. The students are learning how to read for a purpose and organize their note-taking as they gather information from sources.

C. The students are using fiction and nonfiction to learn.

D. The students are learning how to use cohesive ties.

5. The teacher reads aloud an excerpt from an informational book that addresses the topic at hand: baby wolves, or pups. The teacher then closes the book and makes a list of what he remembers about pups on the page for note-taking devoted to the topic of baby wolves.

How can this demonstration help students gain in inquiry skills?

A. The teacher is ensuring students have background knowledge they need.

B. The teacher shows how to preview a text.

C. The teacher can follow up by asking students to copy the notes to use when they write that part of the report.

D. The teacher shows how to take notes without copying the text.

6. A school district wants to monitor each student's abilities in learning to understand and spell commonly confused words. Which of the following types of assessment should be used?

A. Criterion-referenced

B. Norm-referenced

C. Running records

D. Anecdotal accounts

7. Which of the following statements best describes how to foster fluency?

A. Encourage students to recognize the purpose of headings.

B. Provide students reading materials that have challenging words to foster growth.

C. Make sure students can recognize text structure.

D. Provide opportunities for students to read texts again so that the texts are easy in regard to identifying words.

8. In helping a student proofread to develop a final draft, the teacher focuses upon the following sentence:

A delicious cake was baked by the chef.

The student's final draft includes this revision:

The chef baked a delicious cake.

Which of the following aspects of writing does this instruction feature?

A. Dangling modifiers

B. Subject-verb agreement

C. Verb tense

D. Passive and active voice

9. Which of the following represents an accurate analysis of the student's miscue?

    Student: She needs tap to wrap the gift.

    Text: She needs tape to wrap the gift.

    A. The miscue shows the need for instruction in phonemic awareness.

    B. The student's miscue indicates that the student is not paying attention to meaning and needs phonics instruction.

    C. The student needs instruction in reading multisyllabic words.

    D. The student is not paying attention to meaning and not using any visual cues.

10. How can running records provide beneficial assessment?

    A. The teacher can keep a record of books the student has read for independent reading.

    B. The teacher can use the running record to help determine the correct text for students' reading instruction and to analyze students' oral reading errors.

    C. The teacher can determine how well the student reads as compared to other students in the state at the end of the school year.

    D. The teacher can keep a record of whether the student can spell high-frequency words.

11. A student wrote the following:

    I like to play with my cat.

    What stage of writing development is indicated through this writing sample?

    A. Semiphonetic

    B. Phonetic

    C. Transitional

    D. Conventional

12. A language arts teacher has shown students how to identify an unknown word in a sentence by reading the sentence to see what word would make sense and starts with the letter of the unknown word. Which of the following describes the ability the teacher is developing?

    A. How to preview the text

    B. How to use visualization when reading

    C. How authors use foreshadowing

    D. Using context clues and phonics for word identification

Use the student writing sample below to answer the question that follows.

My best friend lives next to my house, we have fun. Last Friday we had a sleep over at her house, we stayed up until midnite.

13. Which of the following is an accurate assessment of the student's abilities in applying writing conventions?

    A. The student does not use correct-subject-verb agreement.

    B. The student knows how to use a period and a comma correctly.

    C. The student needs to learn how to avoid a comma splice.

    D. The student needs to learn about capitalization.

14. Which of the following represents a way a teacher could use a visual organizer to help students think about new terms and see the relationships among terms.

    A. Directed Reading Thinking Activity

    B. Concept Maps

    C. Reciprocal Teaching

    D. Question-Answer Relationships

15. During a mini-lesson, the teacher models rough-draft writing by thinking aloud and saying, "I am not sure about how to spell this word, so I am going to spell it the best I can so I focus on what I want to say. I can check on the spelling later." What is the rationale for this mini-lesson?

    A. Teachers need to provide differentiated instruction in teaching writing so that English learners are not overwhelmed by learning about writing conventions.

    B. Students are likely to not want to write if they have to care about spelling and punctuation.

    C. Through worksheets, students can obtain ample instruction on writing skills they need to learn.

    D. When writing rough drafts, students should do their best in spelling and using punctuation, but they should not be overly concerned about writing conventions.

16. Which of the following pertains to semantics of language?

    A. The study of meaning in a language

    B. How words can be combined in language

    C. Letter-sound relationships

    D. Sounds of a language and how they combine

17. Which of the following statements is accurate in describing demands of reading fiction and expository texts?

    A. Expository text is too hard for students to grasp, so it is best to use discussion and visual media.

    B. Students have a schema for the text structure of expository texts, but they can struggle with the narrative structure of fiction because it is unfamiliar.

    C. If students read fiction, they will be prepared for the text structure of expository texts.

    D. Topics in expository text have a structure that is based upon how the subject or topic is organized, so students need to uncover the text structure as they read expository texts.

18. A teacher observes that a student can identify words when reading, but the student does not read smoothly and does not change intonation when a sentence has a question mark. What type of instruction does the student need?

    A. Structural analysis

    B. Fluency

    C. Visualization

    D. Phonics

19. A teacher presents the following pair of sentences and asks the class to select the one that is correct.

    The majority of the students want to go on the field trip.

    The majority of the students wants to go on the field trip.

    What aspect of writing does this instruction feature?

    A. Dangling modifiers

    B. Verb tense

    C. Subject-verb agreement

    D. Using strong verbs

20. After assessing the students through running records, a sixth-grade teacher determines that some students will experience difficulty when trying to identify words in the social studies textbook. Which of the following is an effective way the teacher could help the students gain in reading content-area textbooks?

    A. The teacher could give the students easy questions to answer for each chapter so students can learn information.

    B. The teacher could avoid using the textbook because it is too hard for the students and they will become discouraged.

    C. The teacher could work with students in small groups and use shared reading with students who cannot read at least 90% of the words.

    D. The teacher could give a test each week so that students read and study information in the textbook.

Use the information below to answer questions 21 to 27.

A sixth-grade classroom includes students who are English learners, as well as native speakers who are reading below grade level. Other students in the class read on grade level or slightly below.

Part 1. During guided reading, the teacher meets with a small group, where students read at the same level (homogeneous grouping). When not working with the teacher, the students participate in learning stations where groups are heterogeneous in reading ability level.

Part 2. At the poetry notebook station, the students read the poems the teacher has presented to the class in a previous week for shared reading.

Part 3. When reading the poems at the poetry notebook station, students read with a partner.

Part 4. At another station, students work in a small group and practice a readers' theater script based upon stories or nonfiction that the teacher knows the students can read.

Part 5. At another station, students listen to audio recordings of books while they follow along and read the book.

Part 6. For the independent reading station, students can select any book for reading, and they record the title on a reading log.

21. Which of the following statements provides a rationale for the teacher's decisions for grouping in Part 1?

A. Homogeneous groups are best for instructional activities so that students receive instruction at a level that meets their needs, whereas heterogeneous groups work best for productive independent work while the teacher works with a small group.

B. Older students do not need small groups for instruction because students can identify words and read at the same level.

C. After forming groups, the teacher will not need to change them.

D. Heterogeneous groups work best for independent work because worksheets can be adapted, and heterogeneous groups work best for small-group instruction to motivate students.

22. In Part 1, how can teachers ensure students read texts that are appropriate for their reading ability level?

A. The teacher could give the students an interest inventory to find books about topics that interest the students.

B. The teacher could examine students' records to determine the correct reading levels for the current year.

C. The teacher can use running records to assess students using benchmark books of various levels to form three or four groups for instruction.

D. The teacher should have students use a text according to the students' grade level so students make progress.

23. In Part 2, the teacher lets the students read poems that the class has read together in a previous week. What is the rationale for the teachers' decision?

A. The activity prepares students to monitor comprehension.

B. The activity prepares students for making predictions.

C. Rereading fosters fluency because students can gain in reading smoothly, accurately, and with expression, making it possible for them to focus on understanding what they are reading.

D. The rereading prepares students for an assignment where the teacher asks the students to memorize the poems.

24. In Part 3, what is a main rationale for the teacher's decision to let students read with a partner?

    A. Students are able to monitor their comprehension and apply "fix up" strategies, as needed.

    B. English learners, as well as other students who struggle in reading, can gain in reading proficiency by reading with a student who can read a text successfully. More advanced students also can gain in fluency.

    C. Students are engaging in a text feature walk as they read together.

    D. Through reading with a partner, the students will gain in the regulatory function of language.

25. In Part 4, the students work in a heterogeneous group as they read readers' theatre scripts together. How can this activity contribute to students' reading development?

    A. The activity prepares students to monitor comprehension.

    B. The activity prepares students for making predictions.

    C. Rereading fosters fluency because students can gain in reading smoothly, accurately, and with expression, making it possible for students to focus on understanding what they are reading.

    D. The rereading prepares students for memorizing the lines of the script.

26. In Part 5, students listen to audio-recordings of books. How can this activity contribute to students' reading development?

    A. Students can experience gains in listening comprehension or word identification.

    B. Students are apt to stay on task so the teacher can work with others.

    C. Students can learn more about root words and derivations.

    D. Students learn to monitor their reading.

27. In Part 6, why does the teacher let students self-select books for independent reading rather than require books of a designated level or length?

    A. Students learn to engage in metacognition where they monitor their reading.

    B. When students select books, they experience authentic reading experiences and are more apt to read.

    C. The students read above grade level.

    D. The students read at grade level.

28. A teacher is providing a mini-lesson to help students learn how to write informal reports. The teacher tells the students that they are going to write an informal report about soccer. The teacher writes "Playing Soccer" in the center of the web, and then adds lines extending from the center as she talks briefly about the following: Starting and Playing, Penalties, Positions. Which of the following rationales best explains why the teacher would provide this mini-lesson?

    A. The teacher is showing students how to take a topic they know about and then create a web to see possible ways to develop the topic through paragraphs or chapters.

    B. The teacher is encouraging students to write about soccer and demonstrating how to get started.

    C. The teacher is showing students how to revise their writing by demonstrating.

    D. The teacher is teaching a unit of study on physical fitness.

29. When teaching phonological and phonemic awareness, which of the following is *not* a guideline for instruction?

    A. Start with easier tasks such as rhyming, and then move to blending, and then segmenting.

    B. Start with stop sounds because they are easier for students to blend.

    C. Phonemic awareness entails listening, but students make gains in phonemic awareness as they encounter print and account for sounds, such as in hearing rhyming words and using "invented" spelling for writing.

D. Start with larger units of language such as words and onset-rime and then move to individual phonemes.

30. A teacher has decided that he will devote additional attention to the following pairs of words for spelling instruction: *passed–past, stationery–stationary, capital–capitol, aisle–isle.* Which of the following is a rationale for grouping such words for students?

A. Each pair represents words that are synonyms and need to be explained.

B. Each pair represents homophones that need to be explained.

C. The teacher can combine spelling and social studies instruction.

D. The teacher can use the words to help students read multisyllabic words.

31. A teacher is focusing upon the following words in working with students: *for example*, *for instance.* Which of the following explains how this instruction could contribute to literacy development?

A. The teacher is showing common affixes used in words.

B. The teacher is teaching antonyms.

C. The teacher is showing how a cohesive tie can be used by writers.

D. The teacher is showing how to use visualization when reading.

32. Which of the following strategies describes anticipating what the text will be about before reading and what will happen next during reading?

A. Summarizing

B. Recalling

C. Predicting

D. Making inferences

33. When teachers require students to read texts independently, the teacher needs to make sure the students can comprehend what they read. Which of the following indicates what percentage of the words students should be able to identify so they can devote attention to constructing meaning?

A. 95%–100%

B. 90%–94%

C. 85%–89%

D. 80%–84%

34. When evaluating whether to use a website, which of the following is a factor that indicates that the website should ***not*** be used for instruction?

A. Most pages present large amounts of information.

B. The site has accurate, understandable content that relates to instructional objectives.

C. The site has multimedia and visual materials that contribute important information.

D. The site is easy to navigate.

35. Which of the following is a type of fiction? Select *all* that apply.

A. Fantasy

B. Mystery

C. Memoir

D. Folktales

36. After students have read a story or book chapter, the teacher and students have grand conversations where they share their personal responses. Which of the following is **not** a way grand conversations can contribute to students' development?

    A. The teacher's contributions can show how a competent reader connects events to arrive at big ideas that emerge from a story.

    B. Sharing personal responses to literature helps students make gains in comprehension as important ideas are brought up for discussion.

    C. These learning experiences can help students be able to know how to use text features.

    D. Students are able to see that their thoughts about literature are legitimate, which can foster confidence when students are asked to analyze literature at subsequent times in their schooling.

37. When reading to learn from expository texts, students can benefit from activating their prior knowledge, setting a purpose for reading, and reviewing content. Which of the following strategies helps students engage in these types of thinking?

    A. Reciprocal Teaching

    B. Think-Pair-Share

    C. Concept Maps

    D. K-W-L

38. Which of the following shows the correct use of a hyphen? Select *all* that apply.

    A. Twenty-five dollars

    B. Ten-year old student

    C. Family-owned restaurant

    D. Very-beautiful sunset

39. Which statement best describes why figurative language can present a challenge for students as they read literature?

    A. Students experience difficulty understanding stories.

    B. Students can have difficulty with word identification.

    C. When figurative language is used, words or phrases do not have the literal meaning students have encountered in their everyday experiences.

    D. Students may not be able to read multisyllabic words.

40. When students learn to write in English, they may use "invented spelling" where they account for sounds in a word, but fail to use conventional spelling, such as *bik* for *bike*. Which of the following is an accurate statement in regard to students' use of "invented spelling" as they write?

    A. Students who use invented spelling do move toward conventional spelling as they are exposed to print, and invented spelling contributes to reading development because phonemic awareness is necessary in learning to read.

    B. Students should not write unless they can spell words correctly because the incorrect spelling will interfere with their growth in spelling.

    C. Invented spelling could make it difficult for students to learn correct spellings because they have practiced writing using incorrect spelling.

    D. Invented spelling is an indicator of difficulty in phonological awareness.

41. A student wrote the following:

    I had to go to the emergency room last summer. Because I broke my arm.

    Which statement accurately describes the student's mastery of writing conventions based upon the writing sample?

    A. The student has difficulty with using verb tenses.

    B. The student does not know that a clause that begins with a subordinating conjunction is not an independent clause.

    C. The student does not know about capitalization of seasons.

    D. The student has difficulty spelling high-frequency words.

42. As part of her reading aloud program, the teacher includes quality nonfiction books the students enjoy. As part of teaching students how to write a report, the teacher reads again the lead-ins of several books. Which of the following statements describes a rationale for the teacher's instruction?

    A. The teacher can ask students to write a lead-in like one in the books.

    B. The teacher is showing students how to preview a book.

    C. Books that students have heard or read can serve as mentor texts.

    D. Students can find it difficult to comprehend nonfiction as compared to fiction.

43. First-person point of view is best defined as which of the following?

    A. The events that take place in the story

    B. Lets readers know what each character feels, thinks, says, and does

    C. Where and when the story takes place

    D. When a character tells the story

44. Which of the following is an effective way to help students navigate expository texts so that they can learn information?

    A. Provide weekly assessments to make sure students know the content.

    B. Make sure students write the definitions of words so they will remember the meanings when they read the chapter.

    C. Ask students to read a small chunk of the text in view of their ability, and let students talk about what they learned before reading the next chunk.

    D. Tell students to read to the end of a sentence when they encounter a word they do not know so they can use context clues to figure out the unknown word.

45. Where in the writing workshop does the teacher help students address spelling, capitalization, punctuation, and usage?

    A. Mini-lessons and small-group work

    B. Writing rough drafts

    C. Proofreading/publishing conferences

    D. Author's chair/whole-class conferences

46. What is a rationale for asking students in a group to retell what they have read before the group has a grand conversation?

    A. The teacher can determine whether the student can make inferences.

    B. The teacher can determine whether the student can evaluate information.

    C. The teacher can determine whether the student is making text-to-self connections.

    D. The teacher can determine whether the student understands at a literal level what was read.

47. A team of teachers has observed that their students have made gains in composing, but not in conventions of writing. Which of the following statements best describes components of an effective approach to guide students' writing instruction? Select *all* that apply.

    A. Students need to have systematic instruction in spelling, punctuation, capitalization, and usage through lessons and usage.

    B. Students need to learn how to apply knowledge of writing conventions to their own writing, and teachers can help them through publishing conferences that prepare students for writing a final draft that is shared with others.

    C. Focusing upon spelling, punctuation, capitalization, and usage is not necessary because what matters most is whether students can communicate ideas.

    D. Students need to look up words in a dictionary to correct their spelling for a final draft.

48. If a student receives a score of 90th percentile on a norm-referenced test, what does this score mean?

    A. The score indicates that the student answered 90% of the questions correctly.

    B. The score means that 90% of the norm group performed at the same level or above the student's score.

    C. The score means that 90% of the norm group performed at the same level or below the student's score.

    D. The student has earned a 90 for the grading period.

49. Which of the following describes affixes?

    A. Another name for suffixes

    B. Another name for prefixes

    C. Root or base words

    D. Prefixes and suffixes

50. How can viewing a video be incorporated effectively as part of a unit of study?

    A. The students could be given a test to make sure they gained from the video.

    B. The students could be asked to find a video online to learn about using digital resources.

    C. Students can discuss what they learned and add information to notes based upon other sources used during the unit of study.

    D. To provide differentiated instruction, the teacher should provide the video for English learners instead of having them read the text.

51. When listening to a student read during instruction, the teacher observes that the student stops reading when seeing the word *father*. Which of the following should the teacher do to provide effective support?

    A. The teacher should ask the student to read to the end of the sentence to determine what the word is, based upon the initial sound of the word.

    B. The teacher should ask the student to "sound it out" to determine the word.

    C. The teacher should ask the student to "look for the little word" in the word.

    D. The teacher should tell the student the word.

52. Which of the following pertains to syntax of language?

    A. The study of meaning in a language

    B. How words can be combined in language

    C. Letter-sound relationships

    D. Sounds of a language and how they combine

53. In teaching students how to write a persuasive essay, Mr. Johnson will provide mini-lessons where he models techniques students need to know. Which of the following is **not** a technique the teacher would model to show effective ways to support a position?

    A. Using statistics

    B. Using facts and examples

    C. Using "I think"

    D. Citing quotes from experts on the topic

Use the information below to answer questions 54 to 59.

Part 1. The teacher meets with students in small groups for reading. In preparing English learners to read a story, the teacher presents the word *exit*. The teacher tells the students that one of the words they will read in the story is *exit*. The students look at the word and say it. The teacher then shows the sentence that appears in the story where the word is used, and the teacher explains what the word means.

Part 2. The teacher shows students a photo of an exit sign above a door in a building, and she discusses that the sign indicates where to exit the building.

Part 3. The teacher then tells students that she is going to exit the classroom and briefly walks out the door and comes back in.

Part 4. After students have read the story silently, they retell the story and share their responses. The teacher brings up the point that the people had difficulty when they tried to exit the building because of the location of the fire.

Part 5. On the next day, the teacher and students talk about the times of the day when they exit the classroom.

Part 6. In a subsequent lesson, the teacher reminds students that they learned the meaning of *exit*. The teacher then shows students the following words: *export and expel*. The teacher and students discuss the meaning of the prefix *ex* and how recognizing a prefix can help students understand the meanings of the words.

54. In Part 1, which of the following is a rationale for the teacher's instruction?

    A. The teacher is helping students preview text features.

    B. The teacher is providing direct instruction for a word that English learners may not understand solely by using context clues when reading the story.

    C. The teacher wants to teach phonics so the students can make gains in word identification.

    D. The teacher is helping students be able to make predictions.

55. In Part 2, which of the following is a rationale for the teacher's instruction?

    A. The teacher is using a visual to help provide a variety of unfamiliar vocabulary that is important to know to understand the story.

    B. The teacher is helping students preview text features.

    C. The teacher wants to teach phonics so the students can make gains in word identification.

    D. The teacher is helping students learn to spell the word by seeing it again.

56. In Part 3, what is a rationale for the teacher's instruction?

    A. The teacher is helping students to develop a concept map.

    B. The teacher is helping students preview text features.

    C. The teacher wants students to be able to use pantomime.

    D. The teacher is teaching vocabulary briefly, but the instruction is in-depth by using multiple ways of showing meaning.

57. In Part 4, in which of the following ways does the teacher contribute to the English learners' literacy development?

    A. When sharing with the whole class, English learners are able to practice their English.

    B. The teacher can grade the students' contributions to the discussion to provide feedback.

    C. The teacher can ask comprehension questions to make sure the English learners understood the story.

    D. Through talking about what took place and sharing personal responses, the students are able to expand their experiences with the story.

58. Which of the following is a rationale for the teacher's decision to focus again on the word *exit* in Part 5?

    A. The students will be able to write the word in their personal dictionary.

    B. Teaching a set of vocabulary words over several days helps English learners master unknown words.

    C. The teacher can use the talking experiences as a basis of students' writing.

    D. Through talking about what took place and sharing personal responses, the students are able to expand their experiences with the story.

59. The teacher's instruction in Part 6 is beneficial because it

    A. helps students to apply phonics generalizations.

    B. helps students prepare for a vocabulary quiz.

    C. prepares students for being able to write sentences using the new words.

    D. builds upon what the English learners know by introducing new words, and the teacher is helping students use morphology to figure out on their own what words mean.

60. A teacher makes sure students engage in independent reading daily as part of classroom instruction, including time when students select what they want to read.

Which of the following is a rationale for this instruction?

    A. Students can make gains in phonics.

    B. To make gains in reading, students need to read connected text and see that they can find books that are rewarding to read.

    C. The teacher can make sure students read required books.

    D. The teacher can give tests to make sure students do read.

61. The teacher listens to a student read a text. The student makes a miscue when reading, as shown below. What type of prompt should the teacher say to help the student become more effective in identifying words?

Student: The boat sailed across the over.

Text: The boat sailed across the ocean.

    A. To help the student self-correct, the teacher should ask, "Does that make sense?"

    B. The teacher should tell the child to "sound out" the word the child missed.

    C. The teacher should not say anything because this could discourage an English learner.

    D. The teacher should tell the child the word she or he did not know so the child knows the correct word.

62. The teacher shows the class the following sentences:

    Each of the players is able to go to the game.

    Either of us is able to help you.

    Everyone rides on the bus.

The teacher is focusing instruction upon which of the following?

A. These pairs of words show a common error in writing a plural form of a noun.

B. The teacher is teaching subject-verb agreement.

C. These pairs of words show pronouns that are plural.

D. The teacher is addressing phonemic awareness.

63. Which of the following strategies describes using past experiences and connecting ideas in the text to understand ideas that are implied in the text, but not stated explicitly in the text?

A. Summarizing

B. Recalling

C. Predicting

D. Making inferences

64. Which statement describes the cloze procedure?

A. Encourage students to recognize the purpose of headings.

B. Students examine the structure of expository texts.

C. Students examine the structure of a story through a graphic organizer.

D. Passages have deleted words, and the reader uses context clues to provide the missing words.

65. A teacher presented sentences to paired students and read each sentence aloud:

*The **object** of the game is to score more points than your opponent.*

*The people did not **object** to the change in the delivery date.*

_____

*People wondered about the **decrease** in attendance at the games.*

*She did not **decrease** the amount of time she practiced for the game this week.*

What is the teacher showing students through the sentences and highlighted words?

A. The teacher is showing how to use a word in more than one sentence to provide more than one example.

B. The teacher is showing derivatives of words.

C. The teacher is showing that some words are spelled the same but pronounced differently, depending upon whether the word is used as a noun or verb.

D. The teacher is providing practice reading a word twice so that students are more apt to remember how to recognize a word.

66. Given that the writing process can be recursive, where in the writing process does the writer devote attention to establishing content as a rough draft?

A. Prewriting

B. Drafting

C. Revising

D. Editing

67. A teacher "publishes" a book that each student has written. These books are added to the classroom library where students use them for their independent reading. How does this experience support the students' writing development?

A. The students gain practice in topic selection.

B. Students gain practice in developing a title for their writing.

C. Students learn about elaborating in their writing to include important details.

D. The students are provided an authentic audience and reasons for writing, including reasons for proofreading a final draft.

68. Which of the following most nearly defines the omniscient point of view?

    A. The events that take place in the story

    B. Lets readers know what each character feels, thinks, says, and does

    C. When the story is told by a narrator from one character's viewpoint

    D. When a character tells the story

69. Mr. Martinez has decided that he will devote additional attention to the following words when he instructs English learners: *rose, bark, spring, trunk.* Which of the following is a rationale for Mr. Martinez's instruction?

    A. Each of these words demonstrates an *r*-controlled vowel for phonics instruction.

    B. The words are commonly misspelled words.

    C. Each of these words demonstrates the initial consonant sound of *r*.

    D. Each word can create confusion as a homonym.

70. Which of the following represents a way to help students understand characterization?

    A. Discussing where the story took place

    B. Discussing the events of the story

    C. Discussing what the author reveals about a person, and the techniques the author used

    D. Asking students to think about the lesson(s) or big idea(s) that emerge from a story

71. Where in the writing workshop can teachers provide students instruction for writing drafts?

    A. Writing and rough-draft conferences

    B. Author's chair/whole-class conferences

    C. Mini-lessons and small-group work

    D. Proofreading/publishing conference

72. Ms. Gabel works with English learners who are emergent readers in English and did not learn to read in their native language. As part of instruction, she and her students read a book together, with the teacher pointing to words as she says each word. The students join in reading with her during additional readings of the book. Which of the following statements provides a rationale for Ms. Gabel's instruction?

    A. Through shared reading, students can learn about directionality and concepts of print as well as increase their sight vocabulary.

    B. The students can preview the text through the guidance of the teacher.

    C. The students are being shown how to monitor comprehension.

    D. The students are engaging in reciprocal teaching.

73. Where in the writing process does the writer devote time to proofreading?

    A. Prewriting

    B. Drafting

    C. Revising

    D. Editing

74. As children acquire oral language, they can use words in a conventional way, such as saying *went.* Subsequently they can say *goed,* but later they return to using the conventional form, *went.*

    This sequence points to which of the following in terms of language acquisition?

    A. The child is acquiring a second language.

    B. Children can overgeneralize.

    C. Children can forget the conventional form of the word, but later are reinforced to relearn it.

    D. Children can be confused at points in language acquisition.

75. Which of the following provide conditions for learning that would support English learners' acquisition of language and content? Select *all* that apply.

    A. Not expecting students to participate in content-area lessons if their language proficiency is not at least at an intermediate level

    B. Using actions and gestures to explain the definitions of words

    C. Letting students talk to a classmate about what they learned after reading a small chunk of information in a chapter before asking students to share with the whole group

    D. Asking students to look up definitions of unfamiliar words in a dictionary

76. Which of the following is *not* accurate in describing what is needed for vocabulary development?

    A. Students should be given time to read daily and read various types of texts.

    B. Teachers need to be intentional in selecting words for instruction that meet students' needs.

    C. Teachers can help students by modeling their own strategies for figuring out the meanings of words.

    D. Teachers need to give vocabulary tests on a regular basis and monitor results.

Use the information below to answer questions 77 to 80.

The teacher is helping students learn about state government, and he also is teaching students how to read and learn by using informational texts. Parts of the unit of study are presented below.

Part 1. Before students begin to read the chapter about the branches of state government, the teacher directs students' attention to the title of the chapter and guides students to notice the chapter headings: *Executive*, *Legislative*, and *Judicial*.

Part 2. The teacher and students read the introduction. Thinking aloud, the teacher says, "The introduction tells us that the chapter will describe what a branch of government consists of or who heads the branch, what the role of each branch is, and what the terms of service are. We can develop questions we will try to answer as we read." The teacher adds questions to a chart that will be developed by the students and the teacher as the students read.

Branch of Government	Executive	Legislative	Judicial
What does the branch consist of or who heads the branch?			
What is the role of the branch?			
How long is the term of office?			

77. Which of the following is a major rationale for Part 1?

    A. The teacher is providing shared reading to help students acquire new information.

    B. The teacher is helping students understand academic vocabulary.

    C. The teacher is helping students develop comprehension monitoring.

    D. The teacher is helping students preview the chapter to gain an understanding of how the overall topic is organized.

78. In Part 2, the teacher shares his thinking about the overview of the chapter and guides students in developing questions. Which of the following best describes why this is an effective approach?

    A. The teacher provides modeling to help students understand what to do in reading to learn from expository text.

    B. The teacher is building background knowledge.

    C. The teacher is helping students be able to complete the table.

    D. The teacher is activating students' prior knowledge.

79. In Part 2, the teacher displays a table the students complete with the teacher's guidance as they learn about each branch of their state government. After reading about the executive branch, the teacher asks students to tell what they have learned, and the teacher adds the information to the table. In the next lesson, the students continue in this way after encountering additional information. How does this approach help students remember new information?

    A. The categories of the table help students organize individual facts in their memory.

    B. Building background knowledge helps students relate the new to the known.

    C. Students can copy the table and complete it.

    D. Previewing headings can help students before reading a text.

80. In Part 2, the teacher does not require students to complete the reading and chart on their own. Which of the following is a rationale for the teacher's approach?

    A. The teacher is providing shared reading to help students who read below grade level.

    B. The teacher knows that the students have difficulty with academic vocabulary.

    C. The teacher is providing ample modeling, which is necessary for students to succeed in learning strategies for navigating expository text.

    D. The teacher is helping students for the first lesson, but students will work on their own after that.

81. Below is what a student said in reading a story, compared to what the text presented. Which of the following represents an accurate analysis of the miscue?

    Student: Where are you going?

    Text: When are you going?

    A. The student's miscue indicates the student is not using all of the visual cues.

    B. The student's miscue indicates the need for instruction in fluency.

    C. The student is not paying attention to meaning.

    D. The student's miscue indicates he or she needs instruction in structural analysis.

82. Which of the following statements does **not** apply to text features?

    A. Text features include headings, captions, illustrations, index, and table of contents.

    B. Students can be prepared for reading expository text by discussing text features and predicting what they will read.

    C. Text features are the parts of the text that are not the body of the text.

    D. Text features pertains to the text structure or patterns of the text.

83. A teacher is listing words the children know to teach a phonics generalization.

    Which pairs represent words that clearly show a diphthong?

    A. toy
       boy

    B. chip
       cheese

    C. she
       ship

    D. them
       this

84. Below is what a student said in reading a story, compared to what the text presented.

    Student: Every morning the children could hear the singing of the birds.

    Text: Every morning the children could hear the sounds of the birds.

    Which of the following represents an accurate analysis of the miscue?

    A. The student is not using language structure cues and meaning cues.

    B. The student is not using any visual cues.

    C. The student is not using an inflectional ending for past tense.

    D. The student is using visual cues and meaning cues, but may not know the word that is the source of the miscue.

85. Which of the following is *not* a way that proofreading/publishing conferences contribute to students' development as part of the writing workshop?

    A. By applying writing conventions as they proofread their own writing, students gain more than they would by just learning the writing conventions apart from their own writing

    B. Students focus on content while writing rough drafts, and they proofread for spelling, punc-

tuation, capitalization, and usage when editing to write a final draft.

    C. Students need to learn how to apply spelling, punctuation, capitalization, and usage as part of the process of writing.

    D. In a proofreading/publishing conference, students complete skills worksheets based upon their individual needs.

86. Which of the following is *not* a coordinating conjunction?

    A. Because

    B. And

    C. So

    D. But

87. How do teachers contribute to students' oral language development when they read aloud quality literature that meets students' needs?

    A. Students make gains in pronouncing words.

    B. Students make gains in word identification.

    C. Students learn how to preview a text.

    D. Students can make gains in vocabulary.

88. A teacher is presenting the following words for spelling instruction: *bridal-bridle, coarse-course, hair-hare, fair-fare.* Which of the following would be a primary purpose of this instruction?

    A. To help students master irregular plurals

    B. To help students learn multisyllabic words

    C. To help students learn synonyms

    D. To help students learn to spell commonly confused words

89. Which of the following statements does ***not*** describe the significance of text organization as students read to learn or study?

    A. Students can use the text structure to help them remember how individual ideas are connected to each other and to major ideas.

    B. Text features include headings, captions, illustrations, index, and table of contents.

    C. A well-organized text is easier for students to understand.

    D. Helping students read smaller chunks of information makes it easier for them to discern how ideas are presented and relate to each other, such as cause and effect.

90. In SQ3R, readers survey the text and turn a heading into a question before reading that section. Why is it helpful for readers to generate questions as they read?

    A. Students are better able to answer questions on tests.

    B. Students can gain in oral language by generating questions.

    C. Students focus on important information, integrate information, and monitor their comprehension.

    D. Students can write answers to their own questions, not questions developed by the teacher.

91. Which of the following words is irregular in spelling?

    A. Stay

    B. Have

    C. Wait

    D. Name

92. The writing process is recursive, but in which part do writers focus on making needed changes to provide elaboration, clarity, organization, and word choice?

    A. Prewriting

    B. Drafting

    C. Revising

    D. Editing

93. A teacher presents a sentence and then shows a second sentence with a revision:

    The group walked slowly back up the hill covered with snow.

    The group trudged back up the hill covered with snow.

    This instruction primarily features the use of which of the following?

    A. Strong verbs

    B. Correct verb tense

    C. Subject-verb agreement

    D. Passive versus active voice

94. Which of the following statements is ***not*** accurate in regard to new literacies such as digital and media technologies?

    A. Students are capable of using computers, so they are not apt to make gains in new literacies.

    B. New literacies need to be offered in classrooms so that all students have opportunities to make gains.

    C. Connections to the internet can provide scaffolding for learning and increasing background knowledge.

    D. Through using laptops, students can learn new ways of how to navigate and find information.

95. A teacher is listing words the students know to teach a phonics generalization. Which of the following pairs represents words that clearly show a long vowel pattern?

    A. Home–bone

    B. For–born

    C. Log–top

    D. Toy–boy

96. Which strategy is being used when the teacher encourages students to scan the text to predict what the reading section will be about, then read a chunk of the text and discuss what they have read, then make predictions about the content they will read in the next text chunk, and then, when they finish reading a whole section, go back to verify or change their predictions?

    A. Reciprocal Teaching

    B. Concept Maps

    C. Directed Reading Thinking Activity

    D. Think-Pair-Share

97. Which of the following represents categories of words that are *not* capitalized?

    A. Seasons

    B. Planets

    C. Specific geographical regions

    D. Titles

98. What percentage of words should a student be able to read so that the text is not too difficult?

    A. At least 85%

    B. At least 80%

    C. At least 90%

    D. At least 70%

99. A teacher is listing words the children know to teach a phonics generalization.

    Which pair represents words that clearly show an *r*-controlled vowel sound?

    A. Brown
       Brick

    B. She
       Ship

    C. Dirt
       Firm

    D. Grow
       Green

100. Which of the following reveals why even advanced readers find reading the expository text of textbooks challenging?

    A. Students are unfamiliar with some types of poetry.

    B. Rather than reading an expository text as they would read a story, students need to use strategies, such as reading manageable chunks and figuring out the text organization to help them remember new information.

    C. Students may not understand that the theme is inferred.

    D. Students need to use story structure to understand what they read.

Practice Test 2 Answer Key

Test Item	Answer	Competency
1.	C.	003
2.	C.	009
3.	A.	009
4.	B.	009
5.	D.	009
6.	A.	004
7.	D.	003
8.	D.	006
9.	B.	002
10.	B.	004
11.	D.	006
12.	D.	003
13.	C.	006
14.	B.	004
15.	D.	007
16.	A.	001
17.	D.	009
18.	B.	004
19.	C.	006
20.	C.	005
21.	A.	005
22.	C.	005
23.	C.	003
24.	B.	003
25.	C.	003
26.	A.	003
27.	B.	003
28.	A.	008
29.	B.	002
30.	B.	006
31.	C.	004
32.	C.	004
33.	A.	004
34.	A.	008

Test Item	Answer	Competency
35.	A., B., D.	005
36.	C.	001
37.	D.	004
38.	A., C.	006
39.	C.	004
40.	A.	002
41.	B.	006
42.	C.	007
43.	D.	005
44.	C.	009
45.	C.	007
46.	D.	004
47.	A., B.	006
48.	C.	004
49.	D.	003
50.	C.	008
51.	A.	003
52.	B.	001
53.	C.	007
54.	B.	004
55.	A.	004
56.	D.	004
57.	D.	001
58.	B.	001
59.	D.	004
60.	B.	005
61.	A.	005
62.	B.	006
63.	D.	004
64.	D.	003
65.	C.	003
66.	B.	007
67.	D.	007
68.	B.	005

Test Item	Answer	Competency
69.	D.	006
70.	C.	005
71.	C.	007
72.	A.	002
73.	D.	007
74.	B.	001
75.	B., C.	001
76.	D.	004
77.	D.	005
78.	A.	009
79.	A.	008
80.	C.	005
81.	A.	003
82.	D.	009
83.	A.	003
84.	D.	002
85.	D.	007
86.	A.	006
87.	D.	001
88.	D.	006
89.	B.	009
90.	C.	005
91.	B.	003
92.	C.	007
93.	A.	007
94.	A.	008
95.	A.	003
96.	C.	004
97.	A.	006
98.	C.	004
99.	C.	003
100.	B.	009

Practice Test 2 Detailed Answers

1. C.

    Option C is correct because the teacher is showing how a Latin root is featured in English words and how this relates to meaning, which can help students also understand other words they encounter. **Option A is incorrect** because phonics is learning about sound-symbol correspondences to identify words. **Option B is incorrect** because phonemic awareness is accounting for sounds in words. **Option D is incorrect** because readers use syntax when they use their knowledge of how words can be combined in a language. **(Competency 003 Word Identification Skills and Reading Fluency)**

2. C.

    Option C is correct because students need support as they engage in strategies associated with writing a research report. If the teacher demonstrates and works with students, they are more apt to be able to write independently. **Option A is incorrect** because before students can develop an outline, they need to first read to get an overview of a topic and plan which areas of the topic to address. **Option B is incorrect** because English learners can participate in writing through sheltered instruction, although practice presenting their ideas orally is useful for all students. **Option D is incorrect** because students need to be shown what to do, not solely told. If students are told not to copy what the text says, they often just change a few words of what is in a sentence. **(Competency 009 Study and Inquiry Skills)**

3. A.

    Option A is correct. Students eventually do need to learn how to locate and evaluate websites, but as novices they can be overwhelmed or use poor-quality sites. Therefore, having preselected materials and websites is essential in the beginning. By using quality sites, stu-dents will come to understand what a quality site is. In narrowing the web search for students, teachers allow students to focus on other skills, such as note-taking, noting sources, and writing a draft. **Option B is incorrect** because criteria on a checklist will not be understood if students are not familiar with the criteria. **Option C is incorrect.** Even if students know how to search for a website, they may not find a quality site. **Option D is incorrect** because students who are novices will not be able to support each other's learning in this situation, even though working in pairs is effective for many types of learning situations. **(Competency 009 Study and Inquiry Skills)**

4. B.

    Option B is correct. The designated questions and topic areas of interest provide structure and purpose for students as they read and record information. **Option A is incorrect** because the teacher is not providing information that students need in order to understand a text. **Option C is incorrect** because the teacher has used solely nonfiction in this situation. **Option D is incorrect** because the concept of cohesive ties was not used in this situation. Cohesive ties pertains to words that connect ideas together, such as *furthermore*, a word that shows addition. **(Competency 009 Study and Inquiry Skills)**

5. D.

    Option D is correct. Note-taking can be difficult for students to learn, but the teacher shows how to read short segments and then write notes without looking at the text so that students see a way to put ideas in their own words with accuracy. **Option A is incorrect** because the teacher has not focused upon building background knowledge in this learning experience. **Option B is incorrect.** Previewing a text entails looking at titles, headings, illustrations, photographs, and captions to prepare for reading. **Option C is incorrect** because if students copy the notes, they are directing their attention to copying, not observing what process the teacher is modeling. Instead, the teacher should continue to model or work together with students to provide gradual release of responsibility. **(Competency 009 Study and Inquiry Skills)**

6.   A.

Option A is correct because criterion-referenced tests can provide information about what students know in regard to a specific set of predetermined outcomes. **Option B is incorrect** because the scores of a norm-referenced test provide information about a student's ranking in comparison to other students, not specific information about what students know and can do. **Option C is incorrect** because running records provide information about a student's oral reading, but not a specific assessment of a listing of commonly confused words. **Option D is incorrect** because anecdotal accounts may not include observing students using commonly confused words in their reading and writing, even though anecdotal accounts can be beneficial in other ways. **(Competency 004 Reading Comprehension and Assessment)**

7.   D.

Option D is correct. Reading fluency is developed when students read materials a second time. This helps them to read smoothly and accurately, along with appropriate intonation to better comprehend what they are reading. **Option A is incorrect** because recognizing the purpose of headings pertains to noting the text structure of expository text. **Option B is incorrect** because students do need to gain in sight vocabulary words to read fluently, but fluency is developed when students can read the words of the text easily and can devote attention to reading smoothly with expression. **Option C is incorrect** because noting text structure is useful for understanding the way information is presented in expository text, which can foster comprehension and learning. **(Competency 003 Word Identification Skills and Reading Fluency)**

8.   D.

Option D is correct. The example shows how to write a sentence using the active voice, where the subject performs the action. **Option A is incorrect** because the student has not placed a word, phrase, or clause in such a way that what is being modified is unclear. **Option B is incorrect** because the subject-verb agreement is correct in both sentences. **Option C is incorrect** because the verb tense is the same—not different—in the two sentences. **(Competency 006 Written Language–Writing Conventions)**

9.   B.

Option B is correct. The student's miscue does not make sense, and the student is not aware of the phonics generalization of how the sound of *a* differs in a CVC pattern (of short vowels) as compared to the VCe pattern (of long vowels). **Option A is incorrect** because phonemic awareness assessment is based upon the student hearing and accounting for sounds in words, not reading words. **Option C is incorrect** because the miscue is not based upon a word with more than one syllable. **Option D is incorrect** because the student uses the visual cues of the initial and final sounds of the unknown word. **(Competency 002 Early Literacy Development)**

10.   B.

Option B is correct. Teachers can use running records along with an assessment of the students' comprehension to form reading groups, monitor students' progress, and teach in view of the miscues. **Option A is incorrect** because a reading log is used by students to record the books they read. **Option C is incorrect** because running records is an informal assessment the teacher uses, not a standardized test. **Option D is incorrect** because a running record is not a record of words the student can spell. **(Competency 004 Reading Comprehension and Assessment)**

11. D.

Option D is correct. At the conventional stage, the student has mostly correct spellings of words. **Option A is incorrect** because in the semi-phonetic stage, the student uses abbreviated spelling whereby a word is represented by a letter, such as *u* for *you*. **Option B is incorrect** because in the phonetic stage the students account for every sound in a word, but their spelling may not be conventional, such as *lik* for *like*. **Option C is incorrect** because the student is not relying on visual and morphological information, such as *liek* for *like*, which occurs in the transitional stage. **(Competency 006 Written Language–Writing Conventions)**

12. D.

Option D is correct because the students are learning to use surrounding words for context clues and the initial consonant sound as part of phonics to identify the unknown word. **Option A is incorrect** because previewing the text takes place before reading to anticipate what the text will convey. **Option B is incorrect** because the teacher is not asking students to create a picture in their minds to comprehend as they read. **Option C is incorrect** because the teacher is not focusing upon words that lead readers to anticipate what is coming later in the narrative. **(Competency 003 Word Identification Skills and Reading Fluency)**

13. C.

Option C is correct. The student has joined two independent clauses together with a comma, which is called a comma splice, and is incorrect. **Option A is incorrect** because the student did use correct subject-verb agreement. **Option B is incorrect** because the student has not used a comma correctly. **Option D is incorrect** because the student has used correct capitalization in the sample. **(Competency 006 Written Language–Writing Conventions)**

14. B.

Option B is correct. Concept Maps are visual organizers that can help students understand the main ideas in content, and how ideas relate to other ideas. **Option A is incorrect.** The Directed Reading Thinking Activity (DRTA) is a comprehension strategy that guides students to ask questions, make predictions, and then read to confirm or refute their predictions. **Option C is incorrect.** In reciprocal teaching, the teacher models, and then students become teachers and use four strategies to have a dialogue about what they have learned: summarizing, question generating, clarifying, and predicting. **Option D is incorrect.** Question-Answer Relationships is a strategy that helps students think about what can be required to answer questions about the material they've read: look in one place in the text, search in more than one place in the text, use what is read in combination with what the reader has experienced, use prior knowledge of the reader. **(Competency 004 Reading Comprehension and Assessment)**

15. D.

Option D is correct. Students will not be able to devote attention to establishing content if their attention is diverted toward a concern for spelling and punctuation they have not mastered. **Option A is incorrect.** Students do need to learn about writing conventions because spelling and punctuation help students communicate clearly and make it easier for someone to read what has been written. Teachers can provide systematic instruction in view of students' needs. **Option B is incorrect** because when writing a final draft, students can be supported through proofreading conferences. **Option C is incorrect** because students need to learn how to apply writing conventions as they write, not solely work on skills in isolation using worksheets. **(Competency 007 Written Language–Composition)**

16. A.

Option A is correct because semantics pertains to the study of meaning. **Option B is incorrect** because syntax pertains to how words can be combined in a language. **Option C is incorrect** because letter–sound relationships pertain to phonics. **Option D is incorrect** because phonemes pertain to sounds of a language and how they combine. **(Competency 001 Oral Language)**

17. D.

Option D is correct. When reading expository or informational texts, students need to discern the text structure to be able to connect units of information. Students typically can read and remember fiction more easily because they have a schema for stories, which makes them easier to remember and retell. **Option A is incorrect** because students can learn how to read textbooks and other expository texts if teachers provide support through modeling and guided practice. **Option B is incorrect** because students have a schema for the narrative structure of fiction. **Option C is incorrect** because reading expository texts makes different demands on readers. Students do make gains in reading fiction that transfer to reading expository texts, but teachers need to teach students how to read and learn from expository texts, not assume that students can. **(Competency 009 Study and Inquiry Skills)**

18. B.

Option B is correct. The student needs instruction in fluency, which entails being able to read smoothly so what is read can be remembered. This will involve prosody because readers understand better when they read with expression and make changes in intonation in response to indicators in the text. **Options A and D are incorrect** because the student does not need word identification instruction. **Option C is incorrect** because the assessment does not focus on visualization, which is used to help students create images in their minds to read actively and comprehend. Comprehension can be affected when students do not read fluently, but a comprehension assessment is not described in this situation. **(Competency 004 Reading Comprehension and Assessment)**

19. C.

Option C is correct. The sentences focus upon an aspect of subject-verb agreement that can be challenging. When using words that show portions (such as *percent of*, *majority of*, *some of*, or *all of*), the noun that comes after the word of determines the verb, such as in this sentence: *Some of the cake is on the table.* However, when words using portions are not used, the subject comes before a phrase that begins with the word *of*, such as in this example: *The box of pencils is on the shelf* (not the plural *are* because *box* is the subject). **Option A is incorrect** because the student has not placed a word, phrase, or clause in such a way that what is being modified is not clear. **Option B is incorrect** because the verb tense is the same in both sentences. **Option D is incorrect** because the use of strong verbs is not featured. **(Competency 006 Written Language–Writing Conventions)**

20. C.

Option C is correct. Through shared reading, the students can participate in reading the textbook because students read with the teacher, which also helps students make gains in word identification. The teacher and students also can use strategies that other students use, such as noticing headings, talking about what they are learning, and using ways to record information. **Option A is incorrect** because answering questions does not help students actually read the textbook. Students could search for answers without reading the sections. **Option B is incorrect** because students need to learn how to read expository texts to participate in subsequent reading experiences in their schooling. Teachers need to modify the textbook or provide scaffolding by using shared reading to help students gain in proficiency and not be discouraged. **Option D is incorrect** because fear of a test does not show students how to read a textbook or help them learn the content. **(Competency 005 Reading Applications)**

21. A.

Option A is correct. Homogeneous grouping of students according to reading ability level works best for instruction activities. Reading at the same level as others keeps students from becoming frustrated at having to read a text that is too hard for them, and as a result not making progress in reading. Heterogeneous grouping based on which students work well together works best for independent work when students of various ability levels can interact. **Option B is incorrect** because just being able to identify words does not ensure that a reader can comprehend, whereas small groups help ensure that teachers meet students' individual needs. **Option C is incorrect** because grouping for instruction needs to be flexible because students may need to be placed in higher or lower levels as the year progresses. **Option D is incorrect** because worksheets are not the focus of the teacher's instruction. Also, heterogeneous grouping for instruction does not motivate students because it will result in many students reading texts that are too hard or too easy. **(Competency 005 Reading Applications)**

22. C.

Option C is correct. A running record provides an informal assessment that teachers can use to determine a student's independent, instructional, and frustration level for texts used for instruction, thereby providing the basis for forming small groups for instruction. **Option A is incorrect** because an interest inventory does not help determine students' reading levels. **Option B is incorrect.** Relying on previous reading levels is not reliable because students can make progress or fall behind when they are not in school, and a previous assessment may not be accurate. **Option D is incorrect** because the grade-level text may be too hard or too easy for the student. **(Competency 005 Reading Applications)**

23. C.

Option C is correct. Students gain in fluency by reading a text multiple times so they can learn to say words automatically, use correct intonation, and observe punctuation, which can make it possible to understand the content. **Option A is incorrect** because the activity does not focus on checking for understanding as students read (even though students might be monitoring comprehension). **Option B is incorrect** because the activity does not focus upon making predictions about what the selection will be about or what will happen next. **Option D is incorrect** because students should be rereading for pleasure as well as gains in fluency and comprehension of the poems—not for being required to memorize poems, which can hamper their enjoyment. **(Competency 003 Word Identification Skills and Reading Fluency)**

24. B.

Option B is correct because all students gain in fluency when they read a text again as the word identification becomes easier and the content becomes more familiar, making it possible to comprehend at various levels. **Option A is incorrect** because the focus of this activity is not on checking for understanding when reading. **Option C is incorrect** because students are not being shown how to examine text features, such as the headings, bold words, illustrations, and captions. **Option D is incorrect** because the regulatory function of language pertains to situations where people use language to request or control, which is not an objective of letting students read with a partner. **(Competency 003 Word Identification Skills and Reading Fluency)**

25. C.

Option C is correct. Students gain in fluency by reading a text multiple times so they can learn to say words automatically, use correct intonation, and observe punctuation, which can make it possible to understand the content. Rereading with others makes it enjoyable for students, and they can learn from others as they practice. **Option A is incorrect** because the activity does not focus on checking for understanding as students read (even though students might be monitoring comprehension). **Option B is incorrect** because the activity does not focus upon making predictions about what the selection will be about or what will happen next. **Option D is incorrect** because readers' theater is a form of drama where students do not memorize lines or engage in actions because the students read from scripts, with the story shared through the readers' voices. **(Competency 003 Word Identification Skills and Reading Fluency)**

26. A.

Option A is correct. By listening to the audio-recording of a book, students gain in listening comprehension if they are listening and not tracking print of a book, and they will make a voiceprint match if they do follow along. **Option B is incorrect** because the purpose of the activity is not to manage the class. Students are more apt to stay engaged if they are shown how to work independently and are provided with engaging reading materials. **Option C is incorrect** because listening to audio-recorded stories does not focus upon morphemic analysis. **Option D is incorrect** because the activity does not focus on checking for understanding as students read. **(Competency 003 Word Identification Skills and Reading Fluency)**

27. B.

Option B is correct. Readers are more apt to read when they select the types of books they want to read. If teachers read aloud, students will know of books they want to read for independent reading, and they'll feel more ownership of their reading. **Option A is incorrect** because the purpose of the activity is not to help students engage in metacognition. **Options C and D are incorrect** because students of all ability levels profit from being able to select books for independent reading. **(Competency 003 Word Identification Skills and Reading Fluency)**

28. A.

Option A is correct because developing a web can help students organize their writing by breaking down a topic they know, and the teacher's demonstration makes this process clearer than solely telling students what to do. **Option B is incorrect.** Students should select a topic because they will be more likely to write when they learn how to draw upon their thinking and experiences. **Option C is incorrect** because revising doesn't take place until students start to establish content. **Option D is incorrect** because the focus of instruction is how to organize ideas for writing informal reports, not how to write about the topic of physical fitness. **(Competency 008 Viewing and Representing)**

29. B.

Option B is correct because teachers actually should start with continuous sounds that are easier to blend and can be held continuously, such as /a/, /e/, /f/, /i/, /l/, /m/, /n/, /o/, /r/, /s/, /u/, /v/, /w/, /y/, /z/. Stop sounds are not held continuously (but rather have an "uh" sound): /b/, /c/, /d/, /g/, /h/, /j/, /k/, /p/, /q/, /t/, /x/. **Options A, C, and D are incorrect** because all are valid instructional approaches and thus are not responsive to a question looking for the opposite. **(Competency 002 Early Literacy Development)**

30. B.

Option B is correct. Homophones can be confusing because they are words that sound the same, but have different meanings and spellings. **Option A is incorrect** because the words are not synonyms, which are words with similar meanings. **Option C is incorrect** because the situation does not indicate that each pair of words is part of social studies instruction. **Option D is incorrect** because not all of the pairs are multisyllabic. **(Competency 006 Written Language–Writing Conventions)**

31. C.

Option C is correct. The words represent cohesive ties that writers can use to indicate examples, and knowing this can help students in comprehending and composing text. **Option A is incorrect** because affixes are prefixes and suffixes. **Option B is incorrect** because the words are not opposite in meaning. **Option D is incorrect** because visualization is a comprehension strategy where students are encouraged to think about what they are reading. **(Competency 004 Reading Comprehension and Assessment)**

32. C.

Option C is correct. Proficient readers use their prior knowledge along with information they see in the text, such as the title, to predict before reading, and they continue to predict and revise predictions based upon what the text presents. **Option A is incorrect.** Summarizing is a strategy that helps readers be aware of what is important in a text and bring together ideas, explaining text in their own words. **Option B is incorrect** because recalling is when students tell what they remember about what they have read, which depends upon their prior knowledge of the topic and the reading level of the text being not too difficult for students to read. **Option D is incorrect** because readers make inferences when they use their past experiences to understand ideas that are implied, but not stated explicitly, in the text. **(Competency 004 Reading Comprehension and Assessment)**

33. A.

Option A is correct because students most likely need to read 95%–100% of the words to be able to comprehend a story. Student texts need to be easy enough to be able to focus on meaning. Being able to read words does not ensure comprehension, so students could need additional support. **Option B is incorrect** because a text is considered to be at a student's instructional level when they can read at least 90%–94% of words, and they will need instructional support to comprehend it. **Options C**

and D are incorrect because when a student reads below 90% of words, the text is considered to be too hard, or at the frustration level. **(Competency 004 Reading Comprehension and Assessment)**

34. A.

Option A is correct because large amounts of information on a page can be overwhelming for students. **Options B, C, and D** present criteria that help ensure that students can gain from a site. **(Competency 008 Viewing and Representing)**

35. A., B., D.

Options A, B, and D are correct because all are types of fiction. Memoirs and other types of nonfiction can be engaging for readers, but the information is not fictional, making **Option C** incorrect. **(Competency 005 Reading Applications)**

36. C.

Option C is correct because students are making gains in listening comprehension, but they are not engaging in study skills or focusing upon text features when sharing their responses to literature. **Option A is incorrect** because the teacher can expand students' comprehension by bringing up important ideas, thereby also modeling how a competent reader thinks about what has been read. **Option B is incorrect** because students can learn from other students' contributions to the conversation. **Option D is incorrect** because the students do gain from being able to see that they can think about literature and formulate ideas, which also is needed to analyze literature. **(Competency 001 Oral Language)**

37. D.

Option D is correct. K-W-L is a strategy where students complete three columns of a chart to activate prior knowledge by stating what they know (K), what they want to know (W), and what they learned (L).

Option A is incorrect. Reciprocal Teaching is where students use four strategies to talk about what they have learned: summarizing, question generating, clarifying, and predicting. **Option B is incorrect.** Think-Pair-Share is a strategy that lets students think about what they have read and learned and talk with a partner as a way of encouraging students to talk as part of their learning. **Option C is incorrect.** Concept Maps are visual organizers that can help students understand how ideas relate to other ideas in expository texts. **(Competency 004 Reading Comprehension and Assessment)**

38. A., C.

Option A is correct because hyphens are used for compound numbers from twenty-one to ninety-nine. **Option C is correct** because a hyphen is generally used when two or more words are a single idea that modifies a noun. **Option B is incorrect** because the age designation – *ten-year-old* – is a noun. **Option D is incorrect** because the intensifier *very* is not hyphenated. **(Competency 006 Written Language–Writing Conventions)**

39. C.

Option C is correct. Students can expect a literal meaning of words, and English learners may be familiar with the literal meanings of words in English, so figurative language can be confusing. **Options A and B are incorrect** because difficulties with figurative language are not due to difficulties in comprehending stories or recognizing words. **Option D is incorrect** because even if students are able to identify words used figuratively, they can still find figurative language challenging to understand. **(Competency 004 Reading Comprehension and Assessment)**

40. A.

Option A is correct. Students who use invented spelling do learn the conventional spellings of words, and by accounting for the sounds of words, students are making gains in phonemic awareness which is neces-

sary in learning to read. **Options B and C are incorrect** because students who use invented spelling eventually will learn more about conventional spellings through effective instruction, and invented spelling actually can help literacy development by fostering phonemic awareness. **Option D is incorrect** because invented spelling shows accounting for phonemes of words or phonemic awareness, a dimension of phonological awareness. **(Competency 002 Early Literacy Development)**

41. B.

Option B is correct. All clauses have a subject and a verb, but a subordinating conjunction such as *because* or *although* creates a dependent clause, which must be joined to an independent sentence to avoid being a fragment. **Option A is incorrect** because this writing sample does not show difficulties with using the correct verb tense. **Option C is incorrect** because seasons are not capitalized. **Option D is incorrect** because there are no spelling errors in the sample. **(Competency 006 Written Language–Writing Conventions)**

42. C.

Option C is correct. Teachers can help students notice strategies and techniques writers use by looking back at works that students have read or heard previously. **Option A is incorrect.** Mentor texts show students options, but they are not used as a model students must follow. **Option B is incorrect** because the teacher is not focusing upon preparation for reading in this situation. **Option D is incorrect.** Students can find it more challenging to read and remember expository text, but the teacher is focusing upon showing students how to write an effective lead-in in this situation. **(Competency 007 Written Language–Composition)**

43. D.

Option D is correct because one character tells the story when first person narrative is used. **Option A pertains to the plot of the story. Option B is incorrect because it pertains to the omniscient point of view. **Option C is incorrect** because it pertains to the setting of a story. **(Competency 005 Reading Applications)**

44. C.

Option C is correct because reading small chunks of information helps students not be overwhelmed by encountering new information. Talking about the information helps students review content and monitor their comprehension. **Option A is incorrect** because assessing students is not providing instruction on how to read to learn. **Option B is incorrect** because students are not likely to understand an unfamiliar concept by writing a definition, whereas time could be devoted to effective vocabulary development to help students understand concepts and how concepts relate. **Option D is incorrect** because this strategy is helpful for word identification, but does not help ensure students can comprehend and learn content. **(Competency 009 Study and Inquiry Skills)**

45. C.

Option C is correct. In proofreading/publishing conferences, students learn to proofread to develop a final draft that would be read by others. **Option A is incorrect.** Mini-lessons are brief demonstrations based upon what students need to know, such as strategies and techniques writers use or procedures of the writing workshop. Teachers can meet with students in small groups to provide further support. **Option B is incorrect.** Writing rough drafts focuses upon establishing content, not writing conventions. **Option D is incorrect.** Through author's chair or whole-class sharing, students experience a whole-class conference when they read aloud their writing. **(Competency 007 Written Language–Composition)**

46. D.

Option D is correct. When students retell, they tell what happened in the story, which is literal level com-

prehension. **Options A, B, and C are incorrect** because retelling does not primarily encourage the student to think at higher levels where students infer, evaluate, or relate what they have read to their own experiences. **(Competency 004 Reading Comprehension and Assessment)**

47. A., B.

Options A and B are correct. The students need systematic instruction to learn writing conventions, but they also need opportunities to apply those conventions in their writing. **Option C is incorrect** because writing conventions are a way of being polite to readers so they can read a text without disruptions. Also, in the workplace, people can evaluate proficiency on the basis of knowing writing conventions. **Option D is incorrect** because looking up words in a dictionary is only one way of fostering spelling development, and spelling is only one part of writing conventions. Additionally, if students have to look up many words, they can become overwhelmed and often will start using only words they can spell to avoid looking up words in a dictionary. **(Competency 006 Written Language–Writing Conventions)**

48. C.

Option C is correct because a score in the 90th percentile means that 90% of the norm group performed at the same level or below the student's score. **Option A is incorrect** because the scores of a norm-referenced test provide information about how the student's achievement compares to other students at national levels. **Option B is incorrect** because a score of 90th percentile means that 90% of the norm group performed at the same level or below the student's score, not above. **Option D is incorrect** because a norm-referenced score is not based upon a student's performance in the classroom. **(Competency 004 Reading Comprehension and Assessment)**

49. D.

Option D is correct. Affixes are prefixes and suffixes that can be added to a base word or root word to form a new word. **Options A and B are incorrect** because affixes includes both prefixes and suffixes. **Option C is incorrect** because affixes are combined with root or base words. **(Competency 003 Word Identification Skills and Reading Fluency)**

50. C.

Option C is correct because this activity helps students learn techniques for selecting, organizing, and evaluating information from an electronic environment. **Option A is incorrect** because students need guidance in learning from the video and ample time for learning new information before taking a test. **Option B is incorrect** because the teacher needs to ensure that the students view a quality video, and students need guidance in locating quality electronic sources. **Option D is incorrect** because all students need to participate in reading the textbook to gain in proficiency, and teachers can provide scaffolding to support English learners so they participate in reading a text. **(Competency 008 Viewing and Representing)**

51. A.

Option A is correct because the teacher is showing how to use context and initial letter sounds to identify an unknown word, which is an effective strategy the student can also use in other situations. **Option B is incorrect** because the word represents an irregular spelling, as do many words in English, so the strategy of "sounding out" will not work for students in many situations. **Option C is incorrect** because using structural analysis or word parts does not work for this word because *fat* is not a root word or part of a compound word in *father*. **Option D is incorrect** because the first response should be to show students how to identify unknown words so that students can be self-reliant in reading. **(Competency 003 Word Identification Skills and Reading Fluency)**

52. B.

Option B is correct because syntax pertains to how words can be combined in a language. **Option A is incorrect** because semantics pertains to the study of meaning. **Option C is incorrect** because letter-sound relationships pertain to phonics. **Option D is incorrect** because phonemes pertain to sounds of a language and how they combine. **(Competency 001 Oral Language)**

53. C.

Option C is correct. Although facts can come from personal experiences, the support for the essay's position must rely upon solid evidence rather than what the writer thinks. **Options A, B. and D are all incorrect**, as they represent ways to support a position when developing a persuasive essay. **(Competency 007 Written Language–Composition)**

54. B.

Option B is correct. If students cannot use context clues to understand new vocabulary, the teacher should ensure students know how to read and understand a word. **Option A is incorrect.** The teacher is not focusing on examining the title, headings, or illustrations of text as ways to enhance comprehension. **Option C is incorrect** because the focus of instruction is on the meaning of a word. **Option D is incorrect** because the focus of this situation is on vocabulary development, not on predicting what will take place in the story. **(Competency 004 Reading Comprehension and Assessment)**

55. A.

Option A is correct. The teacher is strategically using a photo that will help students understand what they will be reading and how they may see the word in other settings. **Option B is incorrect.** The teacher is not focusing on examining the title, headings, or illustrations of text to be able to comprehend. **Option C is incorrect** because the focus of instruction is on the meaning of a word, not on using letter–sound relationships to identify the word. **Option D is incorrect** because the focus of this situation is on vocabulary development, not on spelling. **(Competency 004 Reading Comprehension and Assessment)**

56. D.

Option D is correct. The teacher is using gestures to add to the other activities used to foster vocabulary development. **Option A is incorrect.** Concept maps can help students understand words and how concepts are related, but that is not what the teacher is addressing in this situation. **Option B is incorrect.** The teacher is not focusing on the title, headings, or illustrations of text to aid in comprehension. **Option C is incorrect** because the focus of instruction is on the meaning of a word, not on informal drama. **(Competency 004 Reading Comprehension and Assessment)**

57. D.

Option D is correct because students gain in oral and written language when given the opportunity to talk in authentic ways about what they have read. **Option A is incorrect** because the students are talking in a small-group, not a whole-class situation. **Option B is incorrect** because grading students is not a good way to motivate them. Instead, the teacher should make observations about students' participation. **Option C is incorrect** because the teacher is not asking questions, but is instead using retelling and discussion to enhance comprehension. **(Competency 001 Oral Language)**

58. B.

Option B is correct because students profit from multiple learning experiences across several days when learning vocabulary. **Option A is incorrect** because the teacher is not helping students write in personal dictionaries in this situation. **Option C is incorrect** because while talking is effective for helping students establish content when they write, the students are not writing in this situation. **Option D is incorrect** because in this situ-

ation, the teacher is focusing upon helping students have in-depth experiences with new vocabulary, not on talking about what took place in the story. **(Competency 001 Oral Language)**

59. D.

Option D is correct. Teachers should help students relate new concepts to what they know. Understanding the meanings of prefixes, suffixes, and word roots can help students understand words independently. **Option A is incorrect** because the focus of instruction is on morphology, or word parts, not on phonics. **Option B is incorrect** because research does not show that giving a vocabulary quiz helps students make gains. **Option C is incorrect** because the teacher is not focusing upon writing sentences in this situation. **(Competency 004 Reading Comprehension and Assessment)**

60. B.

Option B is correct. Students need to experience authentic reading experiences in which they select books they want to read, and read daily. **Option A is incorrect** because while students do apply and orchestrate word identification skills when reading independently, applying phonics abilities is not the main rationale. **Option C is incorrect** because requiring students to read certain books for independent reading does not let students learn how to select books they like and see how reading can be meaningful for them. **Option D is incorrect** because tests create anxiety about reading rather than provide motivation. Teachers can assess in other ways, such as through talking with students about what they are reading and asking students to keep reading logs in which they write the title and author of what they read each day. **(Competency 005 Reading Applications)**

61. A.

Option A is correct. The teacher's prompt should help students learn to use language structure (syntax), meaning (semantics), and visual cues (phonics, sight words, morphemic/structural analysis) for word identification. The student's miscue shows that the student is not using meaning cues, and the teacher is reinforcing this by asking if the miscue makes sense. **Option B is incorrect** because sounding out does not work for irregular spellings of English words, so this is not a prompt that helps students for all unknown words. **Option C is incorrect** because teachers should not disregard a miscue since a prompt is an opportunity to help the child learn more about how to identify words. **Option D is incorrect** because the teacher should identify the word only when it is apparent the child cannot figure out the unknown word even with a prompt. The prompt may help the student identify the word independently. **(Competency 005 Reading Applications)**

62. B.

Option B is correct because the teacher is showing pronouns that are singular, which require singular verbs. **Option A is incorrect** because plural forms of nouns is not featured. **Option C is incorrect** because the pronouns are singular, not plural. **Option D is incorrect** because phonemic awareness pertains to hearing words and accounting for sounds of a word. **(Competency 006 Written Language–Writing Conventions)**

63. D.

Option D is correct. Readers make inferences when they understand ideas that are not stated explicitly in the text. **Option A is incorrect.** Summarizing is a strategy that helps readers be aware of what is important in a text. The students bring together ideas and explain text in their own words. **Option B is incorrect.** Recalling is when students tell what they remember about what they have read. This depends upon their prior knowledge of the topic and the reading level of the text (being not too difficult for students to read). **Option C is incorrect.** Predicting is when readers use their prior knowledge along with information they see in the text, such as the title, to predict before reading. They continue to predict and revise predictions based upon what the text

presents **(Competency 004 Reading Comprehension and Assessment)**

64. D.

Option D is correct. The cloze procedure, in which students provide missing words from a sentence, can be used to determine if students understand both a text and its vocabulary. **Option A is incorrect** because helping students recognize the purpose of headings pertains to noting the organization of the information in a text. **Option B is incorrect** because the cloze procedure focuses upon understanding words being read well enough to supply a missing word from a sentence, not the way the information is organized. **Option C is incorrect** because story maps are graphic organizers, which are not related to the cloze procedure. **(Competency 003 Word Identification Skills and Reading Fluency)**

65. C.

Option C is correct. The teacher is showing students that words with the same spelling can be pronounced differently as a noun or verb. **Option A is incorrect** because the sentences do not provide examples of how to use a word because the word is used as a noun in one sentence and a verb in the second. **Option B is incorrect** because the sentences do not illustrate words that are derivatives, but rather show differences in the pronunciation of a word, depending upon whether the word is used as a noun or verb. **Option D is incorrect** because the word featured in each sentence is not pronounced the same way, so the students do not practice reading each word twice. **(Competency 003 Word Identification Skills and Reading Fluency)**

66. B.

Option B is correct because the rough draft is where student writers focus on establishing content, rather than on writing conventions, mechanics, or polishing content. **Option A is incorrect** because prewriting is where writers brainstorm and think about what to write before actually writing. **Option C is incorrect** because revising is where changes are made in establishing content. **Option D is incorrect** because editing is where proofreading takes place, and the focus is on writing conventions and mechanics, including spelling, punctuation, capitalization, and usage. **(Competency 007 Written Language–Composition)**

67. D.

Option D is correct. By sharing their writing with others, students gain a broader, authentic audience and thus are motivated to place more value on the sequenced process involved in achieving correct spelling, capitalization, punctuation, and grammatical expression in a final draft. **Options A, B, and C are incorrect.** Although selecting a topic, developing a title, and elaborating are all parts of the writing process, the experience presented in this item focuses on publishing and sharing writing that students have already done. **(Competency 007 Written Language–Composition)**

68. B.

Option B is correct because the omniscient point of view reveals what all the characters think, feel, say, and do. **Option A is incorrect** because it pertains to the plot of the story. **Option C is incorrect** because it pertains to limited third person point of view. **Option D is incorrect** because it pertains to first person narrative point of view. **(Competency 005 Reading Applications)**

69. D.

Option D is correct. Homonyms can be confusing because they are words that are spelled and sound alike but have different meanings. **Option A is incorrect** because only *bark* is a word with an *r*-controlled vowel, *ar*. **Option B is incorrect** because the words adhere to phonics generalizations and common spelling patterns. **Option C is incorrect** because only *rose* is a word with an *r* in the initial position of a word. **(Competency 006 Written Language–Writing Conventions)**

70. C.

Option C is correct. Authors can reveal a character through describing how a character looks and what a character does as well as through what other characters say about the character. **Option A is incorrect** because it pertains to the setting. **Option B is incorrect** because it pertains to the plot. **Option D is incorrect** because it pertains to theme. **(Competency 005 Reading Applications)**

71. C.

Option C is correct. Mini-lessons take place with the whole class and are brief demonstrations based upon what students need to know. Teachers can meet with students in small groups to provide further support. **Option A is incorrect** because during the writing part of the workshop, students and the teacher write, and the teacher also has rough-draft conferences with students. **Option B is incorrect.** Through author's chair or whole-class sharing, students experience a whole-class conference when they read aloud their writing. **Option D is incorrect.** In proofreading/publishing conferences, students learn to proofread to develop a final draft that would be read by others; so the focus is on writing conventions, not on writing a draft to establish content. **(Competency 007 Written Language Composition)**

72. A.

Option A is correct. When emergent readers read with the teacher and they track print, they gain in concepts of print, such as knowing that print carries the message and that words are separated by white spaces. Students also learn that print moves left to right and top to bottom in English. **Option B is incorrect** because previewing is a strategy for comprehension that takes place before reading. **Option C is incorrect** because the students are not being shown how to monitor their comprehension or check to see if they are comprehending what they are reading. **Option D is incorrect** because reciprocal teaching is a strategy where students work in small groups and assume roles to understand and learn material they read. **(Competency 002 Early Literacy Development)**

73. D.

Option D is correct because editing is where proofreading takes place and the focus is on writing conventions, or the mechanics of writing, which involve spelling, punctuation, capitalization, and usage. **Option A is incorrect** because prewriting is where writers brainstorm and think about what to write before actually writing. **Option B is incorrect** because drafting is where students write a rough draft to start to establish content. **Option C is incorrect** because revising is where students make changes in establishing content. **(Competency 007 Written Language–Composition)**

74. B.

Option B is correct because once children have figured out underlying principles of language from the language they hear, such as *ed* is used for the past tense, they can overgeneralize, such as in saying *goed* for *went*. **Options A and C are incorrect** because over-generalizing is not associated with solely second language acquisition or forgetting. **Option D is incorrect** because studies of children's language acquisition show that overgeneralizing is a predictable part of the process children go through in making sense of how language works, and that "errors" are not random. **(Competency 001 Oral Language)**

75. B., C.

Options B and C are correct because these are effective ways to develop students' language skills while also making it possible for English learners to develop language effectively, while also participating in subject-matter learning. **Option A is incorrect** because English learners do need to participate in content-area learning, and they can do so through sheltered instruction in which they receive the scaffolding and support they need.

Option D is incorrect because while English learners do need to learn to use the dictionary, they are not apt to understand clearly the meanings and use of unfamiliar words by looking up definitions in dictionaries. **(Competency 001 Oral Language)**

76 D.

Option D is correct because research does not show that tests foster vocabulary development because students gain only a superficial understanding of words by memorizing definitions, and they often forget the memorized meanings of words. **Options A, B, and C are incorrect** because they describe instruction that is effective in helping students gain in vocabulary development. **(Competency 004 Reading Comprehension and Assessment)**

77. D.

Option D is correct because students often overlook text features, such as headings, which will help them organize individual facts in memory by understanding the text structure and organization. **Option A is incorrect** because the teacher does not provide shared reading, where the teacher and students read a text together to help students be able to read a text they cannot read on their own. **Option B is incorrect** because the teacher is not focusing upon unfamiliar concepts or terms at this point in the lesson. **Option C is incorrect** because the teacher is directing students' attention to the title and heading, not helping students engage in metacognition where they would check their own understanding as they read. **(Competency 005 Reading Applications)**

78. A.

Option A is correct because teachers can support students' learning by thinking aloud and demonstrating before asking students to engage in a strategy for reading expository text. **Option B is incorrect** because the teacher is not building background needed to understand the text. **Option C is incorrect** because the objective of the instruction is to help students learn how to preview a text and use the introduction as a guide, not complete a table per se. **Option D is incorrect** because the teacher is not activating prior knowledge to help students relate the new information to what they know at this point. **(Competency 009 Study and Inquiry Skills)**

79. A.

Option A is correct because filling out the table will help students understand and remember important details, as well as how those details interrelate. **Option B is incorrect** because the teacher is not building background as the students complete the table, but instead is helping students record information on a table. **Option C is incorrect** because the teacher is writing what the students dictate, and it is best that the students focus on the process and not on copying information. **Option D is incorrect** because previewing headings takes place before reading to help students understand how a topic is organized. **(Competency 008 Viewing and Representing)**

80. C.

Option C is correct because the gradual-release-of-responsibility approach helps students eventually become able to use strategies. Students receive the support they need by first watching the teacher, and then working with the teacher, and next working with other students with the teacher's guidance. **Option A is incorrect** because the teacher does not provide shared reading, whereby the teacher and students read a text together to help students to read a text they cannot read on their own. **Option B is incorrect** because the teacher is not focusing upon unfamiliar concepts or terms at this point in the lesson. **Option D is incorrect** because the teacher should work with students until they can work on their own, and that can require more than one lesson on complex tasks. It is important to remember that students are learning even as they

work with the teacher. **(Competency 005 Reading Applications)**

81. A.

Option A is correct. The student is not paying attention to the final letters of the word *where,* which is a high-frequency word. **Option B is incorrect** because fluency has not been assessed, and the source of the miscue is not using all of the visual cues in word identification. **Option C is incorrect** because the miscue does make sense. **Option D is incorrect** because *when* is a base word, not a word identified by structural analysis or word parts. **(Competency 003 Word Identification Skills and Reading Fluency)**

82. D.

Option D is correct because the text organization pertains to the body of the text and the text structure or patterns used to organize and present information. **Options A, B, and C are incorrect**, as they *do* apply to text features and are therefore not responsive to the question. **(Competency 009 Study and Inquiry Skills)**

83. A.

Option A is correct because *oi* and *oy* are diphthongs. **Options B, C, and D are incorrect** because the words feature a consonant digraph, *ch, sh,* or *th.* **(Competency 003 Word Identification Skills and Reading Fluency)**

84. D.

Option D is correct because the student did use the initial letter sound of *s,* and the miscue does make sense, but the student might not know the word *sounds.* **Option A is incorrect** because the student's miscue shows that the student is using language structure because we could put words together in that way, and the student is using meaning because what the student said does make sense. **Option B is incorrect** because the student is using letters of the word in the miscue. **Option C is incorrect** because the student's miscue does not entail using inflectional endings. *Singing* is a noun, and the student did not attempt to read *sing* in *singing*. **(Competency 002 Early Literacy Development)**

85. D.

Option D is correct because students do not engage in worksheets as part of proofreading/publishing conferences. **Options A, B, and C are incorrect** because they all present rationales for proofreading/publishing conferences where students work with the teacher to check for correct spelling, punctuation, and usage before writing a final draft that would be read by others. **(Competency 007 Written Language–Composition)**

86. A.

Option A is correct because the word *because* is a subordinating conjunction, which creates a dependent clause, which does not require a preceding comma. **Options B, C, and D** are incorrect because they are all coordinating conjunctions, which can be used to combine two independent clauses, and require a comma. **(Competency 006 Written Language–Writing Conventions)**

87. D.

Option D is correct because teachers can read aloud books students are either unable or unwilling to read on their own. Also, literature uses words that students do not encounter in their daily lives. **Option A is incorrect** because students are listening to the teacher, not saying words or reading. **Option B is incorrect** because actual gains in fluency pertain to reading development. **Option C is incorrect** because students are not previewing or viewing the text before reading when teachers read aloud. **(Competency 001 Oral Language)**

88. D.

Option D is correct because homophones are words that are pronounced the same but have different meanings and spellings, so they can be confusing. **Option A is incorrect** because plural forms of words are not featured. **Option B is incorrect** because some of the words have one syllable. **Option C is incorrect** because the pairs of words presented in the question are not alike in meaning and thus are not synonyms. **(Competency 006 Written Language–Writing Conventions)**

89. B.

Option B is correct because this statement pertains to text features, not text organization. Helping students understand how to use text features and text organization are both important, but they are not the focus of this activity. **Options A, C, and D are incorrect,** as they apply specifically to text organization and thus are not responsive to the question, which is posed negatively. **(Competency 009 Study and Inquiry Skills)**

90. C.

Option C is correct. Generating or asking relevant questions can help students read actively with a purpose that helps them read to learn. **Option A is incorrect.** Students who ask questions as they read could do better on tests because they are reading expository text proficiently, and they will be more apt to learn, but the purpose of asking questions as a strategy pertains more broadly to comprehension and learning. **Option B is incorrect.** Students do make gains in oral language development through using language for a variety of functions, but generating questions during reading by examining a heading to think about what information is going to be presented pertains primarily to reading informational text. **Option D is incorrect** because generating questions while reading is not a strategy for written assignments, but rather is a way to help students navigate as they read. Headings can help students learn how to ask good questions to guide their reading. **(Competency 005 Reading Applications)**

91. B.

Option B is correct; the word *have* is irregular in spelling because it does not adhere to the phonics generalization for a long vowel sound where a vowel "says" its name (vowel-consonant-silent *e* pattern). **Options A and C are incorrect** because they show words that do adhere to a phonics generalization (or way to form a long *a* by *ay, ai)*, thereby being regular spellings. **Option D is incorrect** because it also shows a word that features a phonics generalization, or a way to create a long *a* (through the vowel-consonant-silent *e* pattern). **(Competency 003 Word Identification Skills and Reading Fluency)**

92. C.

Option C is correct because revising is where changes are made in establishing content. **Option A is incorrect.** Prewriting is where writers brainstorm and think about what to write before actually writing. **Option B is incorrect** because drafting is where writing a rough draft takes place to start to establish content. **Option D is incorrect** because editing is where proofreading takes place and the focus is on writing conventions, or mechanics of writing, which include spelling punctuation, capitalization, and usage. **(Competency 007 Written Language–Composition)**

93. A.

Option A is correct. Effective writing relies upon using strong verbs rather than adverbs. **Option B is incorrect** because the verb tense is the same in both sentences. **Option C is incorrect** because subject-verb agreement is correct in both sentences. **Option D is incorrect because** the example does not seek to contrast passive voice with active voice. A sentence written in the active voice has the subject perform the action, whereas a sentence written in the passive voice has the subject receive the action. In the example, both sentences use the active voice. **(Competency 007 Written Language–Composition)**

94. A.

Option A is correct because not all students have access to technology in their homes, and new literacies instruction can show all students purposes for reading beyond ones they have already used. **Options B, C, and D are incorrect** because they are accurate statements about literacy instruction with digital and media technologies, and are therefore not responsive to the question. **(Competency 008 Viewing and Representing)**

95. A.

Option A is correct because the words feature the long vowel sound of *o* through the vowel-constant-silent *e* pattern. **Option B is incorrect** because the words feature an *r*-controlled vowel. **Option C is incorrect** because the words feature the short vowel pattern of consonant-vowel-consonant. **Option D is incorrect** because the words feature the diphthong *oy*. **(Competency 003 Word Identification Skills and Reading Fluency)**

96. C.

Option C is correct. The Directed Reading Thinking Activity (DRTA) is a comprehension strategy that guides students to ask questions, make predictions, and then read to confirm or refute their predictions. **Option A is incorrect.** Reciprocal Teaching is where students engage in discussions about what they have read and use four strategies to have a dialogue about what they have learned. **Option B is incorrect.** Concept Maps are visual organizers that can help students understand how ideas relate to other ideas in expository texts. **Option D is incorrect.** Think-Pair-Share is a strategy that lets students think about what they have read and learned, and then talk with a partner as a way of encouraging students to talk as part of their learning. **(Competency 004 Reading Comprehension and Assessment)**

97. A.

Option A is correct because seasons are not capitalized. **Options B, C, D are incorrect** because they represent words that are capitalized. Proper nouns are capitalized, be they names of people, specific places (e.g., Caddo Lake), or things (e.g., TExES test). **(Competency 006 Written Language–Writing Conventions)**

98. C.

Option C is correct because when a student reads below 90% of words, the text is considered to be too hard, or at the frustration level. A text is considered to be at a students' instructional level when they can read at least 90%–94% of words because the students need instructional support to be able to comprehend. Students most likely need to read 95%–100% of the words to be able to read easily. Being able to read words does not ensure comprehension, so students could need additional support, but students do need to be able to read easy texts to focus on meaning. **Options A, B, and C are incorrect** because all the percentages would be considered too hard for students. **(Competency 004 Reading Comprehension and Assessment)**

99. C.

Option C is correct because *ir* is an *r*-controlled vowel, and so is *ar*, *er*, and *ur*. **Option A is incorrect** because the words feature a consonant blend, *br*. **Option B is incorrect,** as the word pair features a consonant digraph, *sh*. **Option D is incorrect** because the pair features the consonant blend *gr*. **(Competency 003 Word Identification Skills and Reading Fluency)**

100. B.

Option B is correct because expository texts make different demands on readers. Students need to be shown they cannot rely upon the approach they have used in reading fiction because expository texts can require understanding how unfamiliar, abstract concepts relate to one another and the broader topic. **Options A, C, and D are incorrect** because they pertain to reading fiction or poetry, which are not expository texts. **(Competency 009 Study and Inquiry Skills)**

References

Adams, M.J. (1994). *Beginning to read: thinking and learning about print.* Boston: MIT Press.

Anderson, R.C., & Pearson, P.D. (1984). A schema-theoretic view of basic processes in reading. In P.D. Pearson, R. Barr, M.L. Kamil, & P. Mosenthal (Eds.), Handbook of reading research. White Plains, N.Y.: Longman.

Atwell, N, (2015). *In the middle: A lifetime of learning about reading, writing, and adolescents.* Portsmouth, N.H.: Heinemann Educational Books.

Beck, I., McKeown, M. & Kucan, L (2002). *Bringing words to life: Robust vocabulary instruction.* New York: Guilford Press.

Calkins, L. (1994). *The Art of Teaching Writing*, 2nd ed. Portsmouth, N.H.: Heinemann.

Cambourne, Brian (1995). Toward an educationally relevant theory of literacy learning: Twenty years of inquiry. *The Reading Teacher*, Vol. 49, No. 3.

Cullinan, B. (2000). Independent reading and school achievement. *School Library Media Research*, 3, 1–24.

Chard, D.J., & Osborn, J. (1998). *Suggestions for examining phonics and decoding instruction in supplementary reading programs.* Austin, Tex.: Texas Education Agency.

Durkin, D. (1978–79). What classroom observations reveal about reading comprehension instruction. Reading Research Quarterly, 14, 481–533.

Echevarria, J., Vogt, M.E., & Short, D.J. (2017). *Making content comprehensible for English learners: The SIOP Model.* (5th ed.) Pearson Education, Inc.

Ehri, L.C., Dreyer, L.G., Flugman, B., & Gross, A. (2007). Reading Rescue: An effective tutoring intervention model for language minority students who are struggling readers in first grade. *American Educational Research Journal*, 44(2), 414–448.

Fisher, D., & Frey, N. (2013). *Better learning through structured teaching: A framework for the gradual release of responsibility.* ASCD.

Graves, D.H. (1983). *Writing: Teachers and children at work.* Portsmouth, N.H.: Heinemann Educational Books.

Graves, D. (1994). *A Fresh Look at Writing.* Portsmouth, N.H.: Heinemann.

Hiebert, E.H. & Reutzel, D.R. (Eds.) (2010). *Revisiting silent reading: New directions for teachers and researchers.* Newark, Del.: International Reading Association.

Lindfors, J.W. (1987). *Children's Language and Learning.* Englewood Cliffs, N.J.: Prentice-Hall.

Moss, B. & Young, T.A. (2010). *Creating lifelong readers through independent reading.* International Reading Association.

REFERENCES

National Reading Panel. (April, 2000). *Report of the National Reading Panel. Teaching Children to Read: An Evidence-Based Assessment of the Scientific Research Literature on Reading and Its Implications for Reading Instruction. National Institute of Child Health and Human Development.*

Fountas, I.C., & Pinnell, G.S. (1996). *Guided reading: Good first teaching for all children.* Portsmouth, N.H.: Heinemann.

Freeman, D. & Freeman, Y. (2008). *Academic language for struggling readers and English language learners.* Portsmouth, N.H.: Heinemann.

Hasbrouck, J. & Tindal, G. (2017). *An update to compiled ORF norms* (Technical Report No. 1702). Eugene, Ore.: Behavioral Research and Teaching, University of Oregon.

Kelley, M.J., & Clausen-Grace, N. (2008). From picture walk to text feature walk: Guiding students to strategically preview informational text. *Journal of Content Area Reading*, 7(1), 9–31.

Kibby, M.W. (1995). The organization and teaching of things and the words that signify them. *Journal of Adolescent & Adult Literacy*, 39(3), 208–233.

Krashen, S.D. (1989). We acquire vocabulary and spelling by reading: Additional evidence for the Input Hypothesis. *Modern Language Journal* 73, 440–64.

LaBerge, D., & Samuels, S.J. (1974). Toward a theory of automatic information processing in reading. *Cognitive Psychology*, 6, 293–323.

Nagy, W.E., & Scott, J.A. (2004). Vocabulary processes. In R.B. Ruddell & N.J. Unrau (Eds.), *Theoretical models and processes of reading* (5th ed., pp. 574–593). Newark, Del.: International Reading Association.

National Reading Panel. (2000, April). *Report of the National Reading Panel: Teaching children to read.* Washington, D.C.: National Institute of Child Health and Human Development, National Institutes of Health, U.S. Department of Health and Human Services.

Palincsar, A.S., & Brown, A.L. (1984). Reciprocal teaching of comprehension-fostering and monitoring activities. *Cognition and Instruction*, 1, 117–175.

Pearson, P.D., & Dole, J.A. (1987). Explicit comprehension instruction: A review of research and a new conceptualization of instruction. *Elementary School Journal*, 88, 151–165.

Pearson, P.D., & Fielding, L. (1991). Comprehension instruction. In R. Barr, M.L. Kamil, P.B. Mosenthal, & P.D. Pearson (Eds.), *Handbook of reading research: Volume II* (pp. 815–860). White Plains, N.Y.: Longman.

Peregoy, S.F., O.F. Boyle, & Cadiero-Kapplan, K. (2017). *Reading, writing and learning in ESL: A Resource Book for K–12 Teachers* (7th ed.). New York: Pearson.

Pressley, M. (2000). What should comprehension instruction be the instruction of? In M.L. Kamil, P.B. Mosenthal, P.D. Pearson, & R. Barr (Eds.), *Handbook of reading research: Volume III* (pp. 545–561). Mahwah, N.J.: Erlbaum.

Rasinkski, T., & Padak, N. (1996). *Holistic reading strategies: Teaching children who find reading difficult.* Englewood Cliffs, N.J.: Merrill/Prentice Hall.

Reutzel, D.R. & Cooter, R.B. (2020). *Strategies for reading assessment and instruction: helping every child succeed* (6th ed.). Pearson.

Ruddell, R.B. (2009). *How to teach reading to elementary and middle school students: Practical ideas from highly effective teachers*. Boston: Allyn & Bacon.

Rosenblatt, L.M. (1978). The reader, the text, the poem: The transactional theory of the literary work. Carbondale, Ill.: Southern Illinois University Press.

Rupley, W.H., Logan, J.W., & Nichols, W.D. (1998). Vocabulary instruction in a balanced reading program. *The Reading Teacher*, 52(4), 336–346.

Snow, C.E., Burns, M.S., & Griffin, P. (1998). *Preventing reading difficulties in young children*. Washington, D.C.: National Academy Press.

Stahl, K.A.D. (2004). Proof, practice, and promise: Comprehension strategy instruction in the primary grades. *The Reading Teacher*, 57(7), 598–609.

Index

G

Grand conversations, 24, 80
Greek roots and derivatives, 55
Guided reading, 58

H

Historical fiction, 80

I

Imitation, in language acquisition, 18
Immersion, for learning language, 22
Independent reading, 57–58
   vocabulary development instruction, 72
Inflectional endings, 53
Informational text, 80
   reading comprehension and, 71–72
Initial consonant sounds, 50
Invented spelling, 31

K

K-W-L strategy, 87–88

L

Language
   assessing speaking and listening ability, 26–27
   components of, 17
   functions of, 20
   knowledge of, and reading comprehension, 69–70
   language acquisition theories, 18–19
   oral language, 15–28
   stages of development, 18
Language acquisition, 18–19
Language Acquisition Device (LAD), 18
Language arts. See English language arts
Language register, 20

Latin roots and derivatives, 55
Letter identification, 45
Limited English Proficient (LEP) students
   assessing English proficiency, 27
   English Proficiency Standards (ELPS), 27–28
Listening skills
   assessing listening ability, 26–27
   fostering development of, 20–22
   oral language development and, 19
   reading aloud, 23–24
   retelling, 24–25
   Speaking and Listening Checklist, 26
   turn and talk, 25–26
Literacy development, 29–46
   alphabetic principle, 33
   analyzing miscues, 43–45
   analyzing oral reading errors, 37–38
   assessment and instruction guidelines, 32
   foundations for, 29–30
   importance of comprehension development, 36
   phonological and phonemic awareness, 30–31
   responding to students' oral reading miscues (errors), 38–40
   role of instruction, 36
   running records, 40–45
   sources of information on proficient reading, 37
   stages of reading development, 34–36
   visual cues, meaning cues and structure cues, 37–38
Literary elements, 80–81
Literature
   fiction, 80–81
   multicultural literature, 79
   nonfiction, 79
   poetry, 80
   role of quality, for students, 79
Long vowels, 51

M

Meaning cues, 44
   analyzing oral reading and, 36, 37–38, 43–45
Memoir, 79
Mentor text, 95
Mini-lesson in writing, 95
Morpheme, 54
   vocabulary instruction and, 74
Morphemic analysis, 54
Multicultural literature, 79
Multimodal literacy, 100–101

N

Nonfiction, 79
Norm-referenced test
   reading assessment, 46
   reading comprehension, 81

O

Open syllables, 54
Oral language, 15–28, 39, 40
   assessing speaking ability, 26–27
   assessment of limited English proficient students, 27
   audience and, 20
   buddy or partner reading, 24
   conditions for learning, 22–23
   cooperative learning, 25
   developing with written language, 23–25
   English Language Proficiency Standards (ELPS), 27–28
   fostering development of, 20–22
   functions of, 20
   grand conversations, 24–25
   imitation, 18
   important factors in schooling for, 19
   language components, 17
   language register, 20
   learned in social settings, 18
   reading aloud, 23–24
   retelling, 25